D1170698

POETRY AND MORALITY

Poetry and Morality

STUDIES ON
THE CRITICISM OF MATTHEW ARNOLD
T. S. ELIOT AND F. R. LEAVIS

By

VINCENT BUCKLEY

With an Introduction by
BASIL WILLEY
FELLOW OF PEMBROKE COLLEGE
KING EDWARD VII PROFESSOR OF ENGLISH LITERATURE
IN THE UNIVERSITY OF CAMBRIDGE

1959
CHATTO & WINDUS
LONDON

Published by
Chatto and Windus Ltd
42 William IV Street
London, W.C. 2

*

Clarke, Irwin & Co. Ltd
Toronto

'There is very little doubt what the great artists would say.
People of that temper feel that the whole thinking man is one,
and that to count out the moral element in one's appreciation
of an artistic total is exactly as sane as it would be (if the total
were a poem) to eliminate all the words in three syllables, or
to consider only such portions of it as had been written by
candle-light. The crudity of sentiment of the advocates of
"art for art" is often a striking example of the fact that a great
deal of what is called culture may fail to dissipate a well-seated
provincialism of spirit. They talk of morality as Miss Edge-
worth's infantine heroes and heroines talk of "physic"—they
allude to its being put into and kept out of a work of art, put
into and kept out of one's appreciation of the same, as if it
were a coloured fluid kept in a big labelled bottle in some
mysterious intellectual closet. It is in reality simply a part of
the essential richness of inspiration—it has nothing to do with
the artistic process and it has everything to do with the artistic
effect. The more a work of art feels it at its source, the richer
it is; the less it feels it, the poorer it is.'

HENRY JAMES: *French Poets and Novelists*

'For, in the long run, whatever the poet's "philosophy", however wide may be the extension of his meaning—like Milton's
Ptolemaic universe in which he didn't believe—by his
language shall you know him; the quality of his language is
the valid limit of what he has to say.'

ALLEN TATE: *The Man of Letters in the Modern World*

CONTENTS

ACKNOWLEDGMENTS

I MUST gratefully acknowledge the help, of various kinds, given to me by the following: Professor Basil Willey, Fellow of Pembroke College, Cambridge, and King Edward VII Professor of English Literature in the University of Cambridge; T. R. Henn, Senior Tutor of St Catharine's College, Cambridge; Dr F. R. Leavis of Downing College, Cambridge; Dr J. B. Broadbent of King's College, Cambridge; Alan Wilkinson of St Catharine's College, Cambridge; Brian Way and David Craig of Downing College, Cambridge; Oliver Rottmann of the English Faculty Library, Cambridge; and Dr Ian Gregor of King's College, London, who kindly lent me the typescript of his new edition of Matthew Arnold's *Culture and Anarchy*.

I am grateful to the following for permission to quote copyright material: the author and Messrs Faber and Faber for passages from the critical works of T. S. Eliot; and the author and Messrs Chatto and Windus for passages from the works of F. R. Leavis.

A*

INTRODUCTION

By Professor Basil Willey

HAVING watched the growth of this book from its beginnings, I am now happy to introduce it to the reading public as something worth most careful attention. I am not writing a publisher's blurb, but I can promise the prospective reader all sorts of good things: candour, lucidity, subtlety, insight, understanding, wisdom—and all enlivened by the freshness of a mind that has not lost its bloom.

It might be thought that, after all the discussions about Poetry and Morality which have gone on for the last two thousand years and more, nothing much remained to be said on this topic. Indeed, when Mr Buckley first arrived in Cambridge from Australia a few years ago, full of his project, I hinted to him some such misgiving. But I very soon saw that it was groundless, and this, the finished book, will triumphantly prove the same thing to others.

Let no one be put off by the title; 'Poetry and Morality'. The reader will find here no jargon, no humbug, nothing weary, stale, flat or unprofitable; he will find no boring historical summaries, and still less will he find any vague uplift or pretentious theorising. All is fresh, first-hand and responsible: the work of a man who is himself a poet and a critic, and who cares intensely for both poetry and morality—cares for them so much, indeed, that he sees with extreme clearness the complexities of their inter-connection.

Mr Buckley has wisely avoided the beaten track of the historian of critical ideas; we are spared the hackneyed themes of academic disputation (Plato, Artistotle, Sidney and the rest). Instead, he analyses and expounds some relevant writings of three modern critics (one dead and two living) whose contributions in this field have been especially important and influential: Matthew Arnold, T. S. Eliot and F. R. Leavis.

Even so he does not merely analyse and expound. Using the charts provided by his three acknowledged masters, he shows that he too possesses a first-rate mind and sensibility, and can take his own bearings and break fresh ground independently.

Anyone who may have been apt to take too simple a view of the relationship between poetry and morality will find his thought becoming deepened and enriched as he reads these pages. And yet, after all the complexities have been surmounted, a new simplicity emerges upon a higher level. Poetry is autonomous, yet it is rooted in life; literary judgments are autonomous, yet they pass into ethical judgments through the 'diagnosis' of emotional quality (cf. Mr Buckley's quotation from Dr Leavis on page 177). Do literary judgments need any 'sanction' beyond themselves? Do they need to be 'completed' by reference to non-literary standards, moral or theological; and if so, how can this be done without danger to the critic's literary integrity? These are some of the themes which are here developed and clarified.

Mr Buckley avows that he writes as a Christian, but in his case this does not mean that he is too much of a Christian to be a good critic. Indeed he not only proclaims, but exemplifies in his own writing, that the Christianity is to appear, not explicitly as 'pastoral' homily, but implicitly as better and profounder criticism. A Christian, or any other man, may come to think other things more important than poetry; if so, he is under no compulsion to go on trying to be a critic. But as long as he practices criticism he must do so as Mr Buckley does—that is, keep his ultimate standards implicit and pervasive, and not apply them precipitately. In fact, he will not 'apply' them at all; they will be to him an informing and living principle, like Dr Leavis's 'sense of health'.

It would be inappropriate to go on discussing or summarising Mr Buckley's argument further; let the reader taste for himself. He will not be disappointed, and he will assuredly want to see more from the same pen.

CHAPTER I

Explanations

MY title should really be something like the following: Poetry and Morality: An Approach to the Question through an Examination of the Work of three Modern Critics. And it might, if this were not enough, carry the sub-title: Is there a Problem at all?

A good deal of explicitness is, in fact, necessary in establishing the theme. For, to establish the theme, one has first to establish the *status quaestionis*. A lot of confusion is immediately apparent in people's minds when one yokes poetry and morality together in the one short phrase. I undertook this work in a university where a sympathetic understanding of the issues involved might be supposed to be widespread. But, in writing it, I was often questioned by wits: 'Poetry and morality? Is there any connection? Shouldn't it be poetry and immorality?' delivered either with an approach to a decadent leer, or with a jolly laugh. Even people who have (as distinct from thinking they have) a real interest in literature, which involves a real interest in other things besides literature, have been puzzled by the project as announced in its briefer title. Some of them took the view that poetry and morality were distinct things which, like East and West, could never really meet, or that their relations could be explored only by an exercise in analytical philosophy, or that no decision could ever be reached on the problem of those relations. One or two even congratulated me on being given the opportunity to write on such a promising subject; they plainly saw me as engaged in a wide-ranging undisciplined 'thinking' about the subject, at a desk pell-mell with diverse books, and with every opportunity to coin *bon mots*, and to indulge, at graver moments, in *obiter dicta*.

So the question asked in my hypothetical sub-title answers itself. There *is* a problem; but it is less a philosophical problem than a problem arising from the ingrained attitudes in most of our minds. That, briefly, is why I have decided to approach it in the way I have done, and to be tentative rather than firm in my enquiries. My aim has not been to give answers to the outstanding questions, but to try to define the *status quaestionis*, and, in doing so, to extend it further than it is normally extended: to establish, not an answer to anything, but a definitive question, and to do even that indirectly. But to show how confused is the range of answers to the question, let me take it for a moment completely in the abstract, and list the attitudes which not only could be taken, but actually are taken. They could almost (so typical they are) be put in the form of a graph:

A. *The view that poetry and morality are not connected at all:*

(i) That poetry is a craft, and has as little to do with moral considerations as any other craft.

(ii) That they are two separate orders of human engagement or activity, both important, and that they retain their importance only by retaining their autonomy: cf. most contemporary minor poets.

(iii) That poetry expresses life at a pre-moral level, morality being only a superficies: cf. the Surrealists and their contemporary offspring.

(iv) That poetry expresses life at a mystical, and hence a post-moral level: cf. l'Abbé Brémond, who seems to me to tend towards this view.

(v) That they may have some connection, but of an accidental or occasional sort, with which criticism has no concern: cf. the great majority of academic critics.

B. *The view that they are intimately connected.*

(*a*) The view from effects:

(i) That poetry exists for direct edification.

(ii) That it exists for the consolation of the reader and for the expansion of his moral attitudes by directly inducing in him certain moral sentiments.

(*b*) The view of what is actually 'realised' in poetry:

(iii) That poetry is necessarily moral in its contact with reality, that it *embodies* moral insight; and that this, and

14

not the presumed effects, is the legitimate concern of the literary critic.

(iv) That poetry is concerned with a moral reality, but only as the reflection of a more important dimension, the religious or metaphysical.

Some of these views could be persuasively defended only by considering exclusively certain types of poetry; others, as for example A (i) and A (ii), could be defended only on *a priori* grounds. But I don't want to discuss any of them in the abstract; I have set down this list only to show how very confused the whole question is. It is confused by the fact that people often don't know what their attitudes are, and that their practical attitudes are often in contradiction to their openly asserted beliefs. So it is possible for critics who are, properly speaking, aesthetes to make hallucinatory passes over the words 'moral' and 'insight' in dealing with works which have no concern for lived moral values at all.

Faced with such confusion and lack of self-awareness, how can one fruitfully raise the question of the moral worth, or status, or reality of poetry? One temptation is, certainly, to treat it as a philosophical question. But, if this is an approach for anyone, it is an approach for professional philosophers; and even if it were within my range, it would still seem too abstract an approach to get us anywhere with an art so concrete, so *incarnational*, as poetry. Another temptation is to adopt the critical rôle which we often think of as characteristic of continental critics, the rôle of a free-lance speculator whose interest in works of literature is an interest in their deepest philosophical affinities and tendencies. Such an approach might be quite useful; but it is clearly less useful in confronting poetry in English than it is in confronting poetry in most other languages. It has the danger, too, of leading us to forget the individual reality of the works before us for the sake of educing high-flown historical generalisations. Despite its grave limitations—limitations which can be fairly called provincial—English criticism has generally been more successful than French or German in keeping its eye on the object. And I should suggest that today, when the reality of human life is threatened by the twin mechanistic principles of too-great externality and too-great subjectivity, keeping an eye on the object is precisely what literary studies need. An essay in free-lance speculation, therefore, would be, in the present circumstances, no more than a pleasant indulgence.

To keep one's eye on the object, then! But what is the object? The object clearly is poetry; but it is 'poetry in general'; and, faced with such an immense, such a diverse human phenomenon as poetry is and has been, how are we to keep our eye on it in any disciplined way? After all, I am writing a book, not an encyclopedia of values. One way would be to take for analysis several admittedly good poems, and several admittedly inferior poems, and to try to define my *status quaestionis* by a process of elaborate cross-reference between my accounts of them. That, in fact, is how the subject first suggested itself. But it has serious defects as a method. In the first place, it offers the temptation to impose on the material which one is considering one's own half-inchoate attitudes to poetry, one's half-conscious expectations and prejudices. In the second place, there is the difficulty of choosing enough poems which are representative enough to enable one to define any question at all. For these two reasons I had to conclude that, despite its disciplined bearing, this method was not disciplined enough.

For the first consideration is, I feel, the necessity of not being random or arbitrary, of finding some method sufficiently disciplined to keep my comments relevant to their alleged subject. And, after all, it is surely quixotic to try to answer the question: 'In what sense, if any, is the goodness or badness of a given poem a moral goodness or badness?' Quixotic if only because that does not seem to me to be the vital question. The vital question can only be approached through a consideration of works of great intensity or pretensions.

That is my first reason for choosing to study not poetry but criticism; though I hope that my study will be also, in a real sense, an indirect study of poetry. It is my first reason, too, for choosing these three critics. It was, first of all, a question of dealing with a subject by examining the work of men who had, each from his own angle of vision and interest, devoted disciplined lives to the study of that subject. Not only do they seem to me to be easily the greatest critics of the last century and a half, but they are critics in an integral sense, not philosophers or *flâneurs*.

It seems to me impossible, as I have said, to give a satisfactory definition of poetry which would establish its moral status. Such a definition would be of the form: 'Poetry is an ethical action or thing of such-and-such a kind.' And even intelligent moralists, like Yvor Winters, who attempt such a definition can't provide a formula which answers adequately to all our experience of poetry. On such a level of formulation, definitions are useless; rather, they may be useful in inciting the reader to meditation of his own, but they are useless as definitions.

Even a definition of morality, which must seem so clearly called for if we are to avoid final and disastrous confusion, won't come just for the calling; and, even if it did, it might not be so useful as we should hope. For the sense of 'morality' which we need to have in discussions about poetry is not an exclusive but an expansive, an adaptable sense. I am not preaching relativism; but I am suggesting that that sense, that understanding, must be a sense for something that touches, on the one hand, standards of behaviour, and, on the other hand, depths of understanding: the knowledge of good and evil as well as decisions on behalf of this or that course of action. And it would touch on, it would have bearings on, much that lies between these poles: on the pieties, the perceptions, and the self-checks, which are equally a matter of morality and of the affections. In saying so, I am not trying to make the term inclusive enough for even the most feather-brained critic to use; I am simply trying to say why an explicit definition of it seems to me inappropriate.

It is interesting that the three critics whom I am considering —Matthew Arnold, T. S. Eliot, and F. R. Leavis—make no attempt at a definition of this kind. Their interest in the moral quality of poetry (to call it that for a moment) comes to a point of definition when they consider either the greatest poetry, or poetry which, because of some revealing eccentricity of vision, exhibits the whole question of poetry and morality in an intense form. But, at such a point of definition, the implicit question arises: 'In what sense is the greatness of poetry a moral greatness? In what sense is the poet's concern with and for his material a concern for something possessing moral vitality and importance?' It is an implicit question, a hidden guiding pre-occupation; and it is interesting that the answer which each of them can be induced, under examination, to make is not made in terms which we should immediately call 'moral'.

The chapters which follow are devoted to demonstrating this judgment, among others. At least, they are not deliberately devoted to it; in each case, the fact emerges naturally from the analysis. I came to each of these critics with as little prejudg-ment of them as one can be reasonably sure of having. And the process of analysing their work showed me, with compelling force, the significance of the things they have in common. These things, too, may be listed:

They are all moralists in one way or another.

None of them is a definer, none is interested in theories which account for poetry-as-a-whole.

Although they have different conceptions of the moral status of poetry, each gives an unusual force and meaning to the word 'moral'.

Each of them finds the moral value co-extensive with the artistic value of any work. There is no attempt, in any case, to set up 'aesthetic' values as a substitute for life.

In each case, the value which is detected in the greatest poetry is seen to pass unobtrusively out of a realm of merely moral discourse and to approach one or other religious conception of life.

All are constantly preoccupied with the same problems, both in literature and in society; and there is a good deal of cross-criticism between them; Eliot criticises Arnold, Leavis criticises both Arnold and Eliot.

Finally, the more we read them, the more we find that these three ardent 'modernists' are rootedly aware of and involved in a tradition, the more we find them striving to bring to light and to justify in actual criticism a conception of the tradition in which they are involved.

The affinities are significant, certainly; and a lesson is there for those of us who care to make use of it. The differences are almost as great; and I hope that they emerge in the chapters on the individual critics. At this point, it must be stressed that I am *not* trying to give an account of the significance or value of each of them as a critic, to take up an attitude to his criticism as a whole. I have simply taken each of them as a subject for study under a single head: that of poetry and morality. Consequently, all my approaches to their work have been made towards this point in it, the point at which some formulation under that head could be found or made. The studies are, in short, essays in exposition; they could not help being so. For Eliot and Leavis, in particular, have been very chary of making formulations which can be taken as definitive, or even used directly at all. My studies of these two men, therefore, will tend to have the appearance of an undisciplined piling-up of examples, an appearance which their own comparative reticence enjoined on me. To have quoted less widely, in the case of Eliot, would have been unjust; for his position, so far as he has a definite position at all, is full of ambiguities and even contradictions. To have quoted less purposively, and even exclusively, in the case of Leavis, would have been to deny expression to my sense of his development. Despite the appearance of a decisive change in his views, a change which we might locate around 1928, Eliot's critical position seems to me essentially all of a piece; it is only certain emphases and certain habits of phrasing which have changed. The essence of his continuing position is the demand that the poet 'surrender' himself, his individual values, to the judgment of an objective presence in history; it is merely the conception of this presence that changes. As for Leavis, despite the appearance of a certain emotional immobility in his judgments, of a certain premature fixing of critical sympathies, there is a real development in his approach. I have tried to characterise this by calling it a development towards a nearly religious conception of the value of great literature.

Because of the very complex presence which all three critics offer to an investigator, my examination of their views has tended to be largely in terms of exposition; and my criticisms and reservations have tended to be incidental and, as it were, *ad hoc*. It could hardly have been otherwise; for it was, as I have said, a matter of fixing the *status quaestionis*, of fixing it by a slow and patient exploration of suggestions, nuances, alternative meanings. And because this approach seemed to me necessary, it was also necessary to let this whole study remain, in a sense, a preliminary one. It is a matter of preliminaries, not of conclusions.

It might seem unfair to offer, even in an incidental way, criticisms of their formulations while refusing to venture my own. This refusal is not due, I hope, to an affectation of the kind of superiority apt to be affected by critics of critics. The point is that, in so far as I do hold some formulation of my own, I hold it in much the way that Leavis, or Eliot at his best, holds it; inwardly and implicitly. If, as I believe, the issue is one on which one ought not to venture too ready an answer, it is also one on which one ought not to rush to declare oneself. Manifestos are not called for; and there would be little point in my trying to excogitate a personal standpoint which would require as much patient reservation as that which I have tried to give to my disengagement of their separate views.

What might be said, however, is this: That any simple form of didacticism seems to me an impossible stance to maintain; for it ignores the complexity, and the complex importance, of what it offers to deal with. The action of history has made certain answers, certain ways even of raising the issue, quite beside the point. Whatever terms we may use, the issue can certainly be seen no longer as an issue between a didactic poetry and the notion of *l'art pour l'art*. There is no such thing as a free, a disengaged poetry; and didactic poetry is generally quite inefficacious.

That this is so can be attested by the fact that the novel has for decades accomplished many of the tasks which poetry had previously done. I mean that the historical development of literary forms has led to an expectation of richness and complexity in the novel going together with an expectation of intensity and of spiritual maturity in poetry. Neither form gives room for a didactic approach. So we find the best of the few remaining didactic critics, Yvor Winters, rejecting the name of didact and attempting to formulate his position in as subtle a way as possible:

> The poem is a statement in words about a human experience. Words are primarily conceptual, but through use and because human experience is not purely conceptual, they have acquired connotations of feeling. The poet makes his statement in such a

way as to employ both concept and connotation as efficiently as possible. The poem is good in so far as it makes a defensible rational statement about a given human experience (the experience need not be real but must be in some sense possible) and at the same time communicates the emotion which ought to be motivated by that rational understanding of that experience.[1]

Here, I suggest, we see the dangers, the inevitable deficiencies, of the approach through open definition. It is made all the more anomalous, in this case, by Winters' being a sort of didact—or, as he would put it, a 'moralistic' critic. His view is that art and the artist are both purposeful; art is the execution of purpose. The aim of a poem is to communicate something; what it has to communicate is a declaration of its author's meaning, and so of his purpose. The purpose of a poem might almost be said to be a declaration of its author's purpose. A declaration stabilised in its 'appropriate' emotion, certainly; but a declaration nonetheless. It is a view of poetry as simple communication. And its view of 'morals' comes to be in itself exaggerated:

> I believe, to be sure, that ethical interest is the only poetic interest, for the reason that all poetry deals with one kind or another of human experience and is valuable in proportion to the justice with which it evaluates that experience. . . .[2]

The import of this is that all acts of 'valuing' are ethical; Winters is suggesting that the only terms in which one can 'value' anything are ethical ones. The term is too wide, the vital question is not being asked. For the vital question is the question what ethical significance can be seen in a poetry in which the author's insights, moral and otherwise, are *realised* as completely as possible in poetic terms. And no one who does not hold a simple communication theory can believe that those poetic terms are identical with terms of open ethical declarations. It seems to me that Winters' laudable attempt to find the intertwining roots of poetry and morality while rejecting a simple didactic account has, in fact, led him straight towards some such account. He is a didact despite himself.

And the didactic writer or critic in a confused and complex

[1] *In Defence of Reason* (University of Denver Press, n.d.), p. 11
[2] *Ibid.* p. 505

world is a thorough anomaly—an anomalous symbol of narrowness. The only responsibility which he recognises towards that
world is the responsibility of teaching it—of teaching it as
directly and persuasively as possible. And what, given his chosen
limits of sympathy and perception, can he teach it? He can
teach it *himself*, a tactic to which the later romantics tended. He
can teach it his personal opinions, which are not likely to issue
in a particularly lively and persuasive art if they proceed from
a man whose engagement with the life around him is no deeper
than that of the self-elected 'teacher'. He can teach it the
beliefs or dicta of his group, his party or his church; but these
again can't come into a living contemporary literature unless
they are personalised; and they can't be adequately personalised
in a man who holds himself apart from the currents of sympathy
which animate his society and his world, and who conceives
it his only duty to teach that world the conclusions of a
corporately held doctrine. I am not saying that poetry has no
relation to truth; but didactic poetry in our age can only be a
technique for personal superiority, for a kind of snobbery. It is
not generally recognised that it is also, as the doctrine of *l'art
pour l'art* is, a technique for becoming dégagé, for resigning
from communal responsibility. As late as the eighteenth century,
the striking, even the full sounding, of the didactic note would
have implied a deep identity with an audience which was
known in advance to be there, and whose moral responses
could be counted on. Today, it would imply not identity but
separation from the audience whom it was intended not to
represent but simply to influence. And a fatal separation; for,
if that note were struck at all, it could hardly help having a
false ring. We can't count on the moral responses of our
presumed audience as even Arnold could.

Didacticism is the extreme form of conceptions of poetry
which demand that it have a directly salutary effect on the
reader. But there are other contemporary views which, because
of their insistence on the direct effect, may be called examples
of disguised didacticism. I. A. Richards' position, for example,
is that poetry directly integrates the personality of poet and
reader alike. A similar position is held by such a critic as J. W.
Saunders, who writes:

Poetry is the art *par excellence* which deals both with co-ordination and with human values. Poetry alone in the arts is wholly concerned with declaring man to man; poetry alone in the sciences is wholly concerned with the co-ordination of analyses; poetry alone among the disciplines, now that Latin and Greek have had their day, can equip the intelligence to bring human order into the complexities of modern life.[1]

This is, for all its rhetorical force, an evasive statement. The casual jamming of poetry into the packed ranks of the sciences comes as something of a surprise. And the co-ordinating of analyses is not something which we normally think of poetry as undertaking. But the writer's last sentence reveals his chief intention: poetry is the only remaining guide in a complex world; and it is a guide to the 'intelligence'; in some sense of the word, it teaches, presumably by a sort of training. It is a guide, probably the only guide, to this complexity for people who are now the unwitting victims of it. It does not teach precisely by *saying*; nor is it simply an *example*, persuasive because it is there and can be resorted to. It is something midway between; it co-ordinates the mind in the midst of those social patterns which lie behind itself.

This is, then, a kind of didacticism, less sophisticated than mechanistic; and it seems to me that it is merely wishful thinking expressed in the language of science. Such views as this represent a garbling of didactic approaches which have been confused, historically, by the immense claims which Romanticism made for poetry. The big difficulty with most of the more exalted theories of poetry is that they see poetry as the chief former, the chief power, the chief illumination, of the reader's mind: It is as though we had no other sources of power, of self-formation, of the inward strength to make truth effective. By brooding on the 'high destinies' of poetry, or of any art, a man is alarmingly likely to attain a single-mindedness which is not at all healthy, and to want to prescribe for that art more than it is capable of effecting. In such a way those theories grow up in which, as Eliot says, poetry is seen as a substitute for something else, or even for everything else. It seems to me foolish

[1] 'Poetry in the Managerial Age' (*Essays in Criticism*, Vol. IV, No. 3, July 1954), p. 278

to ask poetry[1] to console or sustain man, to integrate or
harmonise him, to 'save' him; for each of these ways of putting
it really means to redeem him from the limitations, the im-
potences and terrors, attendant on his actual state in the world.
The end of such views is invariably self-delusion, or disillusion-
ment, or both. People who care seriously for literature would be
saved a great deal of disappointment if they were realistic about
the arts. As James K. Baxter's dialogue has it,

> When Prometheus asks the meaning of Orpheus' song, Orpheus
> replies—'Listen again.'
>   'But,' says Prometheus, 'does it incite men to the practice of
> virtue?'
>   'No, it restores to them the freedom to do good and evil.'
>   'Then, it is not ethical.'
>   'No. But if you want a sermon, the churches are open.'
>   'I was going there in any case, but I wanted to hear from your
> own lips the proof of your immorality.'[2]

This, of course, does not settle any question; but it would do
no harm to begin our thinking with it.

---

[1] I have spoken throughout of poetry, not of the novel. For the novel, as a study
in itself, raises problems (centring around questions of 'characterisation') which I
don't want to deal with. But most of my remarks may be taken, given the relevant
reservations, to deal with imaginative literature generally.

[2] *Notes Towards an Aesthetic* (Salient, Wellington, N.Z., September 1953)

CHAPTER II

Matthew Arnold: Poetry as Religion

HISTORICALLY, Matthew Arnold is perhaps the most interesting of all English literary critics. It is not that he stands apart from, or to any great degree transcends, Victorian literary assumptions, but that he is so firmly rooted in those assumptions, so clearly draws conclusions from them, so finely systematises the insights which he gains into them. For he is, despite all appearances, a systematiser, a synthetic thinker. But what makes him most interesting is the fact that he summarises so much of the Victorian spirit, reconciles (so far as one man can) the opposing terms in the Victorian discussion of artistic value. He is fully of the Romantic tradition of thought—in so far as we can say that it was anything as definite as a tradition— and yet tempers it with constant recourse to the 'classical' spirit. Time and again, his urbane discourse, in development and even in phrasing, parallels Shelley's rapid utterance; yet the final effect of his writing is utterly different from the effect of Shelley's. He draws, too, on Wordsworth for his view of the poet's subject-matter; but he surpasses Wordsworth in subtlety. He is a post-Romantic of a distinctive kind and period: of a cultivated middle-class élite. And he is, in consequence, half a classicist. He could not afford to have a view of the moral reality of poetry as eccentrically ambitious as Shelley's, as unpretentious and in a way provincial as Wordsworth's, or as firmly rooted in a metaphysic as Coleridge's. His virtue is of the Philistine, not the Barbarian, stamp.

He is, too, notoriously difficult to interpret, partly because it is so difficult to see him objectively. Even though the great Victorians have come lately to fascinate a number of younger critics, they still have power to irritate us. And Arnold is the most sensitive—some people would say the most vacillating—of the great Victorian literary men. Yet his basic position is quite simple: it is the notion that poetry is, in some real sense, a religious act. What makes that position so baffling is the variety of his approaches to it. His attempts to specify and enhance the value of poetry show a many-sided concern, and take very different expressions. He wants from poetry teaching and consolation and moral vitality: the teaching and consolation and moral energy which many others in his time, as in ours, expected from religion. But just *what* poetry teaches, and *how* it teaches it, are vexed questions, even for Arnold. And, while we may find his concern with consolation a most subjective one, we can find it baffling that he should so often associate the work of consolation with the work of stimulating and enlarging man's affective faculties, his capacity for sentiment.

Sentiment! There is the weakness of Arnold. It may also have been the weakness of Victorian England; the preoccupation with religion, and the tendency to make religion manageable by reducing it to its 'poetry'—to moral sentiment, in short—strike us, perhaps unjustly, as curiously Victorian traits. In a sense, religion overshadowed the Victorians, instead of penetrating them. Even the Oxford Movement was, on the whole, doctrinal without a metaphysic; hence the charges of ritualism could be made, with some plausibility, against many of its members. And the Victorians generally seem to have concentrated too exclusively on religious devotion as the summation, the natural result, of moral sentiment, far too little on the metaphysical and mystical insight which Christianity embodies, and to which it leads.

Consequently, when we say that poetry for Arnold is a religious act, and that its virtue consists in its being that, we have to be careful to specify further. There is, for evidence, that notorious passage from his earlier work which he quotes at the beginning of 'The Study of Poetry':

> The future of poetry is immense, because in poetry, where it is worthy of its high destinies, our race, as time goes on, will find an ever surer and surer stay. There is not a creed which is not shaken, not an accredited dogma which is not shown to be questionable, not a received tradition which does not threaten to dissolve. Our religion has materialised itself in the fact, in the supposed fact; it has attached its emotion to the fact, and now the

fact is failing it. But for poetry the idea is everything; the rest is a world of illusion, of divine illusion. Poetry attaches its emotion to the idea; the idea *is* the fact. The strongest part of our religion today is its unconscious poetry.[1]

The 'high destinies' of which poetry is to be worthy are those which result from its being made a substitute, if not for religion, at least for much of the work which religion has traditionally done. For 'a religion of preternaturalism is doomed'[2]; and if virtuous conduct and moral sentiment are not to perish with it, poetry will have to take its place in a number of ways. The substitution apparently does not seem to Arnold as hard to achieve; for already religion and poetry have much in common; indeed, 'the strongest part of our religion today is its unconscious poetry'.

This is obviously a contentious notion; and it has been subjected to some sharp analysis. T. S. Eliot, for example, says of Arnold's writings on Christianity:

> They are tediously negative. But they are negative in a peculiar fashion: their aim is to affirm that the emotions of Christianity can and must be preserved without the belief. From this proposition two different types of man can extract two different types of conclusion: (i) that Religion is Morals, (ii) that Religion is Art. The effect of Arnold's religious campaign is to divorce Religion from thought.[3]

The comment is sharp and telling enough; but is it quite accurate? Arnold is not simply concerned to preserve 'the emotions of Christianity . . . without the belief'. He seems also to have the intention of, as it were, redefining religion, so that it is no longer a *bond* between God and man, a bond of which doctrinal formulations are a necessary illumination and expression, but a state of mind. Religion, that is, has its own best guarantee in the state of mind which it is capable of

---

[1] *Essays in Criticism*, Second Series (Scholars' Library edition), p. 1. All further quotations will be from this edition.

[2] *Five Uncollected Essays* (Kenneth Allott [Ed.], 1953), p. 20

[3] Arnold and Pater: in *Selected Essays*, p. 396. Among other very telling criticisms of Arnold's position is that of F. H. Bradley. See in particular the passages quoted by Eliot, *Selected Essays*, pp. 412-14. See also the opinion of a contemporary critic, F. R. Leavis: 'Matthew Arnold as Critic' (*Scrutiny*, Vol. VII, No. 3). Leavis is able to say bluntly that 'Arnold as a theological or philosophical thinker had better be abandoned explicitly at once.'

inducing. In a sense, it *is* that state of mind; and doctrines become redundant in considering or advancing it. It is not precisely an emotion; Arnold is not seeking easy thrills; but his view is nevertheless defective as a conception. It has its root in what we may call a sentiment of the numinous, and it has its active effect in moral sentiment. For Arnold, religion can therefore be defined most nearly in terms of sentiment; and so, as I hope to show later, can poetry. Arnold claims, in other words, to be a refined sort of empiricist, and he shows himself to be a pragmatist of a kind at once subtle and ill-defined.

The various attacks made, by Eliot among others, on Arnold's religious position, and on his apparent confusion of religion with culture, seem to me utterly damaging. And his religious position —in so far as it is articulated as a conscious attitude or belief— must now seem to many of us little short of obtuse. The point of criticising his religious position at all is that his attitude to poetry is so closely associated with it, and gets from it a distinctive colouring. We are not really concerned with him as a religious thinker, but as a thinker about poetry. Yet he does, in some sense, regard poetry as a religious act. That is why I think F. R. Leavis is skirting too perfunctorily about the problem when he writes of the opening passage of 'The Study of Poetry':

> The element that 'dates' in the worst sense is that represented by the famous opening in which Arnold suggests that religion is going to be replaced by poetry. Few would now care to endorse the unqualified intention of that passage, and Arnold as a theological or philosophical thinker had better be abandoned explicitly at once. Yet the value of the essay does not depend on our accepting without reservation the particular terms in which Arnold stresses the importance of poetry in these introductory sentences, and he is not disposed of as a literary critic by pointing out that he was not theologian or philosopher.[1]

This is true; and it needed to be said, if only to refute the scornful view of Arnold propagated by such men as J. M. Robertson. 'The Study of Poetry' *is*, as an exercise in literary criticism, largely independent of the pretensions announced in its opening paragraphs. Yet, in the perspective established by

[1] F. R. Leavis, *Ibid.*

28

my present interest—an interest in Arnold's view of poetry and morality—the stress which Leavis leaves may be misleading. Arnold's claims for poetry are religious claims; and they are intimately connected with his expectations of poetry as a moral force. Consequently they colour not only the degree but the kind of trust which he places in it. The desperation of his moral demands on poetry is a direct result of his defective religious position. And the poets whom he most reveres are in a sense religious poets; they are the poets of an ethical-aesthetic sentiment which is, to Arnold's mind, the core of religion. Or, at least, they are poets who are capable of yielding, in some parts or aspects of their work, the kind of satisfaction which Arnold declares to be moral but which is associated in his mind with religion.

Whatever we may say of his religious position, his view of poetry in this essay is certainly not obtuse. Nor does he, as I have insisted, exactly identify poetry with religion. But his tendency to reduce religion to those elements in it which it shares with some kinds of poetry is a curious way of asserting the value of poetry: curious, if only because it generates an optimism about poetry which the history of this century has made to seem unfounded.

His case, as he announces it in 'The Study of Poetry', seems to be something like this: It is in poetry that the essential religious, moral, and aesthetic sentiments coalesce and compose one thing. In the process, nothing is destroyed; on the contrary each of the three components, however alike they have all come to seem, has its true value enhanced. For, on its own, traditional Christianity stands self-condemned through its reliance on historical fact, through its tendency to derive doctrinal formulae from historical facts; ethical systems on their own are lifeless and incapable of persuading to an action which is not only virtuous but also cultivated; and 'aesthetic' interests, if they are regarded as self-sufficing, lack a certain broadness, a depth of humanity, do not conduce to *life*. But, blended as Arnold would have them blended—in poetry—they provide the contemporary wisdom of the race.

It is obvious, then, that Arnold believes himself to be freeing both religion and morals from impurities, and to be preserving at the same time the central tradition of Western poetry. And we may sympathise with him. Religion and morals and poetry cannot afford to be separated from one another. But neither can any one of them afford to be reduced to either of the others, or to be made a substitute for either of the others. And that is precisely what Arnold unintentionally tends to do.

As well as this, we may find it alarming that he should place so much trust on the *sentiment* of poetry, as of religion and morals. I hope later to justify my own personal unease. Yet it must be noticed here that what he wishes to retain of religion, what he relies on poetry to communicate to the modern world, is the religious sentiment, resting on a vague numinous awareness of God as other than ourselves, and as (in some very mysterious way) making for righteousness: religion without a definite object, without a coherent intellectual formulation, without any spiritual discipline proper to it. Rather, the spiritual discipline will come from the ennobling effects of poetry; in such a conception, poetry becomes the *ascesis* of Arnold's 'religion':

> More and more mankind will discover that we have to turn to poetry to interpret life for us, to console us, to sustain us.[1]

Now, this is really fantastic. It does not answer to the facts of the past seventy years; nor does it, I believe, answer to the facts of the world to which it was announced, to the England of seventy years ago. And it has had, during those seventy years, some unfortunate results; it has influenced Pater and I. A. Richards. As Eliot points out,[2] it is not a far cry from Arnold's moral beauty to its apparent opposite, the Paterian cult of experience. It is not a far cry, either, to Richards' statement: 'Poetry is capable of saving us'—a statement which, in its emotive vagueness, in its blindness to certain relevant facts of modern life, and in its suggestion of a religious feeling and terminology, is little short of irresponsible.

But it is necessary to go beyond an initial notice of Arnold's weakness, to go to other texts besides this controversial paragraph, before we may see what he expects of poetry. In this

[1] 'The Study of Poetry', *op. cit.* p. 2
[2] *Selected Essays, op. cit.*

way, we may see what value he assigns to it. This value is first touched on by the suggestion, made throughout his writings, that poetry is a criticism of life. Perhaps the most moving statement of this position is to be found in his essay on Maurice de Guérin:

> The grand power of poetry is its interpretative power; by which I mean, not a power of drawing out in black and white an explanation of the mystery of the universe, but the power of so dealing with things as to awaken in us a wonderfully full, new, and intimate sense of them, and of our relations with them. When this sense is awakened in us, as to objects without us, we feel ourselves to be in contact with the essential nature of those objects, to be no longer bewildered and oppressed by them, but to have their secret, and to be in harmony with them; and this feeling calms and satisfies us as no other can. Poetry, indeed, interprets in another way besides this; but one of its two ways of interpreting, of exercising its highest power, is by awakening this sense in us. I will not now enquire whether this sense is illusive, whether it can be proved not to be illusive, whether it does absolutely make us possess the real nature of things; all I can say is, that poetry can awaken it in us, and that to awaken it is one of the highest powers of poetry.[1]

Several things about this passage are remarkable: not least its tone, which is very far from that of the brash manifesto or of the arrogant *obiter dictum*. And, despite Arnold's claim to have suggested the nature of only one of the two great kinds of poetry, the poetry of natural evocation, it is fairly clear that here we have the germ of his whole position. Poetry is interpretation, but it is not philosophical explanation or analysis. It is a kind of knowledge, and one which reaches deep into its object; but it is knowledge by sympathy, not by reasoning. It is feeling and thought together. It is a mastering of whatever forces in the world oppress us. It is a power of consoling us, of satisfying us. And it awakens in us a sense and sort of life. These are large claims, and they are claims which are closely linked to one another under the pressure of an unusually focussed mind and sensibility; I hope later to say something about each of them as Arnold develops it.

---

[1] *Essays Literary and Critical* (Everyman's Library edition), pp. 51-2

But he is dealing here with a kind of writing which is not based on moral ideas at all, which has for its genius a power of interpreting the world of 'Nature'. Guérin was not a moralist, and Arnold does not treat him as a moralist, just as, many years later, he is to make a similar distinction in speaking of Keats. Yet how morally satisfying he finds Guérin's 'non-moral' poetry to be! The very movement of his prose, as well as his terminology, testifies that the satisfaction which he expects from this writing is of a moral kind. Arnold finds it morally satisfying because it induces in him—what he seems most to have desired —a kind of stoic calm which has elements of a pantheist exaltation. His position is, plainly, that all fine poetry is moral, whatever its agreed object; it is moral in the manner of its contact with that object, and in its consequent capacity to console the reader. The difference between a moral interpretation and a natural interpretation lies in their objects, not in their moral-poetic value. And all fine poetry is moral not by stating or explaining, but rather by representing its contact with reality.

The first mark of the best poetry, then, is something we may call by the very un-Arnoldian name of realism: that is, fidelity to experience. That is the first thing that ensures its moral content, whether or not it is dealing with a subject (such as the life and rhythm of nature) which seems to be neutral as to moral considerations. It gives the sense, that is, not only of the actuality of things themselves but also of their links with the life of man, and of their existing in some dimension which gives them a more than sensuous importance. It is an important point, though only a preliminary one; and I will not here complain of Arnold's characteristic refusal—in this case admitted—to ask himself what grounds there are for accepting the reality of such a dimension, of his readiness to be satisfied with the sense, the sentiment of contact and to assume the reality of its cause.

His emphasis even on nature poetry is of the most serious kind. We may see its seriousness attested in the very tone of his stern aside; 'greatness can never be founded upon frivolity and corruption'.[1] Yet he insists that the greatest poetry gets its

---

[1] *Essays Literary and Critical, op.cit.* p. 55

authority from a different kind of contact with reality—with a reality which is itself moral rather than 'natural':

> Poetry is the interpretress of the natural world, and she is the interpretress of the moral world.[1]

The second is generally the more significant; and Guérin, as Arnold has said, is the poet of the first. Yet even as he repeats this fact, he slips insensibly over the borderline into a virtual confusion of the two kinds which he has been at pains to distinguish. We must see in this unconscious striving after the fullest possible significance in the work of a favourite poet his own heavily charged preoccupation with morals:

> To make magically near and real the life of Nature, *and man's life only so far as it is a part of that Nature*, was his faculty. [My emphasis.]

Surely a 'moral' activity, if ever there was one.

> To assist at the evolution of the whole life of the world is his craving, and intimately to feel it all.[2]

Surely, in a very real sense of the word, a moral aspiration. And Arnold goes on to speak of Guérin's poetry as expressing 'the physiognomy and movement of the outward world'. A physiognomy is a remarkably human thing for nature to have, at least when it is felt, as Arnold apparently feels it, to express more than a casual similarity and to denote a real identification of the two orders of being.

In fact, when we are faced with these passages, we can't avoid asking some rather perplexed questions: Is Arnold too exclusively preoccupied with morality, in his wide sense of the word: is this his King Charles' head? Do we not find here certainly a view of morals, but a view of morals in itself puzzlingly naturalistic? Is Arnold engaging in a sort of inversion of anthropomorphism, and an inversion which suffers from the fancifulness of that attitude? The questions are not idle ones, but Arnold's attitude is more complex than we realise at first sight. While stressing the moral orientation of Guérin's response to nature, he makes the comment that his management of that response is lacking in moral judgment:

[1] *Ibid.* p. 68   [2] *Ibid.* p. 69

He is thus hardly a moral agent . . . he hovers over the tumult of life, but does not really put his hand to it.[1]

In the context in which it is made, we cannot be sure how to assess this judgment. We cannot find out whether Arnold really thinks the lack of a central judging energy (what might be called explicit moral passion) is a debilitating one for a poet. The essay on Guérin does not even suggest an answer. I feel that what draws Arnold to so intimate a sympathy with Guérin is his feeling of temperamental kinship; and that is possibly why he does not launch any central criticism of what (judging from his other critical essays) he would presumably consider Guérin's deficiency: the lack of any attempt to penetrate beneath his subject to a reality in itself moral.

It is when he analyses such a surely marginal case as Guérin that Arnold's view may seem dubious, or his personal preoccupation excessive. The *idée fixe* is always the danger of the openly moral criterion. But the burden of his approach, when he gets away from the particular even in this essay, is a quite positive one. It is the idea that great poetry deals generally with man, with human destiny:

> [Poetry] interprets by expressing, with inspired conviction, the ideas and laws of the inward world of man's moral and spiritual nature.[2]

Poetry then is not, at its best, a descriptive art, but an evocative one. It presents, by evoking it, the interior life of man—an idea which is made ambiguous by the unexplained association of 'ideas' with 'laws'. But the presentation of interior states is only one of the two ways in which it interprets man:

> In other words, poetry is interpretative both by having *natural magic* in it, and by having *moral profundity*. In both ways it illuminates man; it gives him a satisfying sense of reality; it reconciles him with himself and the universe.[3]

In both ways; but if we look at the development of English poetry we may decide that the ways are more dissimilar than Arnold suggests, are used with very different imaginative frames

[1] *Essays Literary and Critical* (Everyman's Library edition), p. 69
[2] *Ibid.* p. 77   [3] *Ibid.* p. 71

34

of reference. The point is, that he clearly sees them both as having a moral significance and effect. I have already suggested that, for Arnold, even the 'natural magic' is natural and magical only when he can see it suffused with moral meaning. And he always treats moral meaning, of course, in terms of its effects on the reader. Moral is as moral does. Most of us can with difficulty keep the moral substance of poetry (if indeed that is an apt way of describing it) distinguished from its moral effects. Arnold cannot keep them distinguished at all; his interest and interpretation are so subjective, his full insight so difficult to express without resorting to the device of explaining each of them by reference to the other. In the passage quoted, however, such words as 'satisfying' and 'reconcile' have a disturbingly therapeutic air about them; and it may be concluded that they hold good only for Arnold's ambiguous temperament and still more ambiguous spiritual situation. Is it the business of poetry to 'reconcile man with himself and the universe'? Arnold's contemporary, the young lady who 'accepted the Universe', is an absurd example of the same tendency of thought, though in Arnold the whole tone of his statement helps to redeem it.

And he certainly does not want a narrowly didactic poetry. He considers preaching a debasement of the poet's function. In the passage quoted, he speaks of poetry as *illuminating* man; it does not merely *tell* him his place in the universe, but it makes him *feel* it, gives him the sense and sentiment of it. It brings inward life and outward fact together in an expanding movement. Here again is the vaguely stoic note. It is Arnold's very Victorian emphasis on the 'truth of feeling' which makes him distrust didacticism in the sense in which Johnson would have understood and supported it.

There is a philosophy implicit in these suggestions; it is a philosophy of naturalism informed by pantheism and sustained by a Christian sense of duty. It is not that Arnold can be labelled a naturalist, or a pantheist; for his criticism is not hamstrung by his leanings towards an eclectic *Weltanschauung*. It is, however, directed and in a way limited by them. The whole essay on Guérin impresses me as part of Arnold's lifelong meditation on his own vocation, and as a poignant expression of that meditation.

35

His chief positive point is that poetry is a criticism of life. 'Criticism' means a sense for, an interpretation and healing re-presentation. The whole transforming power of poetry is involved in it; and whether its object is the life of man or the life of nature, it is in fact valuable to the extent that it affirms something of the life and nature of man. Good poetry cannot help doing this. And Arnold characterises that life, with a becoming vagueness, as 'moral and spiritual'.

One of the most noteworthy things about this whole tendency in Arnold is the recurrence of the word 'life', and of the suggestion that poetry is a means of vitalising some essential human faculty or inner aspiration. The greatest poetry 'appeals to the great primary human affections: to those elementary feelings which subsist permanently in the race. . . .'[1] It treats them as its subject, and it appeals to them as they exist in the reader. Here, in the reminiscence of Wordsworth, we can see an attempt to reconcile man and nature; we can see, too, that strain in Arnold's thinking which makes him conceive in moral terms the sort of preoccupation with nature that Guérin has. In other places, he changes the emphasis by referring to the laws of man's nature. All the time, he is insisting that the ultimate value of poetry lies in its touching some profound truth of man.

It is in this sense that poetry interprets, and it is in this sense that 'life' is the subject of the interpretation. But the promise of intellectual richness and vigour which is made here is never fulfilled. Arnold is, in fact, very evasive whenever the question arises of the *truth* of an interpretation. He demands that the truth of poetry be comprehensive and healing, not that it be (so to speak) true. Rather, his attitude is at root a complacent one, since it assumes as truth a characteristically Victorian congeries of ideas and attitudes to man, to moral action, and to nature.

However, it should be clear that 'criticism of life' means interpretation, evaluation, feeling for, sympathetic sharing in; it does not mean carping at, or even rational analysis. And the suggestion (more natural to our contemporaries than to Arnold's) that a criticism of life is a criticism of society and its follies is not borne out, either, in his literary essays. What the

---

[1] Preface to First Edition of *Poems*, 1853: *Irish Essays*, p. 286

phrase means can be seen more nearly when we reflect on the number of times, and notably in the essay on Gray, that he speaks of poetry as an 'interpretation of the world'. The immediate function of poetry is a quasi-religious, not a social one. And the remarks on Burns, in 'The Study of Poetry', show us society as an enabling or disabling condition of poetry, not as its chief subject.

It is in some such sense, then, that the criticism of literature is the same as the criticism of life, and not (as Marxist critics are always in danger of supposing) a criticism of a criticism of life. We cannot keep too firmly in mind that Arnold's concern for poetry is a concern for something which existentially preserves and exhibits and enhances the human situation. It is a concern for a kind of life; and it underlies his habit of advancing his view through a consideration of actual poets and actual poems. In considering them he does not look for a 'truth' which offers itself for debate, but for one which consoles and helps man in a more central way. So Wordsworth's 'poetry is the reality, his philosophy . . . is the illusion'[1]; and Arnold dissociates himself from the *Wordsworthians*, for, as he says, the works which these devotees praise are generally those which have a certain hollowness in them: those in which 'the lines carry us really not a step further than the proposition which they would interpret'.[2]

Even in speaking of his 'touchstones'—those mighty shadows of achievement which have met as much misunderstanding as his phrase about 'criticism of life'—Arnold illustrates his central concern. It is a concern to see the object—in this case, the nature of poetry—as in itself it really is:

> If we are *thoroughly penetrated by their power*, we shall find that we have *acquired a sense* enabling us, whatever poetry may be laid before us, to *feel* the degree in which a high poetical quality is present or wanting there.[3]

The attitude which my italics emphasise is at the very antipodes from that mechanical application of standards of which Arnold is so often suspected. His interest, as I have said, is in

[1] *Essays in Criticism*, Second Series, *op. cit.* p. 88
[2] *Ibid.* p. 89
[3] *Ibid.* p. 12. My emphasis.

whatever is living and profound and accessible in poetry; it is this that has moral interest, and a beneficent effect on man's capacity for living.

As he himself insists, his concern for life is a concern for morals; and we shall therefore be interested in what he thinks and feels about life. And here the promise of a dynamic or visionary force in his interpretation of life, of a forceful and metaphysical insight in his interpretation of poetry, is not fulfilled. When he says that poetry is 'the noble and profound application of ideas to life', the ideas are generally moral ones, and the 'life' that part of human experience which offers itself for illumination through moral ideas. We shall have, later, to ask what is the nature or status of these moral ideas on which he is content to rely; here, it is necessary only (and with a certain unease) to take note of their pervasiveness in his writings:

> If it is said that to call these ideas *moral* ideas is to introduce a strong and injurious limitation, I answer that it is to do nothing of the kind, because moral ideas are really so main a part of human life. The question, *how to live*, is itself a moral idea; and it is the question which most interests every man, and with which, in some way or other, he is perpetually occupied. A large sense is of course to be given to the term *moral*. Whatever bears upon the question, 'how to live', comes under it.[1]

This may well be so, but it takes us no further towards any truth about poetry. It is not appropriate here to criticise the remarkable looseness of his language, in which, for example, the question 'how to live' is said to be a moral *idea*. But the objection which Arnold is trying to anticipate is precisely the objection which Eliot brings: That Arnold, in his attempt to affirm two values at once, confuses life with morals. And he is striking at a real weakness in Arnold's position. Unless the meaning of 'moral' is enormously broad, the injunction does not do justice to poetry; unless it is narrow enough to be recognisable as what it is intended to be, then there is no sense in using it at all. And, after all, do men, should men, go to poetry to find out 'how to live'? All that Arnold can say in reply is that 'conduct is three-

[1] *Essays in Criticism*, Second Series, *op. cit.* p. 84

fourths of life', and that Wordsworth is intensely moral because he grapples with the real issues of life:

> We say, for brevity's sake, that he deals with *life*, because he deals with that in which life really consists.[1]

And, again, he is open to objection. We may object that, while he turns an adequately critical eye upon received religion, he does not turn an adequately critical eye upon received morality; for in both cases, what he could take as 'received' was what Victorian England took as received. But part of his dilemma is the need to preserve morals, and moral sentiment, while getting rid of what is bothersome to him in Christianity—its doctrinal content. Consequently, the sharply critical analysis of contemporary religion is possible to him only while he is passive, and even silent, in his criticism of 'the best' contemporary moral thought and feeling. It would be a mistake to assume that *Culture and Anarchy* provides that criticism; it is not that criticism, but a substitute for it. Hence, we may see one reason for the pervasiveness of his concern with morals: that he needs it to replace religion. And if his view is lacking in dynamism, it is also curiously narrow. His choice of the word 'moral' to indicate his concern, and his insistence on it, reflect a lack in him. So, as Eliot insists, does the choice of the phrase 'criticism of life':

> If we mean life as a whole—not that Arnold ever saw life as a whole—from top to bottom, can anything that we can say of it ultimately, of that awful mystery, be called criticism? We bring back very little from our rare descents, and that is not criticism.[2]

Eliot, of course, has apparently misunderstood the sense in which Arnold uses the word 'criticism', yet in so far as his objection is to the choice of that particular word to express what Arnold does mean, he seems to me to have made a telling point.

---

[1] *Ibid.* p. 87. It is a further objection to Arnold's position that we can reasonably ask in what sense conduct is 'three-fourths of life'.

[2] T. S. Eliot: 'The Use of Poetry and the Use of Criticism', p. 111

It is interesting, by the way, to contrast Arnold's social interests to Newman's. When Newman looks about him at the contemporary world, he is immediately and overwhelmingly aware of a metaphysical conflict taking place between Good and Evil. When Arnold looks about him, he sees only a certain deprivation and a certain possibility; he sees anarchy and culture; and while the one is accidental to human life, the other has no more than a human origin and centre.

Whatever poetry is or does, why characterise it by a word like 'criticism'? Its use betrays a lack in Arnold, a certain shallowness which his subtlety of mind and his seriousness of diction serve, unfortunately, to disguise. It is the same lack which we detect in his recurrent use or suggestion of the word 'moral'. There is surely a way in which we experience poetry, a way which the word 'moral' would seem quite incapable of fixing or defining. And it does not matter, in terms of my present discussion, how broadly Arnold claims to use the term. It is its very *choice* that is in question.

Other commentators have been disturbed by the pervasiveness of Arnold's moral preoccupation, and in a couple of cases the grounds of their unease are interesting. James Bentley Orrick, for example, charges him with misunderstanding and even flagrantly misinterpreting Goethe; and he attributes the misinterpretation to Arnold's desire to 'moralise' the views of a man who was one of his literary heroes.[1] Another critic, Edwin Berry Burgum, sees Arnold as so immersed in his moralising that he simply repeats, in a cruder form, the semi-platonic didacticism of Philip Sidney:

> Arnold's conception of the Christian gentleman was only Sidney's ideal of the courtier, with the stress shifted from manners to morality.[2]

Now, I agree that there is a good deal of truth in both of these criticisms. But we must keep the issue in perspective. Arnold's view of virtue, of moral *behaviour*, is very little different from that of his father, or of any other virtuous, thoughtful, and cultivated Victorian gentleman. And if his sense of the moral reality of poetry ended there, he would have very little interest for us as an important literary thinker. But it does not end there. In fact, he does not ask of poetry that it *teach* such truths of behaviour, or stress the necessity of them. His expectation of it,

[1] J. B. Orrick: 'Matthew Arnold and Goethe' (Publications of the English Goethe Society, New Series, Vol. I, edited by J. G. Robertson: Alexander Mooring, 1928). Orrick comments that 'Goethe, however, as we have seen, goes to Greek art for a very different reason, for an escape from the "moral interpretation" which Arnold sees in him and in the Greeks alike': p. 49. Orrick's view seems to be that Goethe and the Greeks are naturalists, while Arnold is a moraliser.

[2] Edwin Berry Burgum: 'The Humanism of Matthew Arnold' (*Symposium*, Vol. II, No. I, Jan. 1931), p. 97

though no doubt limited by the conventional nature of his moral ideas, is of a completely different, a more subtle kind. Certainly, he expects poetry to induce in the reader a capacity for action; and he conceives that action in terms of virtue; but he expects poetry to induce such a capacity by playing not upon the intellect or the will but upon the whole affective personality of the reader. Poetry variously calms and consoles, braces, edifies, ennobles, vitalises, gives joy. It is in its capacity to do such things that its moral reality consists. And it is in its being this sort of moral reality that its quasi-religious character lies.

Arnold's stress upon the power of poetry to 'stay and console' is obviously connected with his recurrent feeling that life (in a different sense from that in which conduct is three-fourths of life) is capable of being an oppressive mystery, and that poetry is the chief way of mastering it. We have already found him praising poetry for its capacity to waken in us a sense of natural things which allows us to be 'no longer bewildered and oppressed' by those things. And he exalts tragedy for a similar reason:

> For only by breasting in full the storm and cloud of life, breasting it and passing through it and above it, can the dramatist who feels the weight of mortal things liberate himself from the pressure, and rise, as we all seek to rise, to content and joy.[1]

In another place, he explicitly associates the notion of mastering a hostile world with the interpretative power of poetry; he speaks of our need 'to master the world and give an adequate interpretation of it'.[2] Here the term 'master' plainly means not only to get imaginative control of, but also to overcome the world's capacity to disturb and oppress. And we must ask in what sense Arnold conceives poetry to be the confronting of a mystery. It seems to me that he does not want it to express an insight into causes, but a sympathetic insight into natural or moral *states*.[3] And he wants, in the poet and the reader alike, a balanced fusion of thought and feeling sufficient to help transcend the vexations of existence and its philosophical

---

[1] *Irish Essays: And Others*, p. 221
[2] *On the Study of Celtic Literature* (Everyman's Library edition), p. 110
[3] v. E. K. Brown: *Matthew Arnold: A Study in Conflict* (Chicago, 1948), pp. 40-1, for a similar opinion.

problems. It is here, in his sense of philosophical *problems*, that he differs from Eliot, with whom this strain in him has otherwise much in common. Yet he conceives the fusion largely in terms of *sentiment*. He wants poetry to induce, as it reflects, *life*, vitality, under the aspect of serenity, disinterestedness, a largely stoic calm. It is in this sense that poetry is to be a 'magister vitae'. But in practice, in his actual critical judgments and in the reasons which he gives for making them, this comes to look very much like ennobling sentiment, a sentiment which is 'bracing and edifying'. If he is a Romantic, it is a self-qualifying, self-moderating Romantic, who desires 'classical' serenity in place of romantic excitement. Such serenity is a means of gaining ground upon the chaos of life:

> No one has a stronger and more abiding sense than I have of the 'daemonic' element—as Goethe called it—which underlies and encompasses our life; but I think, as Goethe thought, that the right thing is, while conscious of this element, and of all that there is inexplicable around one, to keep pushing on one's posts into the darkness, and to establish no post that is not perfectly in light and firm. One gains nothing on the darkness by being, like Shelley, as incoherent as the darkness itself.[1]

The concluding sentence is admirable; but the whole passage leaves quite unresolved the issue of the 'daemonic' element and of what attitude the poet should take towards it. Here is Arnold preferring to reach some personal *answer* to the mystery of experience rather than to keep an intense sense of it and, in whatever way is suitable, to close with it. This is the social Arnold, the Arnold who fits so well into Victorian progressivism, the Arnold of the Enlightenment; for, in fact, his facile metaphor gives us nothing at all that is valuable, either for poetry or for life. But, despite this strain in him, he does not really expect poetry to be a means of enlightenment in the historical sense. The reproach which he made to Clough so early in his literary life represents a constant position:

> . . . all the exacerbation produced by your apostrophes to duty . . . to *solve* the Universe as you try to do is as irritating as Tennyson's dawdling with its painted shell is fatiguing to me to

[1] Letter to his mother, March 3, 1865: *Letters:* [ed.] G. W. E. Russell, Vol. I, p. 249

witness: and yet I own that to re-construct the Universe is not a satisfactory attempt either—I keep saying Shakespeare, Shakespeare, you are as obscure as life is. . . .[1]

Life is obscure, but part of its obscurity is its aspect of a hostile mystery which has to be overcome or resisted. The point made here is, that it is not to be most efficiently resisted through the systematising intellect, but through ennobling sentiment. The best answer to the hostile mystery is not understanding of its causes, but healing and consolation.

It is from a sense of a world to be 'mastered' that the roots of Arnold's interest in the consoling power of poetry grow. The words *heal, stay, console,* are scattered throughout his criticism. Poetry has, it is true, the ultimate aim of steadying men for virtuous action; but its immediate effect is to stay and console. This is, in a way, a negative criterion. It is rescued from sterility in Arnold's criticism by always being associated with, or at least implying, something much more positive: the work of bracing and edifying. In the essay on George Sand, for example, he speaks of Nature as a source of 'healing and delight for all'[2]; and what is interesting in the remark is the open association of healing with delight. Again, he uses of Homer the words 'tonic and fortifying'.

Stated in this way, it all seems to have a very medicinal flavour, and to be, on that account, rather ludicrous. But Arnold intends it to appear medicinal; poetry is spiritual medicine. And it loses its ludicrous side when we notice that he is constantly driving towards the notion that poetry serves man by animating him:

> The cause of its greatness is simple, and may be told quite simply. Wordsworth's poetry is great because of the extraordinary power with which Wordsworth feels the joy offered to us in nature, the joy offered to us in the simple primary affections and duties; and because of the extraordinary power with which, in case after case, he shows us this joy, and renders it so as to make us share it.[3]

[1] *Ibid.* p. 63: Letter to A. H. Clough, 1847
[2] *Mixed Essays* (1880 edition), p. 332
[3] *Essays in Criticism*, Second Series, *op. cit.* p. 91
This is Arnold towards the end of his literary life. But a very similar testimony is offered in *Letters to A. H. Clough*, Nov. 30, 1853, p. 146.

This is a recurrent strain in Arnold, the cleaving to joy as a means of transcending the vexations of life and of attaching us to some deep truth about the world—a 'truth of feeling'. Arnold is drawn to Wordsworth partly because his intimacy with nature allowed him to cut, or to seem to cut, the Gordian knot of the modern world's complexity. If poetry for Leavis is a confronting of complexity, for Arnold it is very largely an avoidance of it.

But the desire for and sense of animation are very important elements in Arnold's criticism, and they are the qualities which go so far to make him a great critic. Despite the suggestion of defensiveness which he often gives us when he speaks of consolation, stay, bracing, or healing, his instinct is for a quickening of the person. He uses this often to insist on the need for virtuous action, but often to insist on the free flow of feeling. His comment on Flaubert is among his sharpest; in Flaubert, the springs of feeling have dried up:

> But *Madame Bovary*, with this taint, is a work of *petrified feeling*; over it hangs an atmosphere of bitterness, irony, impotence.[1]

Because of his incapacity for a sympathetic flow of feeling towards his subject, Flaubert cannot illuminate it in such a way as to console and inspirit the reader. It is an interesting charge, and it may be contrasted to the use Pound and Eliot, among others, have made of Flaubert. For them, he is a master of the analytical report on *la condition humaine*. For Arnold, this is quite insufficient to establish a writer's greatness. Poetry is like obscenity under the present Obscenity Law, in that it is defined by its effects; and those effects ought to be such as to inspirit mankind.

The reason is clear. It is not merely that Arnold has a subjective need for the consolation and bracing of which he speaks; though this is certainly a factor in his attitude. It is rather that he sees the world, ultimately, as a field for moral action, even when that action is of a contemplative cast; and poetry is the chief means of girding us for that world, just as it is the chief means of interpreting that world for us. We cannot forget— Arnold never allows us to forget—that the morality for which

[1] *Essays in Criticism*, Second Series, *op. cit.* p. 161

great poetry steadies us (as it were) is the contemporary morality of Arnold's own class, varied with a fairly cosmopolitan sense of culture and a vaguely progressivist fervour. Poetry strengthens the sense of life and the readiness for living. But three-fourths of that life is conduct, in the ordinary sense in which any moralist is concerned with conduct; and a readiness for living is very largely a readiness for conduct, for the practice of virtue. Looking at the matter in this light, we can see considerable value in Eliot's reluctance to use the general language of morality when speaking of poetry. Arnold, on the other hand, always has a standard in view, a standard of conduct, and we can readily see that his insistence on both the stimulation and consolation to be got from poetry comes from his intense feeling for virtuous conduct, and for its roots in the inner life of the person. I have called poetry the *ascesis* of Arnold's religion; to put the matter another way, poetry is a refreshment of the soul, a re-creating it for that life of which conduct is three-fourths.

So, in the essay on Marcus Aurelius, he praises a translator for dealing with Roman literature 'as food for men, and men engaged in the current of contemporary life and action'.[1] This is a view as eminently possible, and even natural, to a nineteenth-century critic as to Sidney; it is unfortunately not so possible to their twentieth-century counterparts. My remark is intended as a loosely empirical generalisation. I do not think the contemporary influence of poetry is as negligible as most people seem to think it; but it is certainly limited, because it is in a curious way specialised; and it is not chiefly the men of action and affairs who benefit by it. So I mean that such a view as Arnold's is *subjectively* impossible—or, at the very least, difficult—for the modern critic; it was quite natural for Arnold. And that is something we cannot afford to forget when estimating the value of his analyses.

A view so closely related to a notion of conduct may seem a crudely didactic view. Of course, it is nothing of the kind. But what is disturbing in it is the failure to define or to justify that notion of conduct to which poetry is to be linked. There is a weakness in the use or suggestion of the language of conven-

---

[1] *Essays Literary and Critical, op. cit.* p. 189

tional morality; the weakness comes not from the fact that the morality is conventional, but from the fact that the convention is in itself limited. It is a convention limited in its dynamism, and wary of the asking of the most fundamental questions about human destiny.

There are other weaknesses in Arnold's position. To claim for poetry as much as he claims is to show a surely refreshing sense of its necessity; but it is also to claim too much. There are two questions involved, and not one: (1) What is poetic value, the value of any poem or poetry in itself? (2) What is the value of poetry for mankind? The first is the value which a critical reading will see as somehow residing in the poem, whether or not that value comes to be formulated in moral terms; the second is the value of the poem in affecting human conduct, which can be assessed objectively only by claiming the ability to estimate its probable effects, and so to nominate its probable audience. One is an 'aesthetic' question (though it is idle to delimit things in quite these terms); at least it is a question which arises of actual poems which one is confronting, and which remains focussed on them as its centre of interest. The other is a question of a nearly social kind. It is the first which normally concerns men who are enquiring into the relation of poetry with morality or values. The second is raised only by critics such as Arnold, critics with a moralistic and sociological bent; and I feel myself that it is an idle question. Arnold has a very strong and supple, though debatable, position on the question of poetic value; but he has a most exaggerated view of the value of poetry as (so to speak) a social agent. On this question, we need facts, not personal fantasy. Poetry does not do for the vast majority, nor has it done for centuries, what Arnold expects of it. His expectation could only be reasonable among a class of men who were as assured as he was of the primacy of moral conduct, and of the validity of the morals which they themselves espoused; and who were at the same time confident of the usefulness of poetry to 'make moral action perfect'.[1] It can no longer be a reasonable expectation *in those terms*; and that, not because morality is relative, but because the world has grown to a complexity in which it would appear

[1] *Essays Literary and Critical, op. cit.* p. 187

ludicrous to say 'Be good, sweet maid, and let who will be clever', and expect the injunction to have any effect at all.

The reference to a maxim is not as inappropriate here as it may seem. Leavis, for example, has said that the weakness in Arnold's moral grasp consists in its being the kind of morality which can be characterised by, and expressed in, maxims. And Arnold certainly has a weakness for maxims. It will be noticed that the lines which he offers as touchstones, in 'The Study of Poetry', have all a flavour of the maxim about them. And whereas he plainly regards them as being valuable because they are the summation of a rich moral wisdom, he equally plainly sees moral-poetic value as residing in them, their poetic value consisting in their worth as isolated moral utterances. This is a delicate matter, and one may not generalise too easily. But a comparison with Leavis himself may help to clarify it. Leavis also has a penchant for the representative passage, but he always justifies his detailed treatment of it on the grounds that it shows a 'localisation' of a strength with which the whole work is built or imbued. Arnold does not have this justification; he seems to regard each touchstone as valuable in itself, as consoling and delighting by its quality of utterance; and he is led, of course, to present it as valuable precisely because it is capable of being isolated in this way.

Confirmation is lent by an interesting passage in a very late book, *Discourses in America*:

> . . . art, and poetry, and eloquence, have in fact not only the power of refreshing and delighting us, they have also the power— such is the strength and worth, in essentials, of their authors' criticism of life—they have a fortifying, and elevating, and quickening, and suggestive power, capable of wonderfully helping us to relate the results of modern science to our need for conduct, our need for beauty.[1]

It is a curious passage. It is not often that the weakness in his position declares itself so openly as this. Not only art and poetry, but eloquence has these powers. And it is plain that Arnold is not referring to poetic eloquence, eloquence in poetry (which is often unjustly depreciated by modern critics), but to the

---

[1] *Discourses in America* (London, 1885), p. 123

eloquence of the pulpit or the Houses of Parliament. There is almost the suggestion that poetry is no more than a preaching, conceived in a very sophisticated manner. He cannot, of course, mean that; the whole bias of his writing is against it. But it is significant that, when he relaxes his critical terminology, it should be this association he lapses into.

The notions with which he is dealing are, as I have said, of a quasi-religious kind. We can expect 'moral deliverance' of poetry in something like the sense that religion is often thought of as giving deliverance not only from sin, but also from the cares of the world. And the close association of religion with morals in Arnold's writings has already been noticed: 'The paramount virtue of religion is, that it has *lighted up* morality'[1]; and religion is 'morality tinged with emotion'. These stresses mark a distinct weakness, a weakness that is closely connected with the tendency to rely on poetry, as on religion, for its senti-ment. But to give a quasi-religious status to the best poetry is, in fact, to beg the question of the relation between poetry and religion. It is, in an odd way, to devalue both, as Eliot sees very clearly. What *is* the possible relation between poetry and a religion which, being based on something more definite than a sense and sentiment of the numinous, touches life at many more points than the merely 'moral'? Arnold cannot answer, because such a religious conception is represented, not by his assumptions, but by traditional Christianity.

It is to be expected that his quasi-religious conception of poetry will reveal itself, further, in his attitude to religious poetry, to what most people would call a religious poetry. And it is equally to be expected that this, in turn, will reflect his conception of Christianity. His conception is given in a defini-tive passage in *Literature and Dogma*, which it is necessary to quote at length:

> Yes, the grandeur of Christianity, and the imposing and impressive attestation of it, if we could but worthily bring the thing out, is here: in that immense experimental proof of the necessity of it, which the whole course of the world has steadily accumulated, and indicates to us as still continuing and expanding. Men will not admit assumptions, the popular legend they call a

[1] *Essays Literary and Critical, op. cit.* p. 187

48

fairy-tale, the metaphysical demonstrations do not demonstrate, nothing but experimental proof will go down; and here is an experimental proof which never fails, and which at the same time is infinitely grander, by the vastness of its scale, the scope of its duration, the gravity of its results, than the machinery of the popular fairy-tale. Walking on the water, multiplying loaves, raising corpses, a heavenly judge appearing with trumpets in the clouds while we are yet alive,—what is this compared to the real experience offered as witness to us by Christianity? It is like the difference between the grandeur of the extravaganza and the grandeur of the sea or the sky,—immense objects which dwarf us, but where we are in contact with reality, and a reality of which we can slowly trace the laws.[1]

He is speaking of a genuine 'attestation'; but, from his description of it, the thing attested to need be no more Christianity than anything else. Of course, it is to Christianity that he is referring; because it is Christianity that he believes in. But his evocation of its spirit is as applicable to Buddhism or to Mohammedanism as to Christianity; and his pragmatic test of its *truth* could be as easily seized on by a Buddhist or a Muslim as by a Christian. Here is religion etherealised. It is such utterances as this which lead Burgum to say of him, 'the new interest in comparative religion . . . enabled him to say that Christianity was the true religion of nature'.[2] And what is the burden of this paragraph? It is that orthodox Christianity is artificial and (we are given a strong hint) ungentlemanly and even melodramatic. Even Arnold's visual imagination is dominated by his demand for moral sentiment, and by his repugnance for anything which does not present such a sentiment in a pure and uncomplicated form. That is why he prefers the explicitly grand sentiment of Wordsworth to the broader but more factual engagement of Chaucer's imagination. Both of these may be 'moral imaginations'; but one is a morality given through sentiment, the other

---

[1] *Literature and Dogma*, p. 372

It is interesting that Arnold's tone in his religious polemic is markedly different from that in his literary or social. In the latter, where the central issues are often fairly obvious, Arnold affects uncertainty, lack of competence, great urbanity, and an oblique irony. In the former, where the issues are actually very complicated and his definitions of them open to criticism at every point, he is aggressive, speaking with a somewhat hostile affectation of certainty, dull in his insistence, and at times tediously exasperating.

[2] E. B. Burgum, *op. cit.* pp. 92-3

is a morality given through a pattern of manners and a stable
underlying philosophical activity. That is also why the passages
he chooses from Dante are those in which an elevated *conclusion*
is announced.

It is the nature of his moral expectation of poetry that leads
him to a sympathy with writings which are, in the ordinary
sense, religious; a sympathy seen in the significantly entitled
essay, 'Pagan and Christian Religious Sentiment', in his comparison of the poetry of Theocritus with that of St Francis of
Assisi. In Theocritus, he says, we find nothing that is distinctively and explicitly religious; there is no spiritual comfort, no
religious sentiment of the expected kind. Yet there is something
nearly as good, and what there is can properly be called
religious. There is an ennobling symbolism to be drawn out
from the details of the Hymn to Adonis, which Arnold quotes;
and in the manner of its drawing out there is hope:

> Thus he [Adonis] became an emblem of the power of life and
> the bloom of beauty, the power of human life and the bloom of
> human beauty, hastening inevitably to diminution and decay,
> yet in that very decay finding 'Hope, and a renovation without
> end'.[1]

Rather, the point Arnold is concerned to make is that the
power of the Adonis-symbol to touch this quasi-religious
emotion is only imperfectly realised in the hymn as it stands.
It is not thoughtful enough, not inward; and so it is inadequate
as religious poetry. It does not have the power of true religious
consolation because it does not recognise those elements in
experience which make consolation necessary. The world with
which it deals, and to which it appeals, is too exclusively
sensuous. Therefore

> its natural end is in the sort of life which Pompeii and Hercul-
> aneum bring so vividly before us,—a life which by no means in
> itself suggests the thoughts of horror and misery, which even, in
> many ways, gratifies the senses and the understanding; but by the
> very intensity and unremittingness of its appeal to the senses and
> the understanding, by its stimulating a single side of us too
> absolutely, ends by fatiguing and revolting us; ends by leaving us

[1] *Essays Literary and Critical, op. cit.* p. 136

with a sense of tightness, of oppression,—with a desire for an utter change, for clouds, storms, effusion, and relief.[1]

It is, within its imaginative limits, a very fine piece of criticism: all the finer in that it maintains very delicately the balance needed to pass aptly between literature and life. But a certain weakness shows itself when Arnold goes on to speak of St Francis' 'Canticle of the Sun': very different qualities are to be found there from those characteristic of Theocritus. While Theocritus appeals to the senses, St Francis appeals to the heart and the imagination; Theocritus is 'outward, sensible', St Francis 'inward, symbolical'; one admits what is pleasurable, the other admits the poles of human experience, treated with 'spiritual emotion' and with love; the tradition of Theocritus is Epicurean, that of St Francis ascetic.

One may find, beneath his tender sympathy, something obtuse in this view. I don't suppose anyone would want to claim the Canticle as great poetry; it is not offered as such; poetically, it is a *jeu d'esprit*. But surely, in its way, it is as 'sensible' as the 'Hymn to Adonis', and a good deal more joyful. St Francis does not merely state the extremes of experience; he laughingly embraces them. At least, his attitude is one of laughter and embracing, though his poem is developed as a short litany, which does not pretend to develop a fully realised feeling for the world. Yet we may believe him to mean exactly what he says in his praise even of death:

> Praised be my Lord for our sister, the death of the body, from which no man escapeth.

To such an experience Arnold seems to me to be blind. St Francis' emphasis is, in a very real, a very Arnoldian sense, not 'moral' enough. It reaches too openly into the paradoxes of the human situation, and it rests there; it does not seek or induce consolation, because it is the product of a different kind of certainty. Arnold's approach will not admit this attitude. As he insists at the end of his essay, he prefers Sophocles to both Theocritus and St Francis; and it is the Sophocles whom he invokes in 'Dover Beach', the Arnoldian, the cheerfully stoic Sophocles, who satisfies both the 'thinking-power' and the

[1] *Ibid.* p. 137

'religious sense'. In other words, he is seen as the poet of a more elevated sentiment than Theocritus or St Francis can command —which, indeed, neither St Francis nor Theocritus would probably be much interested in.

Whatever Arnold's great delicacy, such an insistence on ennobling sentiment must appear repellently solemn. We have noted his obvious preference for Wordsworth over Chaucer; and it is significant that he finds also in Villon a kind of heightening, a seriousness, that he does not find in Chaucer. But where in Villon does he find it? In one of the most pathetic stanzas of 'La Belle Heaulmiere'. The Villon he prefers to Chaucer is the Villon of a heightened pathos. In fact, Arnold's feeling for 'high seriousness', the feeling which makes him put the moral sentiments of Sophocles above the hymns of Theocritus and St Francis, seems often a feeling for what we might call a sad magnanimity, a composed sense of the finality (not, of course, the uselessness) of human experience. Chaucer does not possess this note at all; he is too genial, even casual, in his sense of human limitations.

In other words, while seeing the dangers in the naturalism of Theocritus, Arnold implicitly criticises the religious feelings of St Francis and Chaucer by comparison with the naturalism of Sophocles and Villon respectively. In each implied comparison, the standard is not a whole work, but a short fragment, a fragment in which the ennobling sentiment is seen to reside. And it is a distinctive, even a peculiar naturalism, a naturalism which is bent on moralising about life in general.

This indicates another trait of his criticism. As both poet and critic, Arnold is in a sense too much of his age. His first great claim for the moral reality and value of poetry is that it deals with a subject that is either explicitly moral (the inner life of man and the laws of his nature), or implicitly moral (the life of Nature). His second claim is that, whatever the subject, poetry is moral in the manner of its contact with that subject. Consequently, he is involved in saying that poetry is valuable because it is in some way *true*. I shall take up this question in the next essay; here it is appropriate to say that he nowhere justifies, or even indicates the nature of, his claim. Whenever the question arises, he slides rapidly into a consideration of the *effects* of poetry, and he consistently confuses the thing with its effects. This is consistent, in a way, since he is, almost despite himself, a sort of pragmatist. He would judge the truth of poetry, just as he would judge the truth of Christianity, by its inward effects, its power to stabilise man and fit him for moral action in the world. Such a view is obviously unsatisfactory beyond a certain point. It is too subjective, and it is too narrow. His grasp of poetry is in terms of a sort of religion; his grasp of religion is in terms of moral effectiveness; his grasp of moral effectiveness is in terms of sentiment, and of the power of sentiment to ennoble or console. He is an odd critic: a great critic whose chief terms run over into one another, and persuade by their very confusion.

CHAPTER III

Matthew Arnold: Poetry, Ideas, and the Age

A<small>RNOLD</small> is no more interested than are the modern critics I am considering in writing a treatise on the value of poetry or on poetic values. He is a practising critic, with a variety of approaches to his central concern; and that concern shows itself not as a fully formulated doctrine but as a constant preoccupation, held with the utmost intelligence and sensitivity. The same is true of Leavis and Eliot. They hold their views in as personal a way as it is possible to hold them, but they do so with as great an objectivity as they can. All three of them work towards the greatest degree of impersonality consistent with an inward, personal engagement with the real issues. And Arnold can be more naturally associated with Leavis and Eliot than with the majority of the critics who preceded him. He is a recognisably modern critic in a sense in which Dr Johnson, for example, was not, and in which even Coleridge was not fully modern. This modernity consists largely in what we may call his representative self-consciousness, in his sense of the age in which he lives as an age both special and historically important. Most sensitively alert men develop this sense when they live in the kind of age which is loosely known as transitional. Arnold has it in a high degree, and is anxious to estimate and represent the spirit of his age, the *Zeitgeist*. In this he is a Romantic; his Romantic apprehension of and concern with the *Zeitgeist* makes of course against provincialism, for it involves a broad and noble desire to derive important ideas from every available source, not to remain content with old forms of thinking and of social organisation, and to co-operate, as it were, with history in making truth effective.

All this is trite enough, when it is stated so baldly; accounts of the nineteenth century are full of this kind of analysis; and I remark this quality here not only because of the positive

MATTHEW ARNOLD: POETRY, IDEAS, AGE

formulations to which it drives men like Arnold, but also because of its limitations. It generates, in a curious way, a provincialism of its own, a provincialism not of place but of time. Arnold is too avidly of his time, as his generalisations about religion show so clearly. Whereas he hits justly and spiritedly at the provincialism of contemporary England, the provincialism which is really middle-class insularity, he is nevertheless provincial in his own thought in a different way. I have already commented on his deficiency in metaphysical awareness, his reluctance to raise, at any but a social level, the deepest issues of human life as they are represented in poetry. But the deficiency also shows itself in his actual placing of poets. His famous judgment on Pope and Dryden, that they are 'classics of our prose', and that they attempt to compose 'in their wits' that genuine poetry which can only be composed 'in the soul', has become notorious to an age like our own which has a good deal more to learn from Pope than from Gray.[1] Then, the list which he gives of the chief English poets of three hundred years is a significantly anomalous one. It includes Gray and Goldsmith, Cowper and Scott and Campbell, but it makes no mention of Dunbar or Donne, Ben Jonson or Marvell, Blake or Christopher Smart.[2] To have made precisely those inclusions, precisely those omissions, is to have been, and in a limiting sense, too much of the age. Living so intensely in the historical present, Arnold lives too exclusively in it, and he reinforces it too eagerly with the stoic past. Thus he says of Wordsworth:

> ... then we understand what constitutes a European recognition of poets and poetry as contradistinguished from a merely national recognition, and that in favour both of Milton and of Shakespeare the judgement of the high court of appeal has finally gone.[3]

Here it is the appeal to the *finality* of the present which is slightly alarming, while in the case of his list of poets it is the complacent use of the conventional evaluations of the present. In both cases, the note of provincialism is faintly but unmistakably sounded; and it is the result of the intensity of

[1] *Essays in Criticism*, Second Series, *op. cit.* pp. 24 and 56-7
[2] *Ibid.* p. 79   [3] *Ibid.* p. 78

Arnold's attempt to engage with the historical present and to win its meaning. Arnold the progressivist is here in evidence.

These elements in his critical thinking have, therefore, a negative side; but it is more than compensated for by the alertness, the positive sense of life and hope, which his historical intelligence leads to. In an age such as that which Arnold inhabited, and which he was unusually aware of inhabiting, it is necessary for the critic to think more critically and clearly than ever; and it is necessary for the poet to have a highly developed critical apprehension of his work.[1] Arnold's awareness of the needs of the age makes him a modern.

It does not make him what is often called an intellectual, and sometimes an 'intellectualist', or even an 'egghead'. The misconception, however, is often made. If one of the commoner mistakes is to regard him as merely a romantic, involved in a dream of restoring the world's lost innocence through a fusion of elevating sentiment with the fervent dutifulness of Rugby, it is a mistake hardly less common to see him as an intellectual relying on poetry to solve, in more or less abstract terms, the problems of the age. Certainly, as we shall see, he regards poetry as confronting a world of ideas; and he sees those ideas springing up from the meeting of alive modern minds with the problems of a specific age. But he does not regard poetry as solving intellectual problems, or even as directly confronting them. His famous reproof to Clough is relevant here:

> to *solve* the Universe as you try to do is as irritating as Tennyson's dawdling with its painted shell is fatiguing to me to witness . . .[2]

and

> but you know that you are a mere d—d depth hunter in poetry and therefore exclusive furiously. You might write a speech in Phèdre—Phedra loquitur—but you could not write Phèdre.[3]

These judgments are from a very early stage of Arnold's literary life, but the great movement of his criticism shows that

---

[1] The essay, 'The Function of Criticism at the Present Time', is a masterly elaboration of these related points.
[2] *Letters to A. H. Clough, op. cit.* p. 63: Letter of 1847
[3] *Ibid.* Letter of May 24, 1848, p. 81

he has never revoked them. He is not an intellectual at all in the Clough sense; nor is he an intellectual in the sense in which Eliot is one; he is driven by no urge to formulate analyses and account for causes; his is not an analytical mind in any full sense; and consequently he does not ask poetry for an *analysis* of society, or an assignment of philosophic and social causes. On the contrary, he is concerned to get people to see the virtue of one central insight into the world, and to see the value of poetry as the best pledge of that insight. That insight is one which demands, in Arnold's formulation of it, to be expressed in terms of sentiment rather than of philosophical analysis. Certainly he finds the universe recalcitrant to his moral sense as also to his imagination.[1] Certainly, too, he sees poetry in the elevated style as a way of transcending, or even of evading, this recalcitrance. But poetry is valuable to him largely because it turns insight into animating sentiment.

The mention of insight brings up the rôle of ideas in poetry, and Arnold's view of poetry as somehow representing the best ideas of the age. His two important essays, 'The Function of Criticism at the Present Time' and 'On the Modern Element in Literature', give us his view. He sees poetry in certain eras as having a special task, that of stabilising and advancing contemporary insight into the significance of a contemporary situation. Such a poetry would need to have special qualities, to be 'modern' in a profound sense; and it would need, as the condition of its 'adequacy' (an important word for Arnold), special qualities of alertness and strength in the characters of its authors. Here is the didactic strain in Arnold's thinking coming out in a very subtle form; it is a didacticism not of the traditional moralist but of the social evolutionist.

We have already seen him criticised for the belief that a poetry which deals with life, life in its deepest reality, is a poetry which deals with moral ideas. Now, in 'The Function of Criticism', we find the remark clarified and justified: poetry deals with moral ideas not directly, as though they were debatable judgments or mere counters of abstract intercourse, but in their social aspect, as an animating atmosphere in which the

---

[1] Vide, in this connection, an interesting comment by G. H. Bantock: *Scrutiny*, Vol. XVIII, No. 1, pp. 39-40.

poet is stimulated to focus his attention on his primary subjects, the life of man and the life of nature:

> Now in literature, . . . the elements with which the creative power works are ideas; the best ideas on every matter which literature touches, current at the time; at any rate we may lay it down as certain that in modern literature no manifestation of the creative power not working with these can be very important or fruitful. And I say *current* at the time, not merely accessible at the time; for creative literary genius does not principally show itself in discovering new ideas, that is rather the business of the philosopher; the grand work of literary genius is a work of synthesis and exposition, not of analysis and discovery; its gift lies in the faculty of being happily inspired by a certain intellectual and spiritual atmosphere, by a certain order of ideas, when it finds itself in them; of dealing divinely with these ideas, presenting them in the most effective and attractive combinations; making beautiful works with them, in short. But it must have the atmosphere, it must find itself amidst the order of ideas, in order to work freely; and these it is not so easy to command. This is why great creative epochs in literature are so rare. . . .[1]

Two points in this passage may be assented to at once: the notion that a poet in a complex age can be an important poet only if he is alert and responsive to that complexity and its causes; and the notion that where that complexity is the result of a people's growth in social and spiritual energy, it can be a stimulation, a help to the poet, rather than a hindrance. But Arnold makes the poet sound like a privileged sponger on the fortuitous bounty of other men's thought, or like a middleman between 'advanced' philosophers and a public which would otherwise prove impervious to them. As I say, there is a curious sort of provincialism here; and a man of our own day might well enquire of those 'best ideas' whether they are *true* as well as stimulating for poetry. Arnold has not made himself clear; and the reason, I think, is that he does not know precisely what it is he wants. He wants modernity, a fully modern responsiveness; but just how that is to manifest itself in the stimulating of poetry through contemporary thought, he cannot say. Nor does he appear certain whether or not he wants to apply his notion of modernity as a criterion for judging the works of all ages. He

[1] *Essays Literary and Critical, op. cit.* p. 3

sees the Greece of Sophocles, and the England of Shakespeare, permeated with thought in this way. But what of the England of Chaucer, the France of Racine, the England of the later eighteenth century? And why, we may ask, is it necessary to define this stimulation in terms of *ideas*? As soon as you choose to do that, you are necessarily involved in questions of truth. Arnold, of course, is intimately concerned, here as elsewhere, with the advancement of truth. But he often seems to find it quite as persuasive, and a great deal easier, to develop his case in terms of modernity rather than of truth.

We are brought back to the word 'life'. In being concerned with the modernity of ideas, and shying off the question of their truth, Arnold is really paying tribute to their freshness, their life. And his insistence on 'ideas' is valuable if we take him to mean that any poetry cannot be adequate for its age unless it has the vigour which comes from the existence in the age of fresh and lively ideas. For this life to be realised in poetry it is necessary for society to have accepted the ideas at a mature level, and for the poet to be inwardly ready for them. So Arnold charges the English Romantics with being, in their inward grasp of their personal experience, unready for the task of converting contemporary ideas into poetry. They were not ready, and the age was not ready. Consequently, they were lacking both in the material and in the stimulation which a fully awake society provides for the poet; and 'a thorough inter-pretation of the world was necessarily denied to it'.[1]

The English Romantics lacked an intellectually mature world, and they lacked a sufficiently mature personal experience of their world in terms of ideas. These were the opportunities which Goethe had pre-eminently:

> ... the grand business of modern poetry—a moral interpreta-tion, from an independent point of view, of man and the world—it is only German poetry, Goethe's poetry, that has, since the Greeks, made much way with.[2]

And

> Goethe's task was—the inevitable task for the modern poet henceforth is—as it was for the Greek poet in the days of Pericles,

[1] *Ibid.* pp. 4-6. The relevant passage is far too long to quote in full, and it cannot be quoted at lesser length without distortion.
[2] *On the Study of Celtic Literature* (Everyman's Library edition), p. 128

not to preach a sublime sermon on a given text like Dante, not to exhibit all the kingdoms of human life and the glory of them like Shakespeare, but to interpret human life afresh and to supply a new spiritual basis to it.[1]

Very few people nowadays would be so optimistic, so irresponsibly optimistic, as to expect poetry to 'supply a new spiritual basis' to human life; but this is the sort of position to which a writer may be driven in following out the logic of demanding not only a poetry adequate to its age (as Dante's and Shakespeare's surely were) but a poetry whose adequacy comes from dealing with ideas 'from an independent point of view'. And, again, what Arnold demands is that the point of view be independent, not that it be true. It is very hard to disentangle the positive insights from the provincial confusions in these passages. Generally, Arnold seems to want the modern poet to use ideas, to be stimulated by them, rather than—as he puts it himself—to 'discover' them. But here, with his emphasis on 'an independent point of view', he seems to expect poets to be their own philosophers, and original ones at that; for surely there is an important sense in which all good poetry is the expression of 'an independent point of view', and that is a sense which Arnold plainly intends to surpass.

But a later essay gives us a hint that the difficulty with these passages comes chiefly from the peculiar nature of his attachment to Goethe, and not from an irremediable confusion in his attitude. His gratitude to Goethe as a 'liberator' is so great that it tends to become confused with a judgment on Goethe's greatness as a poet. In 'A French Critic on Goethe', we find that 'Goethe is the greatest poet of modern times' because he is 'in the width, depth, and richness of his criticism of life, by far our greatest modern man'.[2] Goethe is 'the clearest, the largest, the most helpful thinker of modern times.'

I cannot help finding this very odd. It is the tendency to think in maxims appearing again, but on a new level. Goethe is seen as a sage, a liberator, a poetic philosopher, the archetypal modern man. And Arnold is content to rely on the asser-

---

[1] *On the Study of Celtic Literature* (Everyman's Library edition), p. 130. These two quotations practically summarise the whole intention of that other essay of Arnold's, 'On the Modern Element in Literature'.

[2] *Mixed Essays* (1880 edition), pp. 311-12

tion of these qualities in representing him as a great poet; he never once shows us how this sagacity, freedom, philosophy, representativeness, are made *actual* in poetry. It is, in a way, a literary-critical judgment; but it is made in such a way as to raise a literary issue the relevance of which Arnold seems to see only in the vaguest terms.

But he is interested in affirming whatever in modern poetry is capable of liberating man from the deadness of 'routine thinking'. So he presents Heine as, after Goethe, the most important liberator of the century; and it is in his treatment of Heine that the dual nature of his interest comes out; it is an interest in 'intellectual deliverance' and in 'moral deliverance' together. It is true that an intellectual deliverance is, in a sense, moral, in that it frees man from the routine thinking which tends to deaden him for perfect moral action. But Arnold can never get far away from his own didactic tendency; he wants poetry to free man in a more direct way as well—to free his sympathies, his moral feeling. Heine, while being a great intellectual liberator, does not offer 'moral deliverance'.[1] He cannot offer it, because he is lacking in 'self-respect, in true dignity of character'.

Here is a typically Arnoldian stress which I shall want to consider later. At the moment, it is more important to try to make sense of his view of ideas in poetry. One of the most interesting things in the essay on Heine is the criticism of the English Romantics for their comparative lack of modernity, their failure, partly because of a lack in society, partly because of a lack in themselves, to 'apply the modern spirit'. The result is a kind of spiritual and moral immaturity which can be traced in their works as well as in their lives: a tendency to be over-whelmed by the world, to fail to *master* it, or to withdraw from it.

What, in fact, was the career of the chief English men of letters, their contemporaries? The greatest of them, Wordsworth, retired (in Middle-Age phrase) into a monastery. I mean, he plunged himself in the inward life, he voluntarily cut himself off from the modern spirit. Coleridge took to opium, Scott became the historiographer-royal of feudalism. Keats passionately gave himself up to a sensuous genius, to his faculty for interpreting nature;

[1] *Essays Literary and Critical, op. cit.* p. 125

61

and he died of consumption at twenty-five. Wordsworth, Scott and Keats have left admirable works; far more solid and complete works than those which Byron and Shelley have left. But their works have this defect,—they do not belong to that which is the main current of the literature of modern epochs, they do not apply modern ideas to life; they constitute, therefore, *minor currents*, and all other literary work of our day, however popular, which has the same defect, also constitutes but a minor current.[1]

Now, this is in direct contradiction to Arnold's later estimate of Wordsworth, in which he applies a criterion of value which is of a directly aesthetic-moral kind, of a kind which I looked at in the last chapter. You cannot use two criteria which lead to conflicting results in your estimate of the one poet. Wordsworth is either of pre-eminent value, or he is not. But Arnold developing a general case is always very much Arnold the advocate, the sophisticated and self-convinced barrister of literature. And he is concerned, at the moment, to contrast the relative unreadiness of the English Romantics to the modernity of Heine:

> Heine's intense modernism, his absolute freedom, his bitter rejection of stock classicism and stock romanticism, his bringing all things under the point of view of the nineteenth century, were understood and laid to heart by Germany, through virtue of her immense, tolerant intellectualism, much as there was in all Heine said to affront and wound Germany.[2]

But he does not offer moral deliverance.

It is an impressive conception of the necessity for a new freshness, a new responsiveness, a new intellectual vigour, in modern poetry; but not only can it not be used as a criterion for the judgment of *all* poetry (as Arnold's own critical practice testifies), it does not recommend itself as an analysis in these terms. A modern responsiveness seems to me to have less to do with the *modernity* of *ideas* than Arnold will admit. And he presses so strongly for his own conception because he is so concerned to press a view of the relation of poetry to society, and of the inner integrity of the poet which becomes more than usually necessary in a complex transitional age. There is in it, too, a personal drive towards a kind of contemplative detachment from the spectacle of life, a spectacle which otherwise would

---

[1] *Essays Literary and Critical, op. cit.* pp. 115-16   [2] *Ibid.* p. 116

prove oppressive and imaginatively unmanageable. All of these facets are more or less in keeping with the aspects of his thought which I have outlined in the previous chapter; but there is a certain amount of confusion, and even of contradiction; Arnold is a much more complex literary personality than has often been recognised.

Nevertheless, the driving interest, in his discussion of the rôle of ideas as in his discussion of the healing and animating spiritual influences of poetry, runs towards the necessity of serenity, detachment, freedom in the contemplation of human destiny. It is in the achievement of some such state that Arnold sees man's readiness for perfect moral action. Moral and intellectual deliverance come, in the finest poetry, to the same thing. He recognises this in his discussion of modernity, in 'On the Modern Element in Literature':

> An intellectual deliverance is the peculiar demand of those ages which are called modern. . . .
> But first let us ask ourselves why the demand for an intellectual deliverance arises in such an age as the present, and in what the deliverance itself consists? The demand arises, because our present age has around it a copious and complex present, and behind it a copious and complex past; it arises, because the present age exhibits to the individual man who contemplates it the spectacle of a vast multitude of facts awaiting and inviting his comprehension. The deliverance consists in man's comprehension of this present and past. It begins when our mind begins to enter into possession of the general ideas which are the law of this vast multitude of facts. It is perfect when we have acquired that harmonious acquiescence of mind which we feel in contemplating a grand spectacle that is intelligible to us. . . .[1]

The whole work of this comprehension does not, of course, devolve upon the poet; he is, in a sense, the servant of 'current' ideas as well as their controller; we have seen this already. But the work of reconciling man to the universe becomes here the work of reconciling him, in a serene and detached understanding, to the movements of his contemporary society. It is still a moral task, in the distinctively Arnoldian sense which I have noted. However, as we see in the case of Goethe, it is

[1] *Essays* (Oxford University Press, 1914), pp. 455-6

possible for him, in developing this particular aspect of his critical position, to confuse poetic greatness with greatness as a sort of practical moral philosopher. And this in the midst of his heartening returns to such words and phrases as 'instructive fulness of experience', 'life', 'development', 'vigour', and of his outright rejection of ennui and overweening depression in literature as elements which make against vitality, both in literature and in life. Lucretius is thus seen as inadequate to a 'modern' age because of the strain of morbidity and defeat in him.[1]

The whole essay deals with poetry as the finest interpreter of an age; it interprets through grasping the central problem of that age, and through employing all possible human energies as agents of that interpretation. It is an interpretation of society, not in any narrow sense, but in the sense of historical forces working on society in the shape either of ideas or of aspiring energies. So it comes to be an interpretation of the nature and needs of man as a given age reveals them.

To our contemporaries, such an analysis may seem vague and naïve to the point of wilfulness. But if a man chooses to speak of this subject at all, how can he escape being vague? Arnold's attitude arises, after all, from his intimate personal sense of the complexity and needs of the age; and his expression of it is plainly intended, not to produce a logically perfect thesis, but to persuade his readers of the greatness of their own age, both in its tasks and its possibilities. He is trying to stimulate an attitude of mind, and it is the attitude which is important. On this question, he stands, I suppose, on the opposite side to Eliot; but, though he often seems rather callow compared with Eliot, he is here on the right side. His attempts to deal with the question of a 'true point of view' from which to contemplate the spectacle of modern life get nowhere. But the attitude he is trying to inculcate is a valuable one. And it is fairly closely in harmony with his view of the moral reality of poetry, announced elsewhere. The intellectualism which he seems to press for has a non-intellectual root and effect; the detachment which he recommends is a contemplative detachment which is in itself a readiness for moral action.

[1] *Essays op. cit.* p. 469

The real force of his view, the constant stress, is seen if we complete the foregoing analysis with his remarks about Leopardi, Byron, and Wordsworth. It is precisely in the 'sure and firm touch of the true artist', and in intellectual clarity and maturity, that Leopardi is seen to surpass Byron, and even Wordsworth:

> ... he has a grave fulness of knowledge, an insight into the real bearings of the questions which as a sceptical poet he raises, a power of seizing the real point, a lucidity, with which the author of *Cain* has nothing to compare.

Yet he is deficient in energy, compared with Byron; and, compared with Wordsworth, he is deficient in joy, in hope:

> But as compared with Leopardi, Wordsworth, though at many points less lucid, though far less a master of style, far less of an artist, gains so much by his criticism of life being, in certain matters of profound importance, healthful and true, whereas Leopardi's pessimism is not, that the value of Wordsworth's poetry, on the whole, stands higher for us than that of Leopardi's, as it stands higher for us, I think, than that of any modern poetry except Goethe's.[1]

There is a certain sleight-of-hand here, in the rapid and persuasive linking of 'healthful' and 'true'. And I feel, as so often with Arnold, that the true is seen as a consequence of the healthful, and not the other way round. The pragmatic moralist is at work, not the sternly scientific observer of contemporary currents, not the dedicated philosopher trying to wrest from an historical era the understanding of its laws. By what criterion could Arnold decide that Leopardi's *criticism of life* is less true than Wordsworth's? He offers none, and I think he could offer none. The sense in which 'true' is used is, it seems to me, an utterly pragmatic one. Leopardi is less 'true' because he has the inferior effect upon the reader. He does not stimulate the best sentiments, does not conduce to a state of mind in which there is a readiness for virtuous action and a desire to make that action perfect.

And the question of 'modernity' is, in effect, jettisoned. When it comes to an assessment of the worth of most poets,

---

[1] *Essays in Criticism*, Second Series, *op. cit.* pp. 111-14

even contemporary poets, Arnold cannot use it to any purpose. What he is after, in his talk about intellectual deliverance, is the release of a current of ideas which can stimulate a current of sentiment and sympathy—the *right kind* of sentiment and sympathy. Intellectual deliverance and moral deliverance lead eventually to the same result. But they lead there only when the intellectual encourages and fosters the moral deliverance. And the estimate of Goethe is not so much that he is a great modern thinker, but that he is a thinker-poet whose work is healing, healthful, for a modern age. It is in that sense that he is adequate and Leopardi is not. And, when all is said and done, Arnold does see Wordsworth as being in the major current of the age: at least, in the current which Arnold, with his constant moral preoccupation, really regards as major.[1]

This interpretation of Arnold's position is confirmed time and time again in his writings, by open statements, habitual stresses, uses of phrase. It is seen as early as 1848, when his reference to '*an* Idea of the world' shows what he is after. The much later phrase '*the* true point of view', with the definite article unobtrusively guiding the tone of the discussion, is simply a sign that Arnold has himself come in the meantime to fix on the attitudes which appear to him 'healthful' for the modern age. And they are attitudes, not ideas in any very definite sense of that word. So he writes to Clough:

> They will not be patient neither understand that they must begin with an Idea of the world, in order not to be prevailed over by the world's multitudinousness; or if they cannot get that, at least with isolated ideas: and all other things shall (perhaps) be added unto them.[2]

What he here calls 'an Idea of the world' seems to be very nearly what some critics of our own day prefer to call a 'myth'. It is a structure of belief or of imaginative attitude by reference to which the experience of an individual or a people is seen as patterned and significant. Our contemporary critics, it is true,

---

[1] v. J. B. Orrick, *op. cit.* p. 30

Goethe is a 'dissolvent', whose work stimulates the reader to attain a full and easeful personality in a schizoid and rapidly changing world. He interprets the facts of the world in such a way as not so much to falsify them but to draw consolation from them.

[2] *Letters to A. H. Clough, op. cit.* p. 97: Letter of after Sept. 1848-9

are generally individualistic in their demand for it: or, at least, they demand it for the sake of 'the poet', so that he may have a centre of significance for his writing. And that, too, seems to be Arnold's emphasis, at an early stage of his thinking. Later, as I say, his view becomes more stable and assured through his mature conviction of the moral reality of poetry, a conviction which comes very largely from his view of the moral effects of poetry.

The rôle of society in the stimulation of poetry has been mentioned. It is a point on which Arnold is rather indefinite (as he can't help being); and he seems, in any case, reluctant to insist on it. But, such as it is, it is one side of the coin of which his view of the *inwardness* of the poet is the other. Arnold's view of society is in some sense an organic one; and his analysis of the relation of poetry to society always includes a sharp sense of the way in which society affects the individual: not externally, by a merely mechanical process or set of pressures, but interiorly, in the individual's sensibility as well as his character and intelligence.

The social orientation of his criticism has always been recognised. Twenty years ago, his name was often invoked in support of one side—the Marxist or quasi-Marxist side—in the literary controversies of the day. He was invoked because he had said that poetry was a 'criticism of life'; and because of his social leanings, he was assumed to have meant that it was a critical analysis of society. It was a gross misreading, both because Arnold's 'criticism' means nothing approaching that conception at all, and because he stands, if anywhere, on the opposite side of that controversy—on the side of individual perfection leading to social justice. I have already quoted the passage in 'The Function of Criticism at the Present Time', in which he speaks of poetry as having its unique contact with life through the use of ideas, modern ideas. There, he says

> the grand work of literary genius is a work of synthesis and exposition, not of analysis and discovery; its gift lies in the faculty of being happily inspired by a certain intellectual and spiritual atmosphere. . . . But it must have the atmosphere, it must find itself amidst the order of ideas, in order to work freely. . . .[1]

[1] *Essays Literary and Critical, op. cit.* p. 3

That atmosphere, that order of ideas, is patently a social thing; it is society under one of its aspects, its aspect of a spiritual commonwealth. We know that Arnold holds poetry to have the effect of helping to purify society by purifying the sensibilities of those men who are, in reality, the leaders of society, who are men of affairs and who engage most intensively in moral action. It is a semi-Platonic idea. And we know that he sees society under its aspect of a spiritual commonwealth rather than an economic one. Consequently, a concern for poetry is also a concern for society, and a concern for society a concern for poetry. We may expect Arnold to be interested in analysing society to see what it can offer the poet in the way of stimulating influences, which he calls an atmosphere, an order of ideas. So we get the idea that poets can work at their highest pitch only when the 'spiritual atmosphere' of society is favourable, as it was in Elizabethan England, in the Germany of Goethe, and, above all, in the Greece of Sophocles. A body of poetry can be 'adequate' to represent and interpret its society only when that society is adequate in its interpretation and representation of the nature of man.

This is a generalisation with which most modern critics would agree, in a loose way. But, as it bears on the moral reality of poetry, it can be treated only in an empirical way; and we lack the kind of experience of most past societies which would enable us to make with any confidence an empirical analysis. Many statements about Elizabethan society, for example, contain a wistful and rather question-begging note. And if we want to reach a conclusion about the spiritual energies of Elizabethan England, we can do so largely through a grasp of Elizabethan poetry. The reasoning tends to be circular, and it is a field of enquiry in which it is possible to talk a great deal of nonsense. Arnold does not. He treats the whole question by estimating what disabling effects are had on the range and quality of a poet's work by its being composed in a plainly limited society. So he says of Burns, in 'The Study of Poetry', that he suffers from a different defect from that which limited Dryden and Pope. They lived in an 'age of prose', in a society which needed for its stabilisation the virtues of, as it were, prose thinking, not of poetic exaltation. Burns, on the other hand, suffered from a defect of 'substance', deriving from a deficiency in the world which provided his subject-matter. He suffered from the crudity of the actual social world he inhabited, and which came quite naturally to inhabit his poetry:

> But this world of Scotch drink, Scotch religion, and Scotch manners is against a poet, not for him, when it is not a partial countryman who reads him; for in itself it is not a beautiful world, and no one can deny that it is of advantage to a poet to deal with a beautiful world; Burns's world of Scotch drink, Scotch religion, and Scotch manners, is often a harsh, a sordid, a repulsive world; even the world of his *Cottar's Saturday Night* is not a beautiful world.[1]

The word 'beautiful' has an unsettling effect. But this is not a mere aberration on Arnold's part, a wandering of his attention or wavering of his pen. Nor is he making the irritating suggestion, which we have met so often, that there are certain things which are 'unpoetical', which cannot be mentioned in poetry. It is true that, in the 1853 Preface to his poems, he presses a view of the intrinsically poetic nature of some subjects in poetry; but we can regard that essay as marginal to his work, and a piece of specious self-defence. What he is more usually concerned with, what he is concerned with here, is the necessity of getting a point of view above the chaos of life, an elevated insight into it. And his complaint against the Ayrshire of Burns amounts to a complaint that it could not assist the poet to get such a point of view from which to interpret it, to make his 'criticism of life'.

Yet we may ask in what way Burns' world was insufficient, and in what way it was too repulsive to be represented in great poetry. Burns was not a social realist, and it may seem that the condition of his social world is irrelevant to the quality of his poetry. It may also be that Arnold's phrasing is seriously at fault, that the terms in which he puts his position, and in which we are forced to pose our questions, prejudice the answers. Eliot flatly denies the whole position: 'is it so important', he asks ironically, 'for the poet' to deal with a beautiful world? Beauty in society, or so he seems to be suggesting, merely serves

---

[1] *Essays in Criticism*, Second Series, *op. cit.* p. 26

to hide the metaphysical tensions in the lives of the people who live in it.

Eliot may well be right, but it seems to me that he is not engaging Arnold's real position at all. They are speaking of utterly different things. And an answer to the dilemma which Arnold raises must be attempted, for he is making an important criticism, a criticism which gives point to the analysis of English society undertaken in *Culture and Anarchy* and *Friendship's Garland*. We can see that in those works he is making a reservation about that society from the point of view of the poet as well as from that of the man of general culture.

The answer is this: that the aspirations and values of society are expressed in its 'manners', in a visible pattern of action, preoccupation, and desire; and that the poet, in attempting to penetrate to the hidden aspirations, must take account of the overt manners, and must indeed use them as in some sense his sensible medium. It is from them that he will draw much of the imagery, much of the local detail of his poetry; it is from them that he will draw much of the emphasis, the body, which gives his poetic speech a distinctive quality. And, of course, in them he will find his image of human destiny. Arnold is here being very like Yeats. Yeats' predilection for the Irish landed gentry was due not to their open political rôle in an unstable society, but to the way in which the rhythm of their life established a pattern of manners in itself stable and stabilising: in itself fit to be reflected in poetry of the most exalted kind.

It is a question of *manners*, not of any vague surface loveliness. In criticising Burns, Arnold is acting not as a sociologist of a somewhat priggish kind, but as a literary critic in the strict sense. He is noticing the local detail of Burns' poetry, estimating the degree to which it constitutes a poetic world, and attributing its crudities to the real world which it so obviously expresses. There is no more involved than that; and that seems to be an eminently sensible exercise of the critical habit.

Arnold's view is more robust and satisfying than he perhaps realised himself. The rôle of society in the generation of poetry is not merely the provision of a current of ideas, but is also something of a more direct, a more *sensible* kind. For the ideas, as we see in 'On the Modern Element in Literature', come themselves to take a palpable form, to exist in society as a pattern of manners as well as an order of ideas. It is a *medium* of living and behaviour as well as of ideas; and it is significant that the word 'medium' should have been used at all.

> Burns is a beast, with splendid gleams, and the medium in which he lived, Scotch peasants, Scotch Presbyterianism, and Scotch drink, is repulsive. . . .[1]

Living in such a society, Burns could not attain the point of view, the elevated yet concerned detachment, which would lead to a 'criticism of life' of the highest kind. He could not produce, under those conditions of the imagination, a poetry which would in the full sense console and inspirit the reader. It is not that he could not, or that a poet in a similar circumstance cannot, write good poetry; but it would be only by transcending the limitations of his world that he could do so. And he transcends those limitations by bringing into poetry his inner integrity as a man, by realising and representing in poetry his 'genuine self'. Burns does so at times:

> No doubt a poet's criticism of life may have such truth and power that it triumphs over its world and delights us. Burns may triumph over this world, often he does triumph over his world. . . .[2]

But he triumphs over his world only at times, and then not in the passages which his admirers laud most fervently. The obstacles of his environment have been too big for consistent poetic greatness.

Our experience of poetry, and of the conditions under which it is produced, would seem to bear out Arnold's contention, though the matter is probably more complex than he would allow. On Arnold's own showing, the substance of a poet's work is life and ideas—life as interpreted and evaluated through the focussed lens of ideas; and both life and ideas are available to the poet generally in a social form, as his society shapes and mediates them. And he cannot, with full imaginative power and insight, reach the 'great primary human affections', the laws of human nature, if they are not adequately represented to him by his society.

[1] *Letters, op. cit.* Vol. II, p. 184: Letter to Miss Arnold, Nov. 1880
[2] *Essays in Criticism*, Second Series, *op. cit.* p. 26

Rather, if his society is inadequate, and if he is great enough, he can reach them as they exist in himself. The quality which enables him to 'triumph over his world', the transcendent quality, is a quality of his own interior life. It is an elusive quality. It is not simply poetic or personal energy; it is not simply intelligence; it is not simply goodness in the ordinary sense. Yet it is energetic, and intelligent, and above all moral. We might call it genius under its moral aspect. It is not an attribute of personality, in the sense in which personality is the man as his friends and biographers love to reveal him. It is an attribute of something deeper in him. Arnold calls it by various names. It is 'sincerity'; it is 'high seriousness'; it is a 'voice from the very inmost soul of the genuine (man)': and when the poet does not speak to us with his real, his deepest voice, there is bound to be something 'poetically unsound' in his work. He will not merely miss the accent of the greatest poetry, the 'accent of high seriousness'; he will also introduce into his work touches or notes—of bravado, or hectoring, or preaching, or sentimentality—which ring false, muffle his general tone, and deflect the reader's attention from what is potentially healing and morally stimulating in his meaning. But when the poet holds these virtues, the most profound virtues of his own being, apart from the limitations of his society, he can use them to triumph over those limitations:

> The world of Chaucer is fairer, richer, more significant than that of Burns; but when the largeness and freedom of Burns get full sweep, as in 'Tam o' Shanter', or still more in that puissant and splendid production, 'The Jolly Beggars', his world may be what it will, his poetic genius triumphs over it. In the world of 'The Jolly Beggars' there is more than hideousness and squalor, there is bestiality; yet the piece is a superb poetic success. It has a breadth, truth and power . . . here we have the genuine Burns. . . .[1]

Of course, Arnold is not postulating any essential opposition between the poet and society, an opposition which has been dearly held by many writers in the past century. Even in having a world to 'triumph over', the poet represents that world. 'The accent of high seriousness, born of absolute sincerity',[2] is a

---

[1] *Essays in Criticism*, Second Series, *op. cit.* pp. 30-1   [2] *Ibid.* p. 29

quality of poetry, not of human conduct. But it can exist in poetry only because it exists, in a different form, in the inner life of the poet. It may exist, too, in society; because it is in the personalising of social values (that is, of values held socially, and given a form in *manners*) that the 'substance and matter' of poetry normally arise; it is in a poetry of high seriousness that that process of personalising issues. The mark of the 'genuine' man becomes the mark of the poetry and the guarantee of its genuineness. When it does so, we find a quality of 'diction and movement', a note, a mark, an accent. It is in such strictly 'literary' characteristics that we recognise the moral force of the poet's utterance: his self-utterance.

Now, this is plainly an exalted view of the poet's function, of his relationship to his society and his age, and of his relationship to the depths, the moral possibilities, of his own nature. It is very far from Eliot's idea of poetry as a report on the essential human condition; it is, rather, an idea of poetry as realising the best part of the poet's nature for the consolation and animation of other men. It is a profoundly moral idea; it is an idea of the poet as performing a function which is nearly priestly, hieratic; it is an idea of the great value of style; and it is an idea of poetry as *utterance*, not as *form*.

At this point of his thinking, when he reaches the interior moral dignity of the poet, Arnold is able subjectively to resolve all the elements of his thought which otherwise would be in danger of contradicting one another. In a way, it is the terminal point of his thinking: here the concern for the moral effects of poetry leads back to, and is justified by, a concern for the moral stature of the poet. Anyone who is interested in tracing out the development of this essay, 'The Study of Poetry', will find with what subtle naturalness Arnold's dealing with the various elements of poetry leads up to his vision of the poet as the representative, the priestly man, the liberator of his own deepest sentiments and of his reader's. That is why Goethe is assessed so highly. It is Goethe's inner personality pervading his work that is morally important to us. And that is why the 'high seriousness' of the finest poetry is held in such high esteem by Arnold, and why he sees in it a quality almost of ritual.

Such an approach is obviously in danger of being at once too optimistic and too narrow: too optimistic in its view of the value of poetry in general, too narrow in its assignment of greatness to particular works. It is also in danger of using, instead of an objective view of each poet, the 'personal estimate' which, in this very essay, Arnold deplores. If poetry can be seen as utterance, and if its value as utterance can be traced with such confidence back to the inner life of its author, then there is no reason why we should not leave the attempt to learn from the poetry and try to learn from the life of the poet—or, at least, from what we can speculatively assume of the life of the poet. Whatever we learn, it is something affirmed and affirmative, not something which is a mere analysis of facts or states. It affirms something of the essence of human life, of that life which is 'at bottom' moral. The poet can affirm values because, at some depth of his personality, he lives them. The stress is on interiority, on the poet as discoverer, not so much of ideas or truths, but of values in himself. As I say, it is not merely for Arnold (or for us) a question of the poet's public personality. Wordsworth may be a prig, Villon a ruffian, Byron a self-flagellating exhibitionist; they are not to be judged on such an estimate, but on whatever is true and valuable 'in the very inmost soul of the genuine (man)'.

I have suggested that there is a certain limitation in this noble view of the poet's powers and function: it is the limitation which shows itself in Arnold's tendency to treat poetry as utterance, and to see the greatest poetry characterised by the use of the 'grand style', the impressive *saying*, the ennobling manner and diction. This tendency is associated with, even consequent upon, his stress on the inward personal life of the poet: as though we could ever detect *that*, except as it appears in poetry; and as though we could ever estimate it, even when we did detect it in poetry. In other words, I am suggesting that Arnold's judgments about the personal dispositions of specific poets are not properly literary-critical judgments at all; and that his recurrent liking for such judgments shows, first, an evasion of the business of estimating each poem as a fully *formed* experience or thing, and, second, an unwitting desire to seek poetic virtue in other places besides poetry. These two tendencies together account for his failure to analyse any fairly substantial passage in detail: a surprising failure, in a way, since even Johnson and Coleridge were interested in, and capable of, such an analysis.

It is, again, a quasi-religious emphasis. The very language in which he speaks, in 'The Study of Poetry' and elsewhere, has strong religious overtones; it is the language of spirituality and of redemptive power. The poet is seen as the true representative of his age, his specific society, his readers and, finally, his own inner potentialities; and Arnold speaks of him in terms of the transcendence of personal and environmental limitations. Again, it is not precisely a case of poetry being seen as a religion, but of poetry being expected to do the work, to enact and establish the values, which are usually considered to be the business of religion, and to have a religious justification. The poet is the true representative, but in an almost hieratic sense. He is not a 'legislator', acknowledged or otherwise; Arnold does not possess the mind of the political campaigner, as Shelley does. He is something more than a legislator; and in Arnold's view of his vocation, it is a vocation not merely to *do* something but to *be* something.

Thus we have the open association of personal character with style: and an association in which they are seen as more than mutual analogies—as forces of a moral kind exerting a mutual influence. The judgment on Keats is instructive here. It is a judgment which passes from an estimate of Keats the man to an estimate of Keats the poet, and back again, always employing the same terms:

> We who believe Keats to have been by his promise, at any rate, if not fully by his performance, one of the very greatest of English poets, and who believe also that a merely sensuous man cannot either by promise or by performance be a very great poet, because poetry interprets life, and so large and noble a part of life is outside of such a man's ken,—we cannot but look for signs in him of something more than sensuousness, for signs of character and virtue. And indeed the elements of high character Keats undoubtedly has, and the effort to develop them. . . .[1]

But since Keats died young:

> What we should rather look for is some evidence of the instinct

---

[1] *Essays in Criticism*, Second Series, *op. cit.* pp. 62-3

for character, for virtue, passing into the man's life, passing into his work.[1]

It would be as well for Arnold to add the word 'consequently' after that second 'passing'; for that is what he means. Keats has clearsightedness and lucidity; 'and lucidity is in itself akin to character and to high and severe work'.[2]

If we take the stresses revealed in my last chapter, and look at them beside the implications of these judgments on Keats, we can see the real limitation better. Arnold is, in fact, limited by being too much a moralist, and by expecting of poetry too immediate a moral effect. Here, we find not only an exalted view of the poet's task and opportunities (which a defeatist age like our own might well take notice of, and meditate on), but a virtual identification of the man with his poetry. We have already seen Arnold slipping unwittingly, like an alcoholic, to an inflated opinion of the literary-moral value of Marcus Aurelius' maxims, of Goethe's power to liberate the modern world, of isolated lines of poetry which have the power not only of examples but also of sentiments complete in themselves, and of Guérin's quasi-moral renderings of Nature. Similarly, in all of the later estimates of particular writers, we find Arnold inviting us to learn as much from the man as from his poetry. Why are the accounts of Byron and Keats, of Tolstoi and Amiel, so pervaded by the sympathy with them as persons? Surely because we are being invited to be edified by them as men as well as by their poetry. And if this is so, why should we need the poetry at all? Why can't we simply praise famous men? Is it because the essential virtue which they possess as persons is merely more compressed, more public, and more accessible in their poetry?

That one can even ask such irritated questions is a sign of a weakness in Arnold's grasp. But, to be fair, his own practice as an analyst of poetic value directs us away from this weakness in him—even if much of his actual criticism suggests the weakness to us. In Arnold's view, there can be no substitute for poetry, for poetry is quite *nodal* in its holding, or summing up, of all relevant values. In the first place, if 'character' is a necessary

---

[1] *Essays in Criticism*, Second Series, *op. cit.* pp. 63-4   [2] *Ibid.* p. 67

condition of poetic greatness, it is not a sufficient condition. In the second place, if character is in question at all (and it is), it is nevertheless character in a broad and profound sense; it is not, for example, a question of a trained will; it is, rather, a fusion of moral maturity with that serene contemplative detachment by means of which one can 'master' the chaos of the world, both in oneself and for the sake of others. Arnold's practical judgments operate negatively as well as positively. In his estimate of Keats, where he is trying to indicate a direct relationship between hidden qualities in the man and valuable potentialities in the poetry, he may strike us as naïve and misleading. It is there that his weakness emerges most nakedly. But in his 'limiting judgment' on, for example, Byron, or on *Villette*, his instinct for the relationship between spiritual attitude and artistic value is much sounder, more realistic:

> Why is *Villette* disagreeable? Because the writer's mind contains nothing but hunger, rebellion, and rage, and therefore that is all she can, in fact, put into her book. No fine writing can disguise this thoroughly, and it will be fatal to her in the long run.[1]

In fact, in Arnold's view, the presence of 'fine writing' under such conditions would be an irrelevant decoration over the unpleasant spiritual facts. It would certainly not constitute 'style', in his sense, though it might be loosely described as 'a style'. His judgment on Byron's weaknesses is also illuminating:

> Some of Byron's most crying faults as a man,—his vulgarity, his affectation—are really akin to the faults of commonness, of want of art, in his workmanship as a poet.[2]

This kind of judgment is fairly common in literary criticism. We may compare Arnold's view of Byron, for example, with Eliot's remarks on the artistic greediness of the Elizabethans. And, indeed, there is a great similarity, even in the phrasing, between certain of their judgments. So Arnold continues his account of Byron:

> [Goethe] saw the constant state of warfare and combat, the 'negative and polemical working', which makes Byron's poetry a poetry in which we can find so little rest; he saw the *Hang zum*

---

[1] *Letters, op. cit.* Vol. I, p. 29: Letter to Mrs Forster
[2] *Essays in Criticism, op. cit.* pp. 105-6

Unbegrenzten, the straining after the unlimited, which made it impossible for Byron to produce poetic wholes such as the *Tempest* or *Lear*; he saw the *zu viel Empirie,* the promiscuous adoption of all the matter offered to the poet by life, just as it was offered, without thought or patience for the mysterious transmutation to be operated on this matter by poetic form.[1]

Eliot's recurrent emphasis on the inordinate aspirations which modern literature has so often fostered is strongly fore-shadowed in these passages. Yet Arnold's remarks are very much in keeping with his own general preoccupations, and are coloured by them. He does not, as Eliot does, see poetry as representing, and evaluating, a state of almost metaphysical tension in the world or in the human soul. He is very far, too, from having any sympathy with the insight which made Yeats declare that, while rhetoric came out of the quarrel with others, out of the quarrel with ourselves we make poetry. He raises the question of the 'daemonic' element in life and literature only to shrug it into a practical irrelevance.[2] In his judgment on Byron and others, the stress is on *character,* and on poetry as possessing an authority and integrity similar or equivalent to that of virtuous human character; and, as we have seen, his interest in virtuous character is closely associated with the virtues of serene, informed detachment from the chaos of the merely factual world. It is this which constitutes a readiness for perfect moral action; it is this which comes into poetry as the accent of high seriousness, of perfect sincerity. And it is precisely this, of course, that Byron lacks. He does not have the virtue of rest, and so his poetry is lacking in restfulness. The emphasis is plain. Poetry *teaches* in a way very like that in which we learn from a man's life: by example, as it were. And Byron cannot reconcile his readers to the universe, for he is not himself reconciled with it. Neither, as we have seen, is the author of *Villette.*

It would be as well, at this point, to return for a moment to the notion of the *Zeitgeist* as favouring some poetical epochs while limiting others. The relative immaturity of the Romantics was as much a result of the era as of the individual. Byron lived

---

[1] *Essays in Criticism, op. cit.* p. 109
[2] See p. 56, note 2, Chapter II

in a time unfavourable to the greatest poetry; and so, Arnold suggests, does he himself:

> It is only in the best poetical epochs, (such as the Elizabethan), that you can descend into yourself and produce the best of your thought and feeling naturally, and without an overwhelming and in some degree morbid effect.[1]

It is at this point that the question of form and style is thrust upon us. At first sight, in a critic of Arnold's open-heartedness and comparative simplicity, such a question may seem to have little to do with the question of the moral value or reality of poetry. But Arnold speaks of style much in the same way as the Bloomsbury critics spoke of form, or as some of our contemporaries speak of 'myth' and symbol: as though virtue, or revelation, or the *mana*, resided in the style itself. For Arnold, style is the pledge of character, and its imaginative equivalent.

This seems natural enough, if we grant Arnold's moral conceptions and his sense of the way in which poetry works on the reader to increase a capacity, and to produce a readiness, for moral action. But few modern critics would want to speak about style in this sense at all; and I feel that their reluctance is reasonable; to speak in such a way is surely an unreasonable limiting of the integrity of poetry, of that very integrity which it is Arnold's intention to promote. But he sees integrity as coming directly from the moral integrity (in the ordinary sense) of the poet himself, and as appearing in poetry in a form which allows of a tracing back of influence from the poetry to the poet: so that it is the glimpsed moral life of the poet, as well as the palpable life of the poem, which is an example and inspiration and solace to the reader. Such a conception almost inevitably involves a reliance on style which is no longer of much use to us; the man is the style, and the style creates manliness in the reader. There is certainly a weakness here, and the choice of his touchstones reveals it; it is open to the same objections as I have already advanced against his view of the way in which poetry has its moral effect. The whole position may be summed up by saying that it is a recurrent tendency in Arnold to see poetry not as an incarnational act and art, but as a kind of

[1] *Letters, op. cit.* Vol. I, p. 52: Letter to Mrs Forster. V. also *Letters to A. H. Clough:* Letter 10, p. 73.

utterance which has something in common with eloquence, something in common with maxims.

A recurrent tendency, but not, fortunately, an invariable one—as we shall see. What is fluctuating, however, in his placing of emphases is caused by his reluctance ever to make up his mind about the relationship between substance and form in poetry. In speaking of them, he always sees poetry as an adjustment of style, of tone and movement and diction, to the 'substance', the meaning; but he does not indicate the nature of the relationship between them. This is obviously unsatisfactory, and it is the cause of much that is unsatisfactory, even question-begging, in the famous Preface to the 1853 edition of his poems. But that is an immature essay, which cannot rank with his great pronouncements, and it is in 'The Study of Poetry' that some attempt is made to account for the quality of a poetic style—'high seriousness'—by finding its source and pledge at once in the subject of the poem and in the inner moral integrity—the 'sincerity'—of the poet.

Still, we are not told anything of the nature of the relationship even here; we are only told that a relationship exists. Poetic substance and poetic style are complementary qualities. After citing Aristotle for his remark that poetry is superior to history in high truth and high seriousness, Arnold goes on:

Let us add, therefore, to what we have said, this: that the substance and matter of the best poetry acquire their special character from possessing, in an eminent degree, truth and seriousness. We may add yet further what is in itself evident, that to the style and manner of the best poetry their special character, their accent, is given by their diction, and, even yet more, by their movement. And though we distinguish between the two characters, the two accents, of superiority, yet they are nevertheless vitally connected one with the other. The superior character of truth and seriousness, in the matter and substance of the best poetry, is inseparable from the superiority of diction and movement marking its style and manner. The two superiorities are closely related, and are in steadfast proportion one to the other. So far as high poetic truth and seriousness are wanting to a poet's matter and substance, so far also, we may be sure, will a high poetic stamp of diction and movement be wanting to his style and manner. In proportion as this high stamp of diction and movement, again, is absent from a poet's style and manner, we shall find, also, that high poetic truth and seriousness are absent from his substance and matter.[1]

Well, it is unequivocal enough, in its way; and we may reflect that it is the first time that such a firm and lucid statement of an important truth has been made in English criticism. It is on this depth or aspect of Arnold that both Eliot and Leavis draw, though they turn it to other and more subtle analytic uses. And we should not be too scandalised by Arnold's characteristic reluctance to tell us what he means by truth, that truth which presumably guarantees the 'seriousness' of the substance and matter. I have already suggested where he locates the value of that substance; and I have suggested that, since he is a sort of pragmatist in these matters, the value exists in an effectiveness, a moral, inspiriting effectiveness, which he would not want to submit to the judgment of reasoning. The substantial value of poetry exists, for Arnold, in the moral nature of the poet's contact with reality—whether that reality seems to be merely natural, as in the case of Guérin, or in itself moral, as in the case of Shakespeare. The moral nature of this contact with reality is characterised by a broadness of view, a serenity and detachment, and a consequent animation or joy. It is the contact with reality of a soul mastering the world, becoming reconciled with the universe; and its effectiveness as poetry is connected with its doing the same service for the reader.

In other words, whatever the 'character of truth and seriousness, in the matter and substance' may mean, it is not simply a current of liberating ideas or a special moral faculty in the poet. These things are necessary for great poetry, particularly in the modern age; but they are necessary as *conditions* for the reaching of the moral contact with reality; they lie beneath that contact, enable and stimulate it; but they do not comprise it. Consequently, it should be clear that by 'substance and matter' Arnold does not mean what is often very loosely called the 'subject-matter' of an actual, achieved poem. It is something deeper than these, and it is a blend of elements. In the greatest poetry it is transmuted into—we may almost say it becomes—'style'.

[1] *Essays In Criticism, op. cit.* p. 13

81

It should also be clear that style does not mean what it is often very crudely assumed to mean: a polishing of the surface of a work or a decoration of tensions, or a gilding the pill of meaning. Certainly, it is part of the exercise of a conscious and deliberate act, but it is not arbitrary and detachable; it is, rather, an equivalent and expression of the 'content'. It is, in fact, the means of giving its true poetic stature and meaning to the 'thing said'—a way of evaluating it:

> Style, in my sense of the word, is a peculiar recasting and heightening, under a certain condition of spiritual excitement, of what a man has to say, in such a manner as to add dignity and distinction to it.[1]

There are many remarks on style, on the 'grand style', on high seriousness as a mark of verbal movement; and we are not so much concerned with his conception of the grand style; it is simply symptomatic of his whole approach, and does not add much to what we already know of that approach. But his constant preoccupation with style can be seen in his early letters perhaps as well as anywhere. In the letters to Clough we get, at any rate, a clear statement that Arnold conceives style as not only having a moral source in the deepest integrity of the poet, and so being a verbal equivalent of moral character, but as having, of itself, a moral effect upon the reader:

> Nay in Sophocles what is valuable is not so much his contributions to psychology and the anatomy of sentiment, as the grand moral effects produced by *style*. For the style is the expression of the nobility of the poet's character, as the matter is the expression of the richness of his mind: but on men character produces as great an effect as mind.[2]

I have said that this passage is representative; and so it is in essentials. It is true that, in 'The Study of Poetry' and in others of his late essays, poetry is seen as a more complex and organic thing, and he is incapable of making quite such simple distinctions as he does here. But the passage shows the constant direction of his mind. He does not see style merely as an extra, a decoration; but he does see it as having an effect in its own

---

[1] *On the Study of Celtic Literature* (Everyman's Library edition), p. 107
[2] *Letters to A. H. Clough, op. cit.* pp. 100-1

right. This effect will only be validly and lastingly made when the style is an adequate embodiment of the substance and matter. So that Arnold would presumably consider it absurd for critics who are revolted by the whole attitude, the whole pretension, of such a writer as André Gide to call him a great writer because of his 'style'. The notion of style implied in such a judgment is a notion of something produced in a nearly schizoid way, with the mind and sensibility working on words in a very different way, perhaps a contradictory way, from that in which they work on their experience of the world. And, if it is proper to talk of style at all, we must speak of it as the rhythmic exercise of the mind and sensibility upon an adequate object of experience. If style is anything, it is surely the medium through which a whole personality comes to centre itself on its intelligence, and so to express its insight and perception. It is not merely a result of the artistic process, but part of the process itself. It is, therefore, in Arnold's terms, a moral thing. If a poet apprehends the moral reality of his experience, it is through his style as much as through anything else that he does so.

But I have said that Arnold would *presumably* agree; and I have added the reservation 'if style is anything at all'. In fact, one must be uneasy about Arnold's reliance on style. He is speaking, after all, primarily of one style—the 'grand style', the accent and movement of elevated and elevating sentiment—as the one most suited to great poetry. And this in itself is suspicious. It seems to me that, if my remarks are acknowledged, then the term 'style' becomes misleading. It is still the subject of, or the excuse for, certain gross misunderstandings of the nature of literature and of its value. And Arnold does see a poet's style as in some way detachable, if only for the purposes of explicit criticism, from his substance and matter. There is almost a suggestion that style *is* moral value. Arnold is always in danger of wanting to get the moral meaning and effect of poetry too easily; and we may feel that the composing and elevating effect produced by style alone cannot be really valuable and lasting to a contemporary reader in the great complexity of our time. However backed it is by 'the power to survey the world from a central, a truly human point of view',[1]

[1] *Essays in Criticism, op. cit.* p. 16

the grand style in poetry is not enough nowadays, if it ever was, to 'make moral action perfect'.

It is true that we are not asked to rely for the moral effects of poetry on style alone, though we are certainly asked to give it an inordinate respect. There is also an insistence (less constant, less noticeable) on what Arnold calls *architectonicé*, on what we may call *built form*, as distinct from the *organic form* which Sir Herbert Read has inherited from Coleridge. This power of building is not a matter of mere 'technique'; it too is akin to character, and in some sense a product of character:

> . . . but the true art, the *architectonicé* which shapes great works, such as the *Agamemnon* or the *Divine Comedy*, comes only after a steady, deep-searching survey, a firm conception of the facts of human life, which the Celt has not patience for. So he runs off into technic, where he employs the utmost elaboration, and attains astonishing skill; but in the contents of his poetry you have only so much interpretation of the world as the first dash of a quick, strong perception, and then sentiment, infinite sentiment, can bring you. Here, too, his want of sanity and steadfastness has kept the Celt back from the highest success.[1]

We see that *architectonicé*, built form, is considered as the equivalent and pledge of certain artistic qualities which are as *moral*—in Arnold's sense—as those which find their outcome in style. Just as style is the product of an inner sympathy and nobility working on the substance and matter, so form is the product of 'steadfastness', spiritual and emotional stamina, a kind of artistic fortitude. No doubt Arnold regards poetic form as in some way delightful, as giving us what someone has called the sense of a completed movement; but that is not the aspect of it which he chooses to emphasise. He chooses to emphasise its capacity, as it were, to give moral example. Burgum, in his trenchant and hostile analysis, certainly accuses him of ignoring aesthetic values, and consequently of ignoring form altogether:

> He was more sensitive to style because it is the style and not the form of a poem which is rhetorical and therefore by its nature influential upon conduct.[2]

[1] *On the Study of Celtic Literature, op. cit.* p. 83
[2] E. B. Burgum, *op. cit.* p. 105

84

And

> Since he has refused to discuss design or plot, emotion has
> ceased to be an end in itself in poetry, and has become praise-
> worthy in proportion to its tonic effect upon the reader's moral
> system.[1]

There is some truth in these judgments; but they are not
quite fair. For one thing, Burgum's term 'moral system' is
ambiguous; and even if it is taken in the sense of moral capacity,
it does not do justice to Arnold's delicate apprehension of the
issues. He certainly does not see men as having a moral system
in the same way that they have a nervous system or a digestive
system—a set of responses simply waiting to be 'toned up' by a
good verbal shock or a good dose of poetry. Burgum is certainly
right in considering him to insist on style as the carrier and
pledge of virtue; but, as we have seen, it is virtue in a fairly
complex sense: a flow of feeling, a condition of sentiment and
sympathy which in itself constitutes a readiness for action.
There is, as well, the interest in form, though his later criticism
does not take enough account of it. But it is in the matter of
form that Burgum's interest declares itself. Arnold conceives
form as *architectonicé*, as built form. He is not a devotee of form
as Burgum apparently understands it: the organic form of
Coleridge and Read. In his view of form he claims to be a
follower not of Coleridge but of Goethe. And it is an open
question whether or not the term *organic form* is itself a
misnomer.

The point is, that even in the relatively immature Preface
to the first edition of his Poems, he associates *architectonicé* with
greatness of subject-matter and depth of feeling. So he says
of Shakespeare that he was 'penetrated with' his subject.
Architectonicé may be a limited conception, but it is not a
mechanical one. It too teaches; it too is an element in the
moral effectiveness of the poetry. It teaches not only through
delighting us as form—a most infrequent stress in Arnold's
writings—but also because it displays certain other qualities of
the soul: fortitude, steadfastness, a readiness for the 'prolonged
dealing of the spirit with matter'.

[1] *Ibid.* p. 103

85

It seems to me idle to debate in the abstract the relative importance of 'style' and 'form'. The only conceivable reason for dwelling so much on them here is that they reveal so much of Arnold's view of the moral reality of poetry. His great strength as a critic seems to lie in his awareness that poetry has its roots in a kind of wisdom—which is what he means by 'truth and seriousness'—and its effect in the animation of the reader for the daily business of life: in the encouragement of 'disinterested' intelligence and of the flow of feeling and sympathy. But his weakness as a critic, at least for our time, lies in his account of what intervenes between those roots and that effect. What intervenes, of course, is the poetry itself. And he accounts for this too much in terms of elevated sentiment, of truth turned too easily into feeling, of style. Because of the limitations of his actual vision of poetry, he tends to estimate it too much in terms of its presumed effects; and he can know those effects only as they occur in himself. However he may try to reach a point of complete disinterestedness, his demands are basically subjective, as well as personal. Hence the frequent desire for a consoling sentiment. And I feel also that he sees poetry as reaching a great effect in too simple and easy a manner—by directly stimulating a readiness for virtuous action. Life is conduct; poetry leads to conduct by stimulating a certain kind of life, which is itself a readiness for conduct.

That is why he is, in a sense, a didactic critic. He is quite as much a moralist as Johnson was; but his view is more complex and sophisticated than Johnson's. And that is also why Burgum is able to insist that he echoes Sidney, but that in place of the courtier he puts his idea of the 'Christian gentleman'. He is a moralist of a quasi-religious kind; and I don't think it would be unfair to say that he sees the poet as a priest of the religion of elevated naturalism: a religion in which any supernatural dimension is simply not available to the imagination. It is from some such view that his whole critical position comes; it is such a view which seriously weakens his great critical achievement.

CHAPTER IV

T. S. Eliot: Impersonal Order

ELIOT is the great initiating critic of the twentieth century as Arnold is the great stabilising critic of the nineteenth. And just as Arnold is often held to be the most authoritative mentor of romanticism in a 'romantic' century, Eliot is as often seen as the champion of 'classical' impersonality in a century the general drift of which is to be classical. Each of these judgments is a half-truth; and the two in combination are a sort of quarter-truth. Arnold was not merely a romantic apologist, but the interpreter of, and modifying influence on, a romanticism already plaintively prosperous, and soon to be decadent. Eliot, on the other hand, is not merely the initiator of a way of thinking about our literary past, he is also a refining and modifying influence on a 'classicism' already becoming, in the personal example of T. E. Hulme, coarse and self-defeating.

He has had, as a critic and as a poet, a vast influence not only on contemporary literary taste (in the narrow sense of preference for one work or convention to another) but also on our sense of the value of poetry as a representative human act. He has radically altered twentieth-century conceptions of the kind of reality a poem is, of the relationship between the shaping sensibility of the poet and the world of his time, of the existence of a recognisable and distinctive literary order extending throughout the history of the West, and of the manner in which this order imposes itself as an orthodoxy (both of wisdom and achievement), against which contemporary achievements in art may be judged. He is, then, from the beginning of his critical work, a key text in our discussion of the ideas which have been held during the past hundred years on the moral significance of poetry.

It is interesting and important to compare him with Arnold—

although in what follows the comparison will generally be implied rather than formulated, for this is not an historical analysis. As we have seen, he has twice sharply reproached Arnold with the inadequacy of those ideas which were basic to his criticism; and in other places, notably in his formal essays on the nature of criticism and in his essay on F. H. Bradley,[1] he has maintained a stance of rigorous dissent from Arnold's influence, while conceding his greatness. It is interesting to compare them, for Eliot has always been conscious of representing a tradition and a conception antithetical to Arnold's. He deliberately offers us his range or complex of values as an antidote to those of the century of which Arnold is, in some ways, the most balanced and distinguished representative. He stands in some sense for 'classicism' as against a literature of romantic sentiment, for man in society as against man in nature, for complexity in the realisation of the actual world as against the noble, wide-ranging utterance which Arnold favoured, for an analysis at depth of the human condition rather than a synthetic affirmation of some order that transcends that condition: in other words, for one or another conception of 'orthodoxy' as against Arnold's 'liberalism'.

What set him against Arnold is what set him against the Romantics' century—the nineteenth. His total position is one of reaction against that century, and an affirmation of a scheme of values alternative to it. This might be taken merely as the inevitable rejection of one's father, especially of a father grown rather alarmingly to the status of a Father-figure. But there is certainly more to it than that; and the additional motive is the essential one. Poets in Arnold's day felt less subjective ease and freedom, less certainty in the use of the imagination, than the great Romantics had felt. Yet Arnold as a critic had behind him fifty years of a Romantic ethos which was already a poetic achievement, and in the context of this achievement he was able to take for granted certain basic attitudes and an agreed critical terminology. By 1920, when Eliot's *The Sacred Wood* first appeared, no such agreement could be presumed. For one thing, romanticism as achievement had been debased first into Ninety-ism, and later into Georgian bucolics. For another,

[1] *Selected Essays* (1949 edition)

romantic criticism had devolved, partly through the influence of French Symbolism, upon the notion of 'art-for-art's-sake', and Pater's cult of aesthetic experience. There was a whole undergrowth of perverse theorising and amateur poetics to be cleared.

Eliot's determination to undertake the clearing was reinforced by his rejection of all the 'romantic' assumptions about reality and the poet's attitude to it. Poetry, at the time he started to write, faced a much more complex dilemma than the thinkers of Arnold's generation even conceived—it faced, among other things, the looming spectre of its own irrelevance. To begin to take it seriously again was to undergo considerable intellectual strain; and to begin to assert an anti-romantic tradition was to put oneself in the position of asserting values unfamiliar to one's audience, and of creating a terminology at once more precise and complex than Arnold's. Being less simple and less familiar, these values and this terminology come to us in *The Sacred Wood* as paradoxical and hard to grasp. Therefore, it is only fair to remember that Eliot's early work, when it was undertaken, was one of experimental probing.

Within the terms of our present enquiry, another factor arises to make investigation of his ideas hazardous. I am treating his view of the relationship between poetry and morality; yet he seldom speaks in affirmative terms of the moral value or effect of poetry. This is particularly so in his early criticism, where he never shows any overt interest at all in the moral reality of art. In a way, he is careful not to show such an interest, since his first concern is to assert the autonomy of poetry as a *making*. But, even in his later work, the open use of a terminology of value is occasional and never consistent.

Yet he has given us a critical *œuvre* which enforces a slowly changing conception not only of the value of poetry but also of poetic values. And what he gives us is an analysis of poetry which, like Arnold's, becomes an analysis of life, without losing its specifically literary focus and terminology. Whatever it is that we derive from his work, it is something implied in his pursuit of different literary problems; so any attempt to disengage his view of poetry and morality must risk two dangers: In the first place, there is the danger of feeling it necessary to bring to light not only his insight into this central question of poetry and moral value, but also his whole critical position. In the second place, there is the danger of taking for a declaration of fixed and central attitude what may be no more than an attempt, entered into at varying angles of interest, to re-assess the value which the literary past may have for the literary present. It is in the nature of my attempt that these risks will simply have to be taken.

Eliot's position is, first of all, one of reaction and re-assessment. Consequently it is easy to misconceive the general intention of this reaction. A hostile critic, R. H. Robbins, in a book[1] which is a very monument of incomprehension, sees Eliot's criticism as part of the 'conservative counter-pressure of this century against the liberal achievement of the past three or four centuries'. To discuss such a thesis here would be a self-indulgent dallying. Yet it is true that Eliot has been markedly influenced by men who hated that 'liberal achievement'. Chief among them is T. E. Hulme, whose position should be distinguished from those of the others (Rémy de Gourmont, Irving Babbitt, Pound, Laforgue, and F. H. Bradley are names which recur in scholarly estimates) who also seem to have influenced Eliot.

Hulme is trebly important: his views impinged upon his generation, of whom Eliot was one, as of immediate and prescriptive value; they are stated with great fierceness, though with an unpleasantly compulsive tone; and they show an emphasis and a terminology which both entered very early into Eliot's work.

In the first fifteen years of this century, Hulme set himself to 'the destruction of this conception . . . of the principle of *continuity*'[2] elaborated by so many nineteenth-century figures. The principle of continuity is the principle which found its main specialist expression in the notion of the evolution of species. Mid-century materialism had affected to find a continuity between the inorganic world and the organic, and between biology on the one hand and religion and ethics on the other. One of the effects of such an insistence was the

---

[1] *The T. S. Eliot Myth*: Henry Schuman (New York, 1951), p. 169
[2] *Speculations*, p. 3

debasement of the idea of God and the growing difficulty of finding any valid field for philosophy.

Hulme reacted violently by asserting that man was quite discontinuous from nature. And he was therefore led, by a perverse logic of extremes, to assert an absolute discontinuity between God and man. If the human spirit was immeasurably above the flesh, to the point of severance of mutual relations, the same was true of God's superiority over man. In Hulme's compulsive prose, superiority comes to mean unbridgeable distance. From such a position, he came to press for an art that should be 'classical' in the paradoxical sense of being explicitly anti-humanist, an art set in scornful opposition to ordinary living. Such an art, he insisted, would be truly religious: religious art is anti-humanist, and even anti-human:

> The disgust with the trivial and accidental characteristics of living shapes, the searching after an austerity, a monumental stability and permanence, a perfection and rigidity, which vital things can never have, leads to the use of forms which can almost be called geometrical.[1]

Such an art 'most obviously exhibits no delight in nature and no striving after vitality'[2]; and it comes from 'a feeling of separation in the face of outside nature'[3]—that nature which receives so much of Hulme's exaggerated disgust: 'the messiness and confusion of nature and natural things'.[4]

It is not clear whether he dwells on the antipathy between humanism and religion for the sake of fostering the new 'geometrical' art forms which he believes to be necessary to our moment in history, or whether he promotes new art forms for the imaginative pledge which they may give of his own philosophical and theological leanings. What *is* important is the stress which he places on the need to believe in Original Sin, a doctrine which he seems to regard as the central insight of Christianity. Thus he sees Classicism as, in large part, the creative recognition of the fact of Original Sin. It recognises that man is seriously limited, a 'bucket' and not a 'well'; or, as Hulme goes on to express it, that man is 'essentially bad'.

The new 'classicism', then, is to be not only an assertion of

---

[1] *Ibid.* p. 9 [2] *Ibid.* p. 85
[3] *Ibid.* p. 85 [4] *Ibid.* p. 96

limits to life and art, but a denial of 'vitality', of 'acceptance of life', of personality, and of that naturalistic art which the Renaissance promoted, and which takes pleasure in man, nature and movement. The stress is significant; and it would be easy to elaborate a statement of his position by a selection of the texts which lie abundantly to hand. Two more of these must be cited to emphasise the influence which the view had on Eliot. In a sustained burst of anger, Hulme attacks Renaissance and post-Renaissance thought and art, which 'exhibits the inability to realise the meaning of the dogma of Original Sin'[1]; which introduced 'an attitude of acceptance of life', a new interest in man, and 'in character and *personality* for its own sake'[2]; 'the fundamental error is that of placing Perfection in *humanity*, thus giving rise to that bastard thing Personality, and all the bunkum that follows from it'.[3]

It is here that Hulme's position, muddled and obsessive though it is, touches the quick of Eliot's. In the critical battle against the nineteenth century, the central point of attack will be the conception of personality, and emotion as the chief agent of its inflation. This emphasis passes into Eliot's work and remains relatively constant in it, whatever else varies from analysis to analysis, or even suffers a sea-change in passing from a pre-Christian to an explicitly Christian criticism. Consequently, the aspects of Eliot's position which I want to look at in this essay are those which might be put under the headings of Order and Impersonality.

The whole of Eliot's work is, in a sense, an exploration of the problem of order as it arises in manifold ways. His first and possibly most influential book, *The Sacred Wood*, states this problem by asking the question whether the works of literature which come down to us through the whole Western tradition compose a recognisable and definable order, the existence of which is to affect the creative work of the present. His answer is the famous essay, 'Tradition and the Individual Talent', in which the *present-ness* of the past order is asserted, and the question of its relevance to the present is turned into a complementary yet less obvious question: the relevance of the present to the past.

---

[1] *Speculations*, p. 13   [2] *Ibid.* p. 25   [3] *Ibid.* p. 33

This early and authoritative book has one pressing theme: it is concerned to explore the present possibilities of poetry, to establish its value in the orderly light of the past, to see how some poet, or some poetic form, can truthfully and fully express the needs of the age in the perspective of the tradition. And so he is interested in the problem of whether a relevant criticism can be established at all; while in his later criticism he assumes the relevance of criticism, and comes to use its methods more inertly. So, in the Introduction to the 1928 edition of *The Sacred Wood*, he says:

> It is part of the business of the critic to preserve tradition—where a good tradition exists. It is part of his business to see literature steadily and to see it whole; and this is eminently to see it *not* as consecrated by time, but to see it beyond time; to see the best work of our time and the best work of twenty-five hundred years ago with the same eyes.[1]

The first requisite for 'anyone who would continue to be a poet beyond his twenty-fifth year' is an historical sense, the sense which is so ardently affirmed in the passage I have quoted. It is a sense, ultimately, of the co-presence of past and present. The passage is very famous, and there is no need to quote from it at length. But there are two emphases in it which are quite relevant to the question of poetry and morality. One is the idea that the existence of a traditional literary order, at once in time yet capable of being seen as independent of time, gives value to the work of the contemporary poet:

> No poet, no artist of any art, has his complete meaning alone. His significance, his appreciation, is the appreciation of his relation to the dead poets and artists. You cannot value him alone; you must set him, for contrast and comparison, among the dead. . . .[2]

Taken by itself, this is no more than a pious platitude. But it is not to be taken by itself:

> What happens is a continual surrender of himself (i.e. the artist) as he is at the moment to something which is more valuable. The progress of an artist is a continual self-sacrifice, a continual extinction of personality.[3]

[1] Introduction to 1928 edition, pp. xv-xvi [2] *The Sacred Wood*, p. 53
[3] *Ibid.* p. 53

Such a stress obviously throws reverberations into that other question which I have later to take up, the question of impersonality in art. Here it is important as showing that the relationship of the present to the past, as Eliot sees it, is not simply a matter of preordained law, a static relationship or mechanical state, but is a matter affecting the moral meaning of the artist's attitude to his art. Eliot does not elaborate the point, and it is unnecessary at the moment to do much more than acknowledge its existence.

What he is insisting on is not so much knowledge as consciousness of the past. That is why he is able to assert, with obvious truth, that 'tradition' is an advantage, not a hindrance, to the artist who is genuinely original. At the same time we may see in his distrust of personality the roots of his later position: that the whole human order is more important than the individual insight, so far as that remains merely individual. Such a view is capable of most perverse elaborations; and it is paradoxical that Eliot should later try to insist, in speaking both of Dante and of the Greek dramatists, that a whole culture can become incarnated in a personal *œuvre*. The relation of the individual to his tradition is never stated with any precision, and is, in fact, left as a question not only begged but undefined.

In an essay dated three years later, Eliot takes up again the theme which he has established. Referring, in 'The Function of Criticism', 1923, to his earlier remarks, he says:

> I was dealing then with the artist, and the sense of tradition which, it seemed to me, the artist should have; but it was generally a problem of order; and the function of criticism seems to me essentially a problem of order too.[1]

One might comment that everything does; but what kind of order? First of all, it is the problem of establishing a literary canon by re-assessing the conventional reputations; but deeper than that, and establishing the canon itself, Eliot sees a community of interest, attitude, and self-dedication among the poets whose works compose it:

> There is accordingly something outside of the artist to which he owes allegiance, a devotion to which he must surrender and

[1] *Selected Essays*, p. 23

sacrifice himself in order to earn and to obtain his unique position. A common inheritance and a common cause unite artists consciously or unconsciously.[1]

If his previous statement can be said to be the affirmation of order under the aspect of tradition, this may be seen as an affirmation of order under the aspect of orthodoxy. But the orthodoxy is not yet brought to light and defined. It is not until much later that he comes to see the literary tradition as baptised, so to speak, by the Church, and bearing a Christian meaning. Even despite its character of a generality, however, one wonders how important this early statement is. Does it not have the effect of making tradition seem too external, too unattainable, and the task of the poet too portentous? And why, and in what sense, is the religious word 'sacrifice' used? And in what sense is it 'himself' that the poet is to sacrifice?

Such caveats indicate not positive objections to his formulation, but a feeling of unease about it. There seems little in it definite enough to be objected to; and this in itself contributes to the unease. At any rate, his intention is clearly to show it as extending further into a new sense of order; he sees the communal insight of poets somehow incarnated in a tradition which is recognisably literary. However vague this notion is, he does draw critical conclusions from it. In the essay on Dante, for example, we may note that he does not assign Dante's universality to any individual moral insight at all, but to factors which, so one would normally suppose, lie outside the field of individual choice or impulse altogether. He is plainly taking for a cause what is merely a predisposing condition of Dante's greatness. It is a startling example of his reliance on order and unity, and it has important and not altogether pleasant parallels in his still later works.[2]

The third level at which he examines the problem of order is that of the internal order of individual works or of the *œuvre* of an individual poet. So, in a passage of obvious good sense, which recalls the influence and terminology of Hulme, he insists that any poem or play can be a unity only so long as the

---

[1] *Ibid.* p. 24
[2] *Ibid.* The essay on Dante is dated 1929.

author recognises limits to the expansion of his imagination. This involves an abstraction from actual life:

> It is essential that a work of art should be self-consistent, that an artist should consciously or unconsciously draw a circle beyond which he does not trespass; on the one hand actual life is always the material, and on the other hand an abstraction from actual life is a necessary condition to the creation of the work of art.[1]

It is not that Eliot is removing poetry completely from life by means of a glib generalisation in which he pretends to reconcile them. That is the error which Yvor Winters makes. He notes that, in 'The Function of Criticism', Eliot holds poetry to be 'autotelic', and he comments: 'Art, then, is about itself'.[2] The comment is the result of a wrong-headed refusal to see the vagueness of the word 'about', which Winters uses but Eliot does not. The weakness of Eliot's statement on the self-consistency of art lies elsewhere—in its failure to do more than state that a relationship exists, or to indicate its nature and dynamism. And the weakness of his statement on Ben Jonson lies in the attempt to hold two seemingly contradictory judgments at once without going through the labour of reasoning and analysis which alone could reconcile them, if indeed anything could. The notion of order is being used as a critical cure-all; and the insistence on it leads to a neglect of other elements in poetic reality.

The essay on Ben Jonson is dated 1919, and 'The Function of Criticism' 1923. By the time of the publication of *After Strange Gods*, in 1934, his interest in the question of literature and order has changed its focus, without in any way being diminished in intensity. The sub-title of the volume is 'A Primer of Modern Heresy', an emphasis which I shall look at in the next chapter. And we recall that in *Essays Ancient and Modern*, which appeared two years later, he has an essay on 'Catholicism and International Order'—a title which sufficiently suggests the nature of his new concern. In both these cases the interest in order is an interest in the state of society which conditions

---

[1] *Selected Essays*, p. 111. See also the astonishing and untypical judgment about the superficiality of Ben Jonson's work, *Selected Essays*, pp. 106-17. I do not want to analyse this judgment in detail precisely because it is untypical.

[2] Y. Winters: *The Anatomy of Nonsense*, p. 122

the state of order or disorder in the individual author. What was originally the starting-point has become the end of his critical investigation; and the centre of attention is not now an objectively existing literary order ('tradition'), but an equally objective cultural order on which literature depends.

Eliot confesses that the 'problem' of order as he stated it in 'Tradition and the Individual Talent' is not now such a simple one, 'nor could I treat it now as a purely literary one'.[1]

I am not sure that he ever did treat it as a 'purely literary' question, but it is easy to see what he means; and he spends some five pages establishing his revised view of 'tradition'— now a question of social and cultural continuity and life— before passing on to talk of what is the central concern of these three lectures, the question of 'orthodoxy'.

While earlier he stressed the obligation of the poet to give allegiance to an order outside himself, now he stresses the need for the preservation of an order on which the poet may feed, and by reference to which his insights may be judged. Behind or within such an order, which is social and cultural, lies the life of dogma, preserving and vivifying it at all levels of its existence. The continuing presence of dogma in this way provides an imaginative and intellectual centre (a matter which also exercised Arnold's cultural conscience); the Christian poet should have the sense of a centre, the sense of an objective life; in a poet fully of the Western tradition, we may expect to find an 'orthodoxy of sensibility'.

It is an idea with which we are already familiar, in the writings of Christopher Dawson and others; and it can be more appropriately considered later in this study. What I want to point out at the moment is that the idea itself, in Eliot's formulation of it, always comes back to the evaluation of particular poets and particular works. In his essay on F. H. Bradley[2] he quotes with approval Bradley's satirical treatment of Arnold's 'our best self'. A good deal of his emphasis, in fact, falls on the insufficiency of the conscience as a guide, whether in literature or in life, and whether it is called (with Irving Babbitt) 'the inner check' or (with Arnold) 'the best self'. On

---

[1] *After Strange Gods*, p. 15
[2] *Essays Ancient and Modern*: reprinted in *Selected Essays*.

the level of polemics I should sympathise with him. But it is rather alarming to find this particular emphasis falling so heavily on literary criticism as well as on religion and ethics; for it suggests that the personal vision of the poet is inadequate, not only as a guide to living, but also as the constructing and valuing agent in the making of a poem. The suggestion as it stands is that external standards of truth can be applied to poems and novels, in the name of order; and orthodoxy looms too threateningly above the poet's actual toils.

But it would be wrong to see him as fascinated merely by authority. The whole pressure of his view of order, in its late as in its early form, bears down on the work of the individual poet, his difficulties and his opportunities. It is a matter of the order in a work of art, and of the depth, so to speak, at which the order is realised. Naturally enough, Eliot's early criticism reflects his own creative practice and problems. So we tend to get, in *The Sacred Wood* and in the first few of the Elizabethan essays, an examination of art as *process*, an analysis of the idea of artistic order from the point of view of its production, of the forces of the personality which act upon it to produce unity, and of the way in which these elements are fused under the flame of language and its contemporary conventions. These are matters to be dealt with generally under the heading of Impersonality; but it is necessary to pursue them a little further under the present heading.

He sees in Greek tragedy 'the unity of concrete and abstract in philosophy, the unity of thought and feeling, action and speculation, in life'.[1] For 'behind the dialogue of Greek drama we are always conscious of a concrete visual actuality, and behind that of a specific emotional actuality'.[2]

Here is the question of tradition and order raised on a new level: it is the unity of the Greek ethos which guarantees the unity of Greek drama. Eliot's concern is always with the need for incarnating, making concrete, a vision or view of life. That is one of the reasons for his insistence on tradition; for a living tradition, as he conceives it, provides not only a 'view of life'

---

[1] 'Seneca in Elizabethan Translation', 1927: *Selected Essays*, p. 68

[2] *Ibid.* p. 68. See also, on page 72, the idea that, for the Greek dramatists, 'their morals are a matter of feeling trained for generations'.

in some abstract sense, but a convention of terms, gesture, feeling, moral attitude, in which that view receives first its cultural and then its poetic embodiment. Such a tradition does not merely safeguard the poet from undue subjectivity in belief and eccentricity of moral judgment (which is Eliot's explicit theme in *After Strange Gods*); it actually regulates and supports our reaction to the world of *things*. The insistence on concreteness is, therefore, part of the insistence on order. It derives from an intense feeling for the moral roots of literary order.

The plays of Thomas Heywood, then, 'exhibit what may be called the minimum degree of unity'.[1] The reason is to be found in a failure of moral interest; the plays lack *character*, 'as it would often be called, personality'.[2]

> The sensibility is merely that of ordinary people in ordinary life. . . . Behind the motions of his personages, the shadows of the human world, there is no reality of moral synthesis; to inform the verse there is no vision, none of the artist's power to give undefinable unity to the most various material.[3]

The question of order is, at this level, the question of 'moral synthesis', and one may deduce from a lack of unity in the work (at least a work of some scope) a lack of central moral judgment behind it.

Yet Eliot's investigation of the problems of order in a poem, especially in his early criticism, centres upon its unity; the moral order behind it is seldom invoked. Thus we get the essentially just, and in a way sprightly, statement of all the things that poetry is often supposed to be but which, in Eliot's view, it cannot be if it is not to surrender its own proper reality and claim on the reader's attention.[4] It is not 'emotion recollected in tranquillity'; for that is a personal definition, springing from self-reflection. To call it a 'criticism of life' is to be frigidly inadequate. It is not

> the inculcation of morals, or the direction of politics; and no more is it religion or an equivalent of religion, except by some monstrous abuse of words. And certainly poetry is something over and above, and something quite different from, a collection of psychological

[1] *Selected Essays*, p. 175   [2] *Ibid*. p. 175   [3] *Ibid*. p. 175
[4] Introduction to 1928 edition, *The Sacred Wood*, p. ix

data about the minds of the poets, or about the history of an epoch; for we could not take it even as that unless we had already assigned to it a value merely as poetry.

'Merely as poetry'; yet Eliot's whole intention, in this essay as elsewhere, is to preserve a notion of the dignity and value of poetry. He seems to be insisting that to give it a value different from, and in a sense 'higher' than, its own, is really to devalue it. And, as he says, in the very passage in which he disclaims the possibility of adequate definition, it has 'something to do with morals, religion' and even politics. At any rate, we find the value of poetry to be a value of a moral kind:

> If I ask myself . . . why I prefer the poetry of Dante to that of Shakespeare, I should have to say, because it seems to me to illustrate a saner attitude towards the mystery of life.[1]

Here the idea of order is asserted as spiritual balance. The focus is once more on the unity of the work of art in itself, and on the unity of the view of life which guarantees and sustains it. For we must place the reflection on Dante beside another passage from the same essay:

> It is an artificial simplification, and to be taken only with caution, when I say that the problem appearing in these essays, which gives them what coherence they have, is the problem of the integrity of poetry, with the repeated assertion that when we are considering poetry we must consider it primarily as poetry and not another thing.[2]

Despite a considerable lapse in the quality of his actual critical grasp, there is no reason to suppose that Eliot has since abandoned anything he wrote in this Introduction of 1928. After all, at the time of writing it, he was already in a position to say that, in the years between 1920 and 1928, he had come to give weight to an additional problem: 'that of the relation of poetry to the spiritual and social life of its time and of other times'.[3] The relative importance he assigns to literature may have changed, but his sense of its reality has not, even if he is later to lose much of his capacity to make that sense actual in works of specific criticism; and for my present study, his

[1] Introduction to 1928 edition, *The Sacred Wood*, p. x   [2] *Ibid.* p. viii
[3] *Ibid.* p. viii

formulation of a position is the important thing, not his faculty for exemplifying the virtues of that position.

Whatever moral reality poetry possesses, then, is intimately connected in Eliot's approach with the question of order. His investigation into this question is conducted sometimes on a level which might almost be called epistemological, sometimes by deducing knowledge of a process from the close criticism of a wide range of poems. His approach in this is very different from that of Arnold, who tends to trace a relatively clear line from the quality of a poem *as utterance* to the state of 'soul' of its author, and back again.

If Eliot's view of order is complex and even baffling, it is because he wears so many paths towards the centre of it, and not all of them go the whole distance. At one moment, the question is one of the unity of a whole *œuvre*, a 'world'; at another it is a question of the unity of tradition, or of a view of life held communally in one place at one time; sometimes, it is a question of the unity of a specific play, or of a given poem. In the criticism of the mid-thirties and later, it tends to be a question of 'orthodoxy of sensibility' preserved by dogma. The term 'order', in fact, plays an alarmingly wide, and undefined, rôle in his writings. Consequently, he forces us to examine his views in a loose and synoptic way. But we can at least say that in all cases the concern with order comes from an interest of a moral kind in literature and its roots. Eliot's sense of order is a reflection of a highly charged moral sense, and it is a sense of something possessing moral significance. This is none the less so even when, as in some of his earlier essays, he is impatient of the raising of moral issues. The reason is that there was something to be established before the baffling questions of moral reality could usefully be raised. What had to be established was that complex set of insights which we may consider under the head of Impersonality.

Eliot has always been at pains to reject the legacy of nineteenth-century critical thought, and at the same time to establish an adequate notion of the reality of poetry. The second interest arises out of his sense of the interior order both of a poem and of the poet. In both, his thought centres on (though it is certainly not confined to) the idea of impersonality.

His concern for impersonality in poetry arises immediately out of his concern with order in its various manifestations. The order of art is for him impersonal. But 'impersonality' is a word of uncertain meaning. And you can't settle any question of its literary value simply by invoking the word. Characteristically, Eliot leaves it to us to assign a full meaning to it for him. But it must be emphasised that he does not see order as impersonal in the sense of fixed and dead. It is not a patterned sterility set against life and 'the natural'. He is not interested (as Hulme was) in the kind of impersonality we see in abstract paintings; nor is he interested in the attempt to transmute reality into a structure of symbols. The order which he desires, and in which he sees the true virtue of impersonality, is an ordering of the facts of human life; it is, generally, an ordering of the emotions.

The word 'emotion' plays a much greater, and a more confusing, part in Eliot's criticism than we realise at a first or second reading. It is in fact bafflingly ubiquitous in his prose; he seems to be obsessed with emotion. At least we may say that he is preoccupied with the need for so rendering emotions in poetry as to purge them of whatever quality gives them a despotic hold over human action. He wants, in some sense, to depersonalise them.

From the first, he has shown his distrust for a poetry based on emotions. He has done so for the most part positively, by trying, for example, to account for the verbal and sensuous richness of Elizabethan and Metaphysical poetry through the invocation not of emotion but of 'feeling' and sensibility. There are two elements in his interest: The autonomy and inner regularity of a poem, based on its complexity; and the insistence on a controlled perception of reality as the basis of poetic language. I have mentioned the first under the head of Order; the second may be dealt with in terms of the primacy of feeling/ thought over emotion, and the necessity to objectify emotion for poetic purposes in feeling/thought.

This latter term must be used, however clumsily, as a composite; for what Eliot means by sensibility is obviously something in which feeling and thought are used as dual and inseparable agents not only of perception but also of poetic creation. The association of the two is frequent and constant throughout his early work; and the variety of ways in which he associates them is richly suggestive of his own acute sense of the actuality of a poem:

> In common with the greatest, they [and he names a number of poets] had a quality of sensuous thought, or of thinking through the senses, or of the senses thinking, of which the exact formula remains to be defined.[1]

> Leonardo lived in no fairyland, but his mind went out and became a part of things.[2]

However close this may seem to the emphasis in many parts of Keats' letters, it is qualified and made more precise by further attempts to state the same theme:

> The sonnet of Shakespeare is not merely such and such a pattern, but a precise way of thinking and feeling.[3]

And:

> And, indeed, with the end of Chapman, Middleton, Webster, Tourneur, Donne, we end a period when the intellect was immediately at the tip of the senses. Sensation became word and word was sensation.[4]

And also, and most significant of all:

> A poet like Donne, or like Baudelaire or Laforgue, may almost be considered the inventor of an attitude, a system of feeling or of morals.[5]

Such a conjunction of feeling and morals cannot be ignored, though it ought not to be taken for an identification. And the conjunction of all these passages is a necessary way of establishing Eliot's view of the primacy of feeling/thought in the *process* and shaping of poetry before passing on to consider his insistence on the primacy of emotion as a *subject* of poetry, and as the (slightly disreputable) pressure behind it. Taken together, they are a valuable commentary on what, at this stage, Eliot himself found most significant in poetry: not intellectual insight so much as intensity of the poet's direct experience of the world, and of the poetic realisation of that experience: the word and

[1] *The Sacred Wood*, p. 23   [2] *Ibid.* p. 27   [3] *Ibid.* p. 63
[4] *Ibid.* p. 129   [5] *Selected Essays*, p. 292

the poet's grasp on the world fusing, as though naturally, into each other; for:

> . . . every vital development in language is a development of feeling as well.[1]

It is not merely the world of *things* that receives the play of the poet's sensibility, but the world of human emotions and even ideas themselves:

> The material of the artist is not his beliefs as *held*, but his beliefs as *felt* (so far as his beliefs are part of his material at all).[2]

To multiply quotations in this way is usually a labour-saving device characteristic of certain attempts at scholarship. Here it may be useful, however, as showing how pervasive the account of feeling/thought is in Eliot's early criticism, and how many applications he is able to find for it. The close association of the two terms, which romantic poetry on the whole notoriously failed to hold together, or held together only in a desperate mechanical partnership, probably has its roots in a precise philosophical notion which it is beyond my powers to disengage or discuss.[3]

Nevertheless, the close association of the terms, and their use as an agent of criticism, imply a good deal about Eliot's view of the value of poetry. It is difficult to deny that it shows an attempt to connect the autonomy of poetry with its relation to the objective world, and so (one would think) to some order of truth. It is a statement of the way in which the poet's sensibility apprehends the actuality partly of the world outside him but partly also of the emotion inside him, and makes that actuality part of his creative capacity. Poetry is a structure of feeling/thought in which the whole of the poet's relevant experience (the cognitive nature of which is at every point suggested, but never clearly formulated) is established in a world of *fact*. Or, rather, the world of fact comes sublimated into the poem in such a way as to make it a structure of feeling/thought. There is not a great deal that is startling in this. But it must have been

---

[1] *The Sacred Wood*, p. 129
[2] *The Use of Poetry*, p. 136
[3] See *Essays in Criticism* (Vol. 2, No. 2) for an interesting discussion, between Eric Thompson and F. W. Bateson, on the derivation and intention of Eliot's idea.

startling to the Georgian poets and reviewers, because it avoids mention of the importance of 'the great primary human affections', which Arnold inherited from Wordsworth, and of poetry's capacity for 'consoling and sustaining' the reader. Yet there are difficulties, internal difficulties, in Eliot's statement of it. In what sense 'feeling' is used it is hard to decide. It is certainly an agent of the whole personality engaged in an activity at once cognitive and affective; and it certainly seems to be one side of the coin of which 'thought' is the other side. Yet sometimes it seems to be synonymous with sensibility; sometimes it seems little more than an acute sense of the visual and tactual properties of things. This shift in meaning does not of itself cause much bafflement; it is a necessary consequence of the fact that every distinguished critic can't help using a terminology which is a sort of shorthand approximation to his whole position. The difficulty comes, rather, in seeing what rôle feeling/thought plays towards emotion. Is it simply a poetic agent superior to emotion? Is it a deliberately fabricated expression of an emotion which already exists? The notion of the objective correlative, which I shall glance at shortly, would seem to suggest so. Or is it a substitute for emotion (specifically, the emotions of 'life'), and a substitute which generates an emotion of its own (the emotion of art)? The difficulty of the whole question comes from the attempt to assert at once the autonomy of poetry and its rootedness in actuality. This is a process which many readers still find exasperatingly para-doxical. Yvor Winters, for example, accuses Eliot of holding the doctrine of *l'art pour l'art*, and of basing his criticism on love of sensation without intellect.

He quotes the passage from 'The Function of Criticism' on the autotelic nature of art, and continues:

> One is confronted here with several problems. How, for example, can an artist perform a function better for not knowing what it is? Is Eliot assuming an automatic, or unconscious art, an art which is an extreme form of romantic mysticism?[1]

This is to misunderstand the whole tendency of Eliot's thought, and actually to misread the text out of exasperation

---

[1] Yvor Winters, *op. cit.* p. 121

with the complex variations in which that tendency is expressed. Whatever Eliot is advocating, it is certainly not 'romantic mysticism'; for his whole criticism is a denial of the poetic usefulness of such a mysticism. And what he actually says is: 'I do not deny that art may be affirmed to serve ends beyond itself; but art is not required to be aware of these ends, and indeed performs its functions, whatever they may be, . . . much better by indifference to them.' He does not deny to the *artist* awareness of his function—his function is, seemingly, to bring his resources of feeling, thought, and language to bear on his subject in such a way as to produce a self-contained reality. He is concerned with the *reality* of his poem, and his function is to ensure it. But it is not his job to know what is the *end* of his activity, the function of his own concern with function, or what use is to be made of it by others, or at what point it is to enter and affect the body of society. Poetry is important enough to be treated in its own terms, as a separate thing. Therefore, Eliot refuses for the time being to speculate on the results which poetry may have in society in general or in human affairs at all.

But the problem remains, and it seems to come from Eliot's view of the function of emotion in poetry. What he seems to suggest is that emotion should be generally part of the subject-matter of poetry, and not an informing and shaping power in the poetic formulation of the subject-matter. But even here the question is complicated. He praises Dante for the sanity of the 'view of life' which lies behind his poetry, and Shakespeare for his 'emotional maturity'. So it appears that emotion may lie behind the poem, not so much as a positive pressure on feeling and language, but rather as a kind of balance in the poet's inner life, preserving him from eccentricity of one kind or another. Again, it may be a kind of shaping power, to be admitted as such only in a disguised and, as it were, neutralised form. The importance of the process Eliot is trying to analyse (and which, in the end, perhaps reconciles such discordant uses of the word 'emotion' as I have pointed to) is that it drama-tises emotions, externalises them, by submitting them to the influence of something else and something poetically more valuable: to the sensibility acting as judge and maker.

His chief account of the necessity to dramatise emotion in

this way is given in the famous passage on the 'objective correlative':

> The only way of expressing emotion in the form of art is by finding an 'objective correlative'; in other words, a set of objects, a situation, a chain of events, which shall be the formula of that *particular* emotion; such that when the external facts, which must terminate in sensory experience, are given, the emotion is immediately evoked. If you examine any of Shakespeare's more successful tragedies, you will find this exact equivalence; you will find that the state of mind of Lady Macbeth walking in her sleep has been communicated to you by a skilful accumulation of imagined sensory impressions. . . . The artistic 'inevitability' lies in this complete adequacy of the external to the emotion. . . .[1]

'The only way'; the dogmatic abruptness of the phrasing demonstrates how great is Eliot's determination to get away from the direct utterance of emotion in poetry. Emotion is to be objectified, in a sense dramatised; it is to be dramatised by the exercise of *feeling*, which replaces it as the agent of poetic creation and which, indeed, turns it into a subject of poetry rather than an agent. Emotion should not be enacted in its own terms, but in terms of feeling. And feeling must include not only an apt sense of emotional tone and a sense of language, but also a sense of the actuality, the sensuous qualities, of things. Feeling is here a capacity for 'sensory experience':

A similar emphasis can be found in the equally famous passage on the poet as catalyst:

> The other aspect of this Impersonal theory of poetry is the relation of the poem to its author. And I hinted, by an analogy, that the mind of the mature poet differs from that of the immature one not precisely in any valuation of 'personality', not by being necessarily more interesting, or having 'more to say', but rather by being a more finely perfected medium in which special, or varied, feelings are at liberty to enter into new combinations.[2]

The poet's mind is like a shred of platinum, assisting at the combination of other chemical elements while itself remaining unaffected. This mind

> may partly or exclusively operate upon the experience of the man himself; but, the more perfect the artist, the more completely

---

[1] 'Hamlet': *Selected Essays*, p. 145   [2] *The Sacred Wood*, pp. 53-4

separate in him will be the man who suffers and the mind which creates; the more perfectly will the mind digest and transmute the passions which are its material.[1]

The experience, you will notice, the elements which enter the presence of the transforming catalyst, are of two kinds: emotions and feelings. The effect of a work of art upon the person who enjoys it is an experience different in kind from any experience not of art. It may be formed out of one emotion, or may be a combination of several; and various feelings, inhering for the writer in particular words or phrases or images, may be added to compose the final result. Or great poetry may be made without the direct use of any emotion whatever: composed out of feelings solely.[2]

It is an interesting passage. One could use it to argue that Eliot sees the human intelligence as a mere enabling condition of the production of a poem, that is, as essentially passive. And one could argue the opposite case: that he assigns a snobbish superiority to intelligence or 'mind', seeing it as a privileged power which controls elements without itself being influenced by its activity. On this reading, the mind would be like the author in Stephen Dedalus' aesthetic—'refined out of existence . . . paring his fingernails', godlike and mysterious. In fact, there is no need to take either reading. The passage does not imply a complete withdrawal of art from life, nor of the artist from his own life; it implies a withdrawal of the artist's forming and judging power from that in his experience which is the material of his art, and which, therefore, offers itself to be judged and formed. The 'more completely' the man as artist is withdrawn from man as experience, the better integrated the poem is likely to be: because such a withdrawal lessens the chance of emotion entering in an undisguised form, and disrupting or deflecting the feelings in their patient assembling.

Now, whatever we think of the truth of this analysis, it is patent that Eliot sees the emotions as separate, or at least separable, from the other experiences of the person; he sees them as providing something of the impulse *towards* poetry, but will not admit them as an impulse *within* poetry; and the reason for this insistence is that he fairly clearly regards them as

---

[1] *The Sacred Wood*, p. 54   [2] *Ibid.* p. 54

despotic, as exercising a despotism over mind and feelings. Art is, then, in some sense an avoidance of the despotism of the emotions; it is also, recurrently but not ubiquitously in Eliot's view, an escape from the reality of emotions.

If we accept such an interpretation of his position, we may find something repellent—and significantly repellent—in his use of such terms as 'catalyst' and 'tantalus jar' to define the poetic process. These terms indicate a desire for a kind of art in which the impulsiveness of the artist will be sterilised, or purged, or reduced to a controllable mechanism, though we should not forget that it is the 'mind' of the poet, and not his whole being, which is to play the rôle of a catalyst. And Eliot's whole criticism shows a number of points at which the emotions are openly separated from feelings:

> . . . poetry, however intellectual, has to do with the expression of feeling and emotion; [that] feeling and emotion are experienced in the language of daily life; and [that] feeling and emotion are particular, while thought is general.[1]

It is worth taking such a recent pronouncement on the subject, since it is all the more impressive an endorsement of remarks in 'Tradition and the Individual Talent', and in the paper on Dante. From first to last, he distinctly separates feeling and emotion, but he never clearly distinguishes their *natures*. What appears certain is that feeling has elements of perception and sensation, has a kind of continuity in personal life which emotion lacks. Eliot speaks, in this essay, of 'modes of feeling' possessed by a whole people; and such modes are surely a matter of continuous exercise or possession.

As we shall see, the conception of the rôle of emotion is a most ambiguous one. On the one hand, he wants to insist that poetry greatly transcends the emotions out of which it arises, and that its value is proportionate both to the strength and depth of the emotions and to the degree of transcendence. But, on the other hand, he seems to restrict poetry to the feeling for and dramatisation of emotion; and he seems therefore to find its moral meaning there. The note of transcendence is struck often:

> We have to communicate—if it is communication, for the word may beg the question—an experience which is not an experience

[1] 'The Social Function of Poetry': *The Adelphi*, July-September 1945, pp. 157-8

in the ordinary sense, for it may only exist, formed out of many personal experiences ordered in some way which may be very different from the way of valuation of ordinary life, in the expression of it.[1]

Here, if anywhere in contemporary criticism, is a 'classical' view: but a classical view influenced by the experiments and terminology of the French Symbolists. It does not, as Yvor Winters suspects, imply that art is 'about itself', but that a work of art comes out of a continuous living of experience and is in some sense continuous with that living: so continuous, at any rate, that the process of art cannot be accounted for in terms of 'experiences'. He seems plainly right. But one must say 'in some sense continuous'; for a large part of his writing on this point is devoted to stressing the view of the *discontinuity* of art with life; the presence of the catalyst is always shading his pages.

In whatever ways he puts it, we are continually reminded that poetry is a re-creation of, or a limitation of, or an escape from, the pressure of emotion. For Eliot, poetry concerns chiefly the reality of emotions, is a report on what it means (and not merely what it is like) to have certain emotions. The mind 'creates', but the man 'suffers', endures; and what he suffers is his own emotional life; living, in that sense, is suffering. Poetry, then, will probe and exhibit the emotions, but the condition of its doing so artistically is that it rob the emotions of their force as emotions. The beginning of art is the distancing of oneself from one's own emotions, and seeing them truly: looking into the Shadow, in fact. Consequently, emotion is seen by Eliot always as a state, never as a movement; and the dynamic activity of the whole person in which emotions *act* is never really seen by him at all. He is fascinated by emotions only while they can be fixed and transmuted; and the process of transmutation seems to be, for him, an artistic and moral purging.

I am anxious not to misrepresent a critic so honest and valuable; but it is necessary to insist on the ambivalence of his attitude, in so far as that attitude can be understood clearly at all; and the only way of insisting on it will involve the appearance of oscillating hesitantly between what is positive in that

[1] *The Use of Poetry*, p. 30

attitude, and what is negative or sterile or afraid. Certainly, it is necessary to insist once more, before further documentation of the 'negative', that the attitude is by no means a tissue of negatives. The probing of emotional states is not merely a sort of delayed catharsis of what is interiorly oppressive, a purging as it were by remote control, it is also to be a profound aware- ness, a feeling for the meaning of one's own states, and the states of others:

> It [poetry] may make us from time to time a little more aware of the deeper, unnamed feelings which form the substratum of our being, to which we rarely penetrate; for our lives are mostly a constant evasion of ourselves, and an evasion of the visible and sensible world.[1]

But these are feelings, not emotions, and they are feelings existing at such depth that they provide a permanent sub- stratum of the experiencing person. No doubt it is only the finest poets who will penetrate so far, and they will do so through a probing and evaluating of their emotions. So their work, as I shall attempt to show in the next chapter, is a report on the human condition, on what it means to be existentially human.

Passages of this sort—and there are many more in Eliot's criticism—present a valuable insight into the nature of poetry and its links with reality. They remind us that the primary place in which poetry engages life is the interior life of the writer himself, is that life seen at depth and without illusions, and seen as representative of a general state of humanity. Have we the right to expect anything more of the poet than this? And if we do expect more, are we expecting of poetry something which religion alone is capable of giving? The answer will depend on the terms in which a particular poet re-creates his awareness, for it is those terms which will enforce a conviction of value. But one can say, no doubt with too much crudity, that man is not only a state, he is also a process; that the poet, like any other man, will gain his insight into values by feeling not only what in himself is permanent or oppressive, but also what is growing. Poetry deals with growth as well as with fixity;

[1] *Ibid.* p. 155

and it is the product of growing more than of fixity. It is this positive and dynamic quality in human life that Eliot seems afraid to take account of.

At this point, we may notice an even more worrying stress on impersonality: a stress which is found in the earlier rather than the later criticism, and is found particularly in the essays, 'Shakespeare and the Stoicism of Seneca', and 'Ben Jonson'. One example will represent several references:

> Shakespeare, too, was occupied with the struggle—which alone constitutes life for a poet—to transmute his personal and private agonies into something rich and strange, something universal and impersonal. . . .[1]

This is surely a view which would limit the range of a reader's responsiveness to poetry. How, for example, could we approach the work of Chaucer, or of Blake, with such a preoccupation? But for Eliot 'the man' suffers, is unresolved and dark; poetry creates, clarifies, gives form, dramatises and transcends the stress of being a man. He indicates the superiority of Shakespeare to Jonson by positing the existence in Shakespeare of 'susceptibility to a greater range of emotions, and emotion deeper and more obscure'.[2] Emotion is in itself not only oppressive, but formless and dark; the direct expression of emotion in poetry continues the formlessness and endorses the darkness; escape must come from clarification, and clarification from the process of dramatising: the process of poetry is a tortuous one.[3]

What, then, does the celebrated impersonality amount to in Eliot's criticism? It begins in a certain attitude to human emotions, and is confused and complicated by that attitude. On the one hand, there is the tendency to regard poetry as a release from interior oppression. On the other, there is the desire to see it as the clarification and even completion of human 'suffering', of suffering understood because it is truly felt. On the one hand the discontinuity of life with art; on the other, continuity between them. In so far as Eliot's position is

---

[1] *Selected Essays* (1949 edition), p. 137
[2] *Ibid.* p. 157
[3] See also *Selected Essays*, p. 297, where the remarks on Gray and Collins give, in germ, Eliot's whole position.

baffling to us, and even seriously suspect, it is because the note of discontinuity is so often harped on. Impersonality as such (taking his sense of it) is no more a virtue than tradition is. If, as I shall later insist, tradition is valuable to the extent that it is personalised and lived, surely the virtues which Eliot sums up under the head of Impersonality can be realised only to the extent that *they* are personalised and lived. But that is a paradox which, while Eliot would no doubt assent to it, does not appear conspicuously vital in his actual criticism.

In so far as his stress on Impersonality seems to me valuable, it is because he sees poetry as clarifying what in human experience could not be otherwise clarified. And to clarify is to evaluate. To dramatise the emotional pressure is to present in some way the meaning which that pressure has for man. Sometimes, indeed, Eliot does state quite clearly that he intends personal life not to be depersonalised, but given a universal force. He says that the greatest art

> is impersonal, in the sense that personal emotion, personal experience is extended and completed in something impersonal, not in the sense of something divorced from personal experience and passion.[1]

It is certainly no doctrine of *l'art pour l'art*, as a moment's reflection will show. Nor does the fascination with emotions in Eliot's work lead on to such a doctrine. His attitude is hard to characterise. It would be false to imply that the interest in Impersonality arises solely (though it does arise mainly) from a concern with emotions: it arises too from a conception of the rôle of *ideas* in poetry, and from a desire to establish the primacy of feeling/thought. Nothing must be allowed to deflect poetry from its natural growth; for, as Eliot often stresses, a poem is an unpredictable thing, which is a long time coming to birth:

> The poet's progress is dual. There is the gradual accumulation of experience, like a tantalus jar; it may be only once in five or ten years that experience accumulates to form a new whole and finds its appropriate expression. . . . The development of

---

[1] Preface to *Le Serpent*, by Paul Valéry, translated by Mark Wardle, 1924. I have been able to find this reference only in Matthiessen's *The Achievement of T. S. Eliot*. See also 'Yeats', p. 201 in the Penguin collection of Eliot's *Selected Prose* (Ed. John Hayward).

experience is largely unconscious, subterranean, so that we cannot gauge its progress except once in every five or ten years.[1]

This says what every poet knows: that the process by which one's experience makes itself ready for artistic expression is a mysterious one, for it is concerned ultimately with human mysteries, and that attempted short-cuts are a way of falsifying it. Eliot is not denying the poet responsible control of his own experience. He is, on the contrary, insisting on control and responsibility; he is merely denying the usefulness of short-cuts —what we might call the activist approach to poetry.

In doing so, he is striking a blow at the notion of poetry as *expression*—expression of 'self', or of emotion, even of ideas (despite his perhaps undue emphasis on 'mind' in his analysis). Poetry is the presentation of experience refined and transmuted by the very means of its expression. Emotion is refined and evaluated by being objectified through feeling; and 'mind' is the unobtrusive controller of feeling. Nor have we the right to easy 'ethical' judgments:

> For it is not the 'greatness', the intensity of the emotions, the components, but the intensity of the artistic process, the pressure, so to speak, under which the fusion takes place, that counts.[2]

Counts for what? The answer can only be given if we recall the beginning of Eliot's analysis. He began by offering to differentiate the mature poet from the immature by casting light on the artistic process itself. Therefore, we answer: Counts for maturity. Greatness is of poems, not of emotions. 'Sublimity', that catchcry of a semi-ethical criterion of poetry, has relevance only if it is seen as applying to the finished work. Sublimity of emotions is of little relevance, for emotions are merely part of the subject-matter.

The difference between emotion and feeling (though extremely difficult to specify from Eliot's work) would seem to be that the former is simply a temporary response to experience, while the latter is something by which the person becomes attached to actuality. It is thus both a *way* of experiencing the actual world, and a capacity for keeping that experience constant.

[1] Introduction to *Selected Poems* of Ezra Pound, p. 16
[2] *The Sacred Wood*, p. 55

But the question I am raising is a vexed one, and it admits of no easy answer. Some writers (Yvor Winters is one) consider that the moral reality of poetry stems mainly or solely from the consciousness, the deliberateness, of the artist's judgment of his experience. In such a view, the deliberation of judgment guarantees the *manner* in which moral meaning comes into the poem, and the manner in which it resides there. So morality tends to be reduced to the morality of statements (no matter how the control of these statements is held to modify or consolidate them poetically); and we are dangerously close to the notion that moral reality comes from the conscious moral intention of the poet. I can't accept this notion, because it denies that the whole person of the poet is, in the acts of composition, the agent producing this moral reality. That reality, whatever its nature, seems to me plainly the product of the whole of the poet's faculties as they are creatively engaged: faculties affective as well as cognitive. So Eliot's position, however many loose ends it leaves us, seems preferable. He seems to be saying something like this:

If the poet's experience is to get into poetry in the most formed and convincing way, it can only do so if he refrains from insisting too early on what shape it is to assume, and on what elements in his past experience are to be found relevant to this shaping. What is to be relevant is not a matter for *a priori* decision, but for a condition of equipoise, of waiting, of poised attention, which may look like inertia. If the poet is not a man 'expressing' his emotions, and thus engaging in a form of self-indulgence, neither is he a man *declaring* what is to be seen as relevant in his past experience. He waits, and he makes; and what he makes expresses and declares the things which, had they been more directly expressed or declared, might have come to be truncated and false. Poetry is not 'emotion recollected in tranquillity' (as Eliot elsewhere insists), but past experience working forward unobtrusively to give body, concreteness, a play of feeling, to a present apprehension of reality: which is perhaps what Wordsworth really meant. In the process, subjectivity becomes somehow objectified, and is thereby judged: though the judgment may be in no way overt.

It is impossible to over-emphasise the importance of feeling/

thought in the establishment of the idea of Impersonality. Even in *The Sacred Wood*, though much more openly in *After Strange Gods*, he sees the whole romantic tradition vitiated by the insistence on 'private judgment', allied as it is to the doctrine of 'private inspiration'. This issues in a reliance on personality, on poetry as the release ('expression') of emotion, and on the sufficiency of the individual conscience as a guide in life. Its final results are the cult of originality, the canonising of random sensation, and an impressionistic criticism, like that of Swinburne. All of these things lead to a denial of the autonomy of poetry, because they lead us to see poetry as primarily a highway into the personality of its author. Consequently, they tend to debase not only the autonomy, but also the specific reality of the poem.

If I am right in believing that the moral reality is not a part of a poem, but exists to the limits and in the depth of the whole poem, then it is possible that expressionism debases our idea of the moral reality of a poem as well. Eliot does not suggest this in *The Sacred Wood*, but he does in *After Strange Gods*. It is difficult to see how a unified moral reality can inhabit a poem formed merely by the expression of emotion, or by a reliance on personality. Rather, it seems to be possible only if an open moral meaning is declared or asserted by the poet as part of his process of self-expression. In that case, the morality comes into the poetry as a set of tenets, offering themselves to be debated; the reader's moral judgment of the poem (which should be not only inseparable from the artistic judgment, but one with it) becomes one side of a debate, in which the poet presumably asserts the opposing side: or it becomes, at best, an endorsement of the poet's *ideas*. What Eliot wants (although he does not put it in these terms) is a poetry which demands a judgment at once artistic and moral.

So far, then, I feel that Eliot is right, though it needs a good deal of exploration to disengage his position at all. *His* emphasis is on sensibility: on sensibility as an awareness both of actual things and of emotions. In that awareness there are elements of thought and of feeling. He insists that the reality of poetry comes from the contact of the sensibility with actuality. But how much of life is comprised in that term 'actuality'? It does not necessarily include certain spiritual states, whether refined and exalted or lowered into what he elsewhere calls 'the abyss'. What has 'feeling' to do with such states? Is it sufficient to apprehend them? He gives an answer in *After Strange Gods*, certainly, but, for reasons which I shall suggest later, I do not find it an entirely satisfactory one. And in *The Sacred Wood* he shies away from the question entirely. Even in *After Strange Gods*, the orthodoxy which he affirms is one of 'sensibility'.

The other difficulty which arises comes from his refusal to allow any positive power to emotion. I fail to see why emotion must be restricted to lying behind poetry, or being the subject of it, or being objectified in it in the modes of feeling. Surely it is the case that, in the finest poetry, a powerful emotion provides part of the impulse, the motivating force, even to the process of its own judgment or objectification. And if joy is an emotion as well as a state, surely Eliot's emphasis has the effect of excluding or depreciating a poetry of joy.

This may seem no more than a minor caveat; but there are certain relevant facts. The first is, that Eliot speaks approvingly of 'emotional maturity' as the interior condition of the production of Shakespeare's best works; and while he does not say what he means by this, it would seem to mean a state of emotional life which readily offers itself to the clarification of poetry. On this basis, his judgment of *Hamlet* is a judgment that the play is immature in a disabling sense. The second fact is, that there is throughout his work a curious association of emotions with *ideas*, so that his reasons for reprehending a poetry which is a direct expression of emotion are also reasons for reprehending a poetry which is a direct expression of thought. I say that this is curious; but it is curious only because it is unexpected; and there is a rationale behind it. As we shall see, the expression of emotions and the expression of ideas are, for Eliot, complementary agents in the aggrandisement of personality. In trying to analyse this attitude, he falls at times into an odd phrasing:

> The poet who 'thinks' is merely the poet who can express the emotional equivalent of thought. But he is not necessarily interested in the thought itself. We talk as if thought was precise and emotion vague. In reality there is precise emotion and there

is vague emotion. To express precise emotion requires as great intellectual power as to express precise thought.[1]

I am not clear what 'precise emotion' might be, nor why a critic should want to attach the word 'precise' to it. And the first sentence comes oddly from a writer the general tendency of whose work is to insist that emotion should find in poetry an equivalent in feeling/thought. Whatever the exact meaning of Eliot's statement, it is surely misleading to imply that 'thinking' is something that can't be carried out in poetry unless it finds an emotional equivalent. If we were to take this literally, we must see it as an exact inversion of the notion of the objective-correlative. For that reason, and because the continued weight of Eliot's emphasis is against it, we can't take it literally; and if we can't take it literally, I don't see how we are to take it.

As we shall see, his criticism of Hardy links 'ideas' with emotion, and sees the literary result as a blending of emotionalism with private and eccentric judgments of life. In fact, we are informed that the emotionalism comes about *because* Hardy's ideas are private, because they are not the product of tradition, have behind them no communal sanction.[2]

It is only in a very limited sense that Eliot can be said to be invoking here the criterion of truth. Certainly, he holds that Hardy's metaphysics are perverse; but his criticism of Hardy claims to be not a metaphysical but a moral one. And in fact he refuses, except in a very limited sense, to consider truth as a criterion of judgment at all. I hope to show later in what sense I mean.

We recall, for example, his statement that beliefs—that is, 'beliefs as held', beliefs believed in—are not relevant to a poet's work. In the essay on Dante we find that:

> . . . we can make a distinction between what Dante believes as a poet and what he believes as a man . . . his private belief becomes a different thing in becoming poetry.[3]

We have seen a similar view before in Eliot's work, in 'Tradition and the Individual Talent'. But there he was

---

[1] *Selected Essays*, p. 135
[2] This occurs in *After Strange Gods*, which, so one guesses, may not be the most reliable record of his opinions. However, one must adhere to the text.
[3] The whole passage should be consulted: V. *Selected Essays*, pp. 257-61, 269-71.

concerned to differentiate the experience ('suffering') of the man from the activity of the artist; here, he is concerned to distinguish between two operations of the intelligence: the operation of 'believing', which is essentially private, and that of making, of conversion or transformation of belief, which is essentially public and in a real sense impersonal. It is an insistence on poetry as a public mode of existence which must not be identified in any way with its roots in the private experience of the poet. If the poet enters this public existence at all, he must do so as a dramatic entity, modified by his self-given context, and not as a subject, a mere self, using the poem to gain attention for himself or his ideas:

Or his ideas. For:

> Or, rather, did Shakespeare think anything at all? He was occupied with turning human actions into poetry.[1]

And:

> In the Nineteenth century another mentality manifested itself. It is evident in a very able and brilliant poem, Goethe's *Faust*. Marlowe's Mephistopheles is a simpler creature than Goethe's. But at least Marlowe has, in a few words, concentrated him into a statement. . . . Goethe's demon inevitably sends us back to Goethe. He embodies a philosophy. A creation of art should not do that; he should *replace* the philosophy. Goethe has not, that is to say, sacrificed or consecrated his thought to make the drama; the drama is still a means.[2]

The eccentricity (if it is an eccentricity) which he is reproving is the one which we might call 'inadvertent didacticism'. Goethe may not intend to preach; but he is so concerned with his thought as such, that it never becomes adequately dramatised; 'the drama is still a means', even when it is not a consciously manipulated means. Eliot's phrasing is again slightly paradoxical. He complains that 'Goethe's demon . . . embodies a philosophy'; but what he seems to mean is that Mephistopheles does *not* embody a philosophy, but merely represents one. The difference is important. If 'thought' receives its proper incarnation in poetry, it becomes something which we are forced to deal with in more complex terms than

[1] *Selected Essays*, p. 135   [2] *The Sacred Wood*, p. 66

those of thinking. In Goethe's case, so Eliot would maintain, the desirable sea-change has not happened. And so drama becomes a sophisticated kind of self-indulgence, in which it is a love of ideas, not of emotions, that is indulged.

Such a position seems unequivocal enough and persuasive enough. But what, in fact, is positive in it? In the essays I have mentioned, and in 'The Social Function of Poetry', he suggests that whatever ways ideas may be considered to be relevant to poetry, they are best assimilable when they are not original to the poet, when in fact they are to a large extent a *donnée*. Consequently, a poet fully in and of the 'tradition' would probably not want to insist on his 'ideas' at all; not only would they not strike him as being specifically *his*, they would exist in him not as ideas but as sensibility: a sensibility which is ultimately moral.

It is a striking conception, and one is inclined to accept it. But large issues are involved. It is probably true that the most intelligent poetry comes about within an accepted order of truth. But in the first place, one must ask whether we have not the ability, or the right, or even the duty, to choose among differing orders of truth: a query which Eliot would probably meet with the surely unsatisfactory answer that for the Western world there is only one order of truth, and that that is incarnated in the tradition; and we are *in* the tradition, whether we know it or not; all that we can do is to choose to be either more or less *of* it. Such an answer seems unsatisfactory. And, in the second place, Eliot's conception does not at all help us to see the rôle of thought in the process of poetry, or to gauge the sense in which a poem is valuable because it is *true*. Here the notion of tradition becomes an evasive abstraction, as we see when it deflects his critical attention in *After Strange Gods*. The looseness of that book obviously comes to some extent from the strain of trying to hold and to actualise a bafflingly involved view.

Such questions cannot possibly be debated in a study of this length.[1] What is certain is that Eliot has given us no persuasive answer to them. His position may, at the risk of considerable misunderstanding, be called a formalist one; for he plainly sees

[1] For an opposing view, see Erich Heller: *The Hazard of Modern Poetry*, p. 24.

poetry as a liberation not only from the oppression of emotion
but also from the eccentricity of ideas. It is in this sense, I think,
that he insists that the use of the critical faculty is necessary to
creativity.

In all this, I am sure that he is, in one way, quite right. His
whole position is a protest against the use of poetry as a means
to self-indulgence of any kind whatever. But while it would be
unfair to retort that his own view of poetry as a purging and
dramatising of emotion is merely a more sophisticated example
of the same vice, we may suggest that he casts his censor's net
too wide, and is prepared to exclude from poetry too many
sources of vitality. What is valuable in his view is the sense it
conveys of the integrity of poetry:

> We cannot simply *use* poetry to express our thought or feeling,
> and we cannot simply seek for knowledge or experience, for the
> sake of writing poetry.[1]

For, in the great poets:

> their learning and thought, as well as their experience of men and
> actions, [should] have been assimilated by their sensibility. And
> for this to happen, the experience must come on its own terms,
> the intellectual study must be pursued for its own sake.[2]

Art, he suggests, is vitiated if its chief effect is to call attention
to the emotions or ideas which it contains, or to the personality
of its maker. The satisfaction so gained is an illicit one, or, at
least, an inartistic one.

If thought and experience must be 'assimilated by sensibility',
however, this can only happen satisfactorily within the 'tradition'. Tradition is the chief positive which Eliot offers, as
personality is the chief destructive force. Personality and tradition are enemies, as we have already seen. And:

> No artist produces great art by a deliberate attempt to express
> his personality. He expresses his personality indirectly through
> concentrating on a task.[3]

In *After Strange Gods*, Eliot sees the two streams blending: the
reliance on personality, and the reliance on the expression

---

[1] 'The Social Function of Poetry': *The Adelphi*, July-Sept., 1945, p. 155
[2] *Ibid.* p. 155
[3] 'Four Elizabethan Dramatists': *Selected Essays*, p. 114

of 'ideas'. But now he sees them blending to enforce views of life which are eccentric and unorthodox within a tradition—the Romantic—which encourages eccentricity in the artistic equivalent of private judgment. He complains that contemporary novelists have been:

> more concerned than their predecessors—consciously or not—to impose upon their readers their own *personal view of life*, and [that] this is merely part of the whole movement of several centuries towards the aggrandisement and exploitation of *personality*.[1]

He sees them using the forms of art for an ulterior motive—the imposition of private and hence eccentric views—which is not generally recognised as ulterior, because the past hundred and fifty years have disposed most readers to associate art with personality in an inseparable union.

We must remember that Eliot is speaking in this book avowedly as a moralist, and not as a literary critic. It goes without saying, however, that the two functions of a reader's (or a lecturer's) response can't really be separated at all, where actual literary works are the subject of discourse. So we must judge his statement as the expression of a view of the nature of literature.

He finds the insistence on personality, and the imposition of a personal view of life, connected with issues which are directly moral. The aggrandisement of the personality, of the personal view, is the result or concomitant of the erection of individualistic morals.

The pages on the novels of Thomas Hardy are at the core of his actual criticism in this book: and although he refers here to fiction, his remarks apply more or less directly to poetry as well. For reasons of clarity, I shall look at certain aspects of his position here, and at others in the next chapter.

His criticism of Hardy is an attempt to expose the eccentricity in the novelist's view of life, and so in the means which he adopts to reveal character and its destiny; for Eliot, Hardy's eccentricity is closely connected with the inordinate assertion of personality through a kind of emotion which becomes emotionalism; Hardy wrote

---

[1] *After Strange Gods*, p. 53

as nearly for the sake of 'self-expression' as a man well can; and the self which he had to express does not strike me as a particularly wholesome or edifying matter of communication.[1]

The tart and moralising tone of this comment should be remarked, for it is evidence that Eliot is not so much estimating Hardy as attacking him. But to see the intent and quality of his criticism, I shall have to quote him at length:

> In consequence of his self-absorption, he makes a great deal of landscape; for landscape is a passive creature which lends itself to an author's mood. Landscape is fitted too for the purposes of an author who is interested not at all in men's minds, but only in men as vehicles for emotions. It is only, indeed, in their emotional paroxysms that most of Hardy's characters come alive. This extreme emotionalism seems to me a symptom of decadence; it is a cardinal point of faith in a romantic age, to believe that there is something admirable in violent emotion for its own sake, whatever the emotion or whatever its object. But it is by no means self-evident that human beings are most real when most violently excited; violent physical passions do not in themselves differentiate men from each other, but rather tend to reduce them to the same state; and the passion has significance only in relation to the character and behaviour of the man at other moments of his life and in other contexts. Furthermore, strong passion is only interesting or significant in strong men; those who abandon themselves without resistance to excitements which tend to deprive them of reason, become merely instruments of feeling and lose their humanity; and unless there is moral resistance and conflict there is no meaning.[2]

Several things about this passage are worthy of notice. In the first place, it begins by offering (implicitly) an analysis of Hardy's work in certain terms, but quickly changes to a kind of sermon. In the second place, a prejudice is immediately invoked by the repeated use of the word 'landscape'. The fact is, Hardy does not deal only with landscape, he deals with nature—a word which has connotations of positive quickening and liveliness which Eliot wants to avoid in stressing the inertness, the use-ability, of nature as mere landscape. Third, there is the suggestion, thrown casually down to colour the discourse,

[1] *Ibid.* p. 54   [2] *Ibid.* p. 55

that Hardy uses characters only for the purpose of self-expression; the term 'vehicles for emotions' means, of course, 'vehicles for Hardy's private emotions', which ought not to intrude on the novels at all.

The burden of the whole passage is that a 'personal view of life' tends towards emotionalism; and emotionalism is the release of emotion in art without the stiffening of spiritual awareness of human beings, and without the *relevance* which comes from its being the product and concomitant of a feeling for moral struggle. Therefore, it is emotionalism which accounts for Hardy's recurrent and unfocussed rhapsodising, for his self-indulgence in the use of 'landscape', and for his self-indulgence in the treatment of character. In this last, Eliot finds a rather horrifying moral flaw. He says that some of Hardy's scenes

> seem deliberately faked. And by this I mean that the author seems to be deliberately relieving some emotion of his own at the expense of the reader.[1]

And in Hardy's group of short stories *A Group of Noble Dames*, the emotional eccentricity (amounting, I suppose, to sado-masochism) which Eliot detects in, for example, *Far from the Madding Crowd*, is seen as becoming a love of cruelty directly dependent on Evil:

> I do not object to horror: *Oedipus Rex* is a most horrible plot from which the last drop of horror is extracted by the dramatist; and among Hardy's contemporaries, Conrad's *Heart of Darkness* and James's *Turn of the Screw* are tales of horror. But there is horror in the real world; and in these works of Sophocles, Conrad and James we are in a world of Good and Evil. In *Barbara of the House of Grebe* we are introduced into a world of pure Evil. The tale would seem to have been written solely to provide a satisfaction for some morbid emotion.[2]

I have said that we have the right, at least in a study of this sort, to treat *After Strange Gods* as a work of, or implying, or deriving from, literary criticism. Yet the effect—and perhaps the intention—of this account of Hardy will be not to send readers back with some illumination to the novels, but to persuade them to avoid them altogether. It seems to me to be

---

[1] *After Strange Gods*, p. 56   [2] *Ibid*. p. 58

attack in the service of defence: defence of modern readers from certain 'corrupting' influences in modern literature. To the extent that it is this, and therefore to some extent a work of polemics, it is the worse criticism. But its emphasis is clear; and it is a literary emphasis. Hardy is unbalanced as an artist because his sensibility is unbalanced. His sense of the actual world and his sense of moral issues are far weaker than his desire to express himself, his private emotions, and his 'ideas'. The unhealthiness of the emotions, and the idiosyncrasy of the ideas, are signs that he does not possess an orthodox sensibility.

The emphasis is still on sensibility, as it always was: sensibility as the guarantee of impersonality in poetry. But where sensibility was once estimated by criteria of strength and immediacy, now it is estimated according to its orthodoxy. Although I shall be saying something on this point in the next chapter, some mention may be made of it here.

The phrase must be taken as a whole: 'orthodoxy of sensibility'. The term 'orthodoxy' by itself does not properly indicate the direction of Eliot's thought. Therefore, it is inappropriate for D. S. Savage to object to his judgment of Joyce as 'the most ethically orthodox of the more eminent writers of my time' by saying:

> Though was he, as a matter of fact, a believer at all.[1]

For, as Eliot himself says:

> We are not concerned with the authors' *beliefs*, but with orthodoxy of sensibility and with the sense of tradition, our degree of approaching 'that region where dwell the vast hosts of the dead'.[2]

Orthodoxy of sensibility is shown to us as an ethical quality. It is the capacity for *feeling* human life and the actual world in such a way as to *feel* as well their moral implications. In the case where emotions are the subject of a novel or poem, it would presumably operate not only through an intense awareness of the reality of those emotions, but through an awareness of their place in a whole scheme of life and of what they are likely to lead to, in action or achievement of a spiritual state.

---

[1] *The Personal Principle*, p. 105   [2] *Op. cit.* p. 38

But against what criterion, within what scale, is this awareness to get its sanction, its certificate of health, as it were? Eliot's answer would be: Within the perspective provided by the wisdom of the race. And by this he means a communal experience, moral and spiritual and even sensuous, delivered by Greece and Rome, preserved and enriched by Christianity. In *After Strange Gods*, Christianity is seen as the specific test. And a man's fiction or poetry is likely to have balance, order, intactness, impersonality (all the values, in fact, for which Eliot has always contended), only if it has behind it the pressure of this tradition, actualised in the Christian sense of Good and Evil.

The literary values, then, remain what they have always been in Eliot's criticism. At least, they seem to remain constant, for it is obvious that he does not now possess a sufficient sense of literature to be the great critic which he once was. But what was once an emphasis on the poetic *process* as the guarantee of those values is now an emphasis on ultimate sanctions and enabling conditions. Eliot's moral interest and sense have not increased; it is only his explicit—and rather disproportionate— insistence on them that has done so. For such a sense, deriving power from a sense of a whole culture and tradition, is present in 1924. Then, Eliot says that the philosophy of the Elizabethan dramatists

> may be summarized in the statement that Duncan is in his grave. Even the philosophical basis, the general attitude to life of the Elizabethans, is one of anarchism, of dissolution, of decay. It is in fact exactly parallel and indeed one and the same thing with their artistic greediness, their desire for every sort of effect together, their unwillingness to accept any limitation and abide by it.[1]

He would probably not go so far as to say (what Arnold clearly implies) that a 'style' is a moral thing. But he says here that moral corruption and artistic disorder are not only analogous but may be 'one and the same thing'. Moral order, and the feeling for it, lead in art into a recognition of limits, propriety in the deepest sense and on the largest scale.

This stress has its complement in his view of the way in which

---

[1] 'Four Elizabethan Dramatists': *Selected Essays*, p. 116

poetry should be received. A genuine impersonality will lead to an art, not, certainly, divorced from life, but bearing life within it in a form at once concentrated and impersonal:

> The aim of the enjoyment of poetry is a pure contemplation from which all the accidents of personal emotion are removed; thus we aim to see the object as it really is and find a meaning for the words of Arnold.[1]

For this very reason, because of his certainty that great art is impersonal, he reproves those who expect poetry to do too much: to be a vehicle of unacknowledged legislation, or to save us, or even to interpret life for us, to console and sustain us. With Romanticism, he quotes Rivière as saying

> the literary art came to be conceived as a sort of raid on the absolute, and its result as a revelation.[2]

If this is true, we might add that, with the much punier neo-Romantics of the past two decades, it came to be conceived as a sort of raid on the deeper, less conscious layers of the personality, which came in turn to be conceived as an absolute. For, since 'we are still in the Arnold period',[3] 'the current tendency is to expect too much, rather than too little, of poetry'.[4]

It is a reliance on personality and emotion which leads to the growth of this expectation. In reply to it, Eliot offers a conception of the poem as a *communion* (to use Allen Tate's phrase) rather than a communication:

> *If* poetry is a form of 'communication', yet that which is to be communicated is the poem itself, and only incidentally the experience and the thought which have gone into it.[5]

Eliot shows us how a feeling for (not only a conception of) the due impersonality of poetry can lead to a balanced sense of its value. It is obvious from our perspective in literary history that all talk about what poetry is to *accomplish* (to edify or to save us, to promote peace of mind or social revolution) presupposes an answer to the cardinal and begged question who

[1] *The Sacred Wood*, pp. 14-15   [2] *The Use of Poetry*, p. 128
[3] *Ibid.* p. 129   [4] *Ibid.* pp. 148-9
[5] *Ibid.* p. 30

is the poet's audience; besides, it loses sight of the reality for the sake of a fantasy of possibilities. It is, of course, a different thing to say that good poetry can't help having an important effect upon the responsive reader's sensibility and sense of life. Such a statement, though by no means of a scientific order, is sufficiently rooted in our communal experience to be persuasive. Yet, for that very reason, it can't afford to claim too much.

It is part of Eliot's value (as of Arnold's) that he realises that his notion of impersonality leads to one of communion. Yet Arnold's view, though it scorns the 'personal estimate', does not really include a feeling for impersonality. For Eliot, it is the key to his whole view of the value of poetry. And his ambiguous way of affirming it, his use of mechanical or sterile images to define it, is the chief cause of the unease which I for one feel with that view.

CHAPTER V

T. S. Eliot: The Question of Orthodoxy

A DISCUSSION of value in terms of impersonality is more characteristic of Eliot's earlier than of his later writings. In the earlier, his whole approach is made through an intense realisation of the reality and autonomy of poetry, the recognition that poetry is something in its own right, and not an equivalent of or substitute for something else. And his insistence on the poet's mind as a 'medium' (dangerous term) in which meaning assembles and is shaped ensures that he treat poetry alone, poetry largely as process, and not something else. Such an approach is perhaps too close to the object to see its full value; and it no doubt needs to be completed by an approach from a different angle. What is in doubt is the terms in which he later chooses to complete it.

The later criticism, that from at least 1932, is less concerned to affirm impersonality than to pass censure on the literary uses of personality. It reveals an open moral concern, even a moralistic one; for Eliot is plainly interested, both in *After Strange Gods* and in the essay 'Religion and Literature', to find some means of protecting the modern sensibility against certain unhealthy factors as they receive a literary form in contemporary novels and poems. His concern is therefore a pastoral one. It amounts to what we may call a negative didacticism, for he is seldom positively didactic, seldom engaged in the direct teaching of virtue. As many commentators, chiefly in the review *Scrutiny*, have remarked, his critical capacity has suffered, possibly not from the presence, but at least from the relative strength of this concern. He seems no longer capable of driving the scalpel of his finely discriminating intelligence into the very fibre and tissue of a literary work seen as a living whole; and he is too quick to take up questions (such as the theological orientation of a poet or novelist) which are certainly important, but which in his hands come to seem the central ones and to overshadow others quite as important.

In a paper, 'Religion and Literature', published in 1936, he affirms:

> Literary criticism should be completed by criticism from a definite ethical and theological standpoint. In so far as in any age there is common agreement on ethical and theological matters, so far can literary criticism be substantive. In ages like our own, in which there is no such common agreement, it is the more necessary for Christian readers to scrutinize their reading, especially of works of imagination, with explicit ethical and theological standards. The 'greatness' of literature cannot be determined solely by literary standards; though we must remember that whether it is literature or not can be determined only by literary standards.[1]

And he offers, in a footnote, Theodor Haecker's book on Virgil as 'an example of literary criticism given greater significance by theological interests'.

It is worth while scrutinising this passage. The third sentence in it is merely a repetition of the first, and I discuss the issues raised by it, in an appendix[2] dealing with a similar question. As for the second sentence, there are probably very few genuine critics who would want to contradict it; at the moment it is other things about the passage which seem most interesting.

It is a seemingly forthright declaration of principle, buttressed as it is by the use of words like 'definite' and 'explicit'. But it does not really tell us much at all. We find the relevance of theology to criticism asserted, but we find it asserted as an 'interest' or, at the very best, a 'standard'. If the theology becomes relevant to criticism merely as an additional interest, then it is difficult to see how it can become very relevant at all. And we find Eliot suggesting that there are two operations in the work of criticism—one to determine literariness ('whether it is literature or not'), and the other to determine stature ('greatness'). That this greatness is literary is not at all clear from the context; but if it is not, what else could it possibly be? The suggestion that there are two operations, two judgments involved, seems impossible to exemplify, much less to justify, in

---

[1] *Essays Ancient and Modern*, p. 93   [2] See Appendix A

actual criticism. And Eliot makes it because he seems to see literature existing as it were on two levels. The statement, seemingly so forthright, is really a most evasive one, concealing its indirection beneath a rhetoric of forthrightness. The proof is that, in the remainder of the essay, he makes no consistent attempt to defend or to elucidate the position just announced, but merely gives moral, or more properly pastoral, reasons for making it at all.

What underlies the passage, as I shall try to show later, is a feeling that Christianity, conceived as dogma or standard, is merely a sub- or super-structure to experience, and not an implicit vision of life to be actualised in daily experience or in poetry.

The same emphasis occurs in *After Strange Gods*, which I have already subjected to some analysis. This is an interesting book, particularly in its grave deficiencies. It comes at a time when Eliot is consolidating his allegiance to Catholic Christianity and revising (but not inverting) his whole approach to literature in the light of that allegiance. It comes, too, at a time of international crisis when Eliot was becoming increasingly preoccupied with the problems of social rather than poetic order. It does not claim to be literary criticism, but moral comment. The essay 'Religion and Literature' was originally a paper delivered to a specifically Christian audience; and its author might claim, with some justice, that he suited his tone and terminology to the needs of that audience. In the case of *After Strange Gods*, no such explanation can be offered. It consists of three public lectures, given on a public occasion. It may therefore be held to be part of a profession of faith to the secular world. As I have already tried to show, that faith (when one considers the subject of discourse) cannot be seen only as theological, it must be seen also as literary; we find this necessary even though Eliot warns against taking it as such:

> The three lectures which follow were not undertaken as exercises in literary criticism. If the reader insists upon considering them as such, I should like to guard against misunderstanding as far as possible. The lectures are not designed to set forth, even in the most summary form, my opinions of the work of contemporary writers: they are concerned with certain ideas in illustration of

which I have drawn upon the work of some of the few modern writers whose work I know. . . . I am uncertain of my ability to criticise my contemporaries as artists; I ascended the platform of these lectures only in the role of moralist.[1]

It is a conceivable undertaking, if it is backed by a sufficiently critical reading of the texts; and what primarily concerns us here is not the difference which he invokes between literary and moral criticism, not the estimate which he holds of the moral influence of any writer, but his views on the relation of poetry to morals, as these are revealed by his analysis.

In a review in *Scrutiny*, R. O. C. Winkler reproves Eliot for undergoing the shift of attention at all. He feels that Eliot went searching after the underlying assumptions of 'Tradition and the Individual Talent', and in the process became a moralist. But he does not say whether Eliot *found* those underlying assumptions; it is part of my thesis that he did:

> And the avowed object of *After Strange Gods* was to produce a Revised Version of *Tradition and the Individual Talent*. . . . Mr Eliot is distracted by the ethical generalizations he wishes to consolidate, and his object is no longer to understand, but to convert.[2]

There is animus here, and I think it leads its possessor astray. I have suggested that Eliot's intention is not to convert, but to protect; he is acting as a pastor, not a proselytiser. If this is so, then it is unfair to say that he no longer wishes to understand the object of his study. The trouble is that he is concerned too much with understanding one part or aspect of it; and it is an 'object' which cannot be divided into parts in this way. It is interesting that critics like Winkler attack quite angrily—and often justly—Eliot's rhetorical procedure, his loss of sensibility and precision; but the anger and distaste help to conceal the fact that they do not try to meet his position, or even to understand it in the dimension and the terms in which Eliot offers it. It is not a sufficient answer to such a position to say: 'Your thought is wrong; for the sensibility through which you illustrate it is deficient'.

The position can only be understood and met if we consider the view of reality on which it rests. For my present purpose,

---

[1] *After Strange Gods*, pp. 11-12   [2] *Scrutiny*. Vol. X, No. 2, p. 196

this can best be done by briefly estimating Eliot's view of the relations of poetry to reality; for he can make good his judgment, even his stance, only by assuming such a relation. I would suggest that his view of the moral reality of poetry comes directly, as Arnold's does, from such an assumption. It is one side of the coin of which the notion of Impersonality is the other.

We have seen that, in *The Sacred Wood*, Eliot considers Impersonality through an examination of the poetic process, and that this examination centres on the relation of the poet to his poetry. The moral reality of poetry is satisfactorily created mainly when a certain distance is maintained between them. But since Eliot in this book is plainly raising critical questions which bear on his own creative practice, he is concerned to ask only the preliminary questions about the way in which poetry engages reality: the reality of a whole literary order extending over centuries, the reality of the external world, and the reality of the poet's emotions which, in a maturing artist, become more and more the subject, not the motive, of his art. Hence the great emphasis on the integrity, and even the relative autonomy, of poetry.

I have already hinted, in the previous chapter, that Eliot's early view is one in which the term 'reality' might almost be superseded by the term 'actuality'. He sees the poet dramatising and objectifying his own emotions by placing them deliberately within the play of feeling/thought; and he sees that feeling/thought playing on the external world, dramatising it. We can understand better what is meant by this if we reflect that Eliot the critic is also the Eliot of 'Portrait of a Lady'.

But the external world seems, as a poetic subject, secondary to the emotions; it is the emotions which alternately fascinate and repel Eliot. Thus we find him trying to account for some lack of intelligibility, of integrity, in *Hamlet*, by positing a failure on the poet's part to bring something of himself into the light of consciousness, there to be judged and objectified:

> It is not merely the 'guilt of a mother' that cannot be handled as Shakespeare handled the suspicion of Othello, the infatuation of Antony, or the pride of Coriolanus. The subject might conceivably have expanded into a tragedy like these, intelligible, self-complete, in the sunlight. *Hamlet*, like the sonnets, is full of

some stuff that the artist could not drag to light, contemplate, or manipulate into art. . . .[1]

That 'stuff' is unrealised emotion, complicated by a feeling inarticulate or unassociated with thought. The metaphorical language in this passage is interesting, because it suggests what has always seemed to Eliot the relation of art to human inwardness: art is clear, light, a sunlight; the human being is dark, complex, inarticulated. The impersonality of art is necessary to express the value of man's inner life, in terms superior to those of his own emotions—and this, it seems, is the condition of his making them articulate at all.

Articulation is a process not only of bringing to light but of dramatising:

> The really fine rhetoric of Shakespeare occurs in situations where a character in the play *sees himself* in a dramatic light.[2]

And what the poet does is similar or analogous: he brings his past experience and his present emotion to the point where they can be dramatised, and he with them.

But his view of poetry as engaging (almost as with an enemy force) the reality of the emotions is seen most sharply, for instance, in 'Baudelaire in Our Time', 1928:

> No man was ever less the dupe of passions than Baudelaire; he was engaged in an attempt to explain, to justify, to make something of them, an enterprise which puts him almost on a level with the author of the 'Vita Nuova'. *The irritant of cruelty*—did Baudelaire 'bring' it, or did he not merely examine it . . . And hysteria! Was anyone ever less hysterical, more lucid than Baudelaire? There is a difference between hysteria and looking into the Shadow.[3]

The reality of a poem (and hence its moral stature) is connected with the reality which the poet investigates; and that reality is largely the actuality, the immediacy, of his own emotions. By 1928, he has begun to erect into an open standard the notions that lie behind (for example) his criticisms of Arnold and P. E. More in the *Sacred Wood*. He attacks the term 'criticism of life', as embodying a concept at once shallow and

---

[1] *The Sacred Wood*, p. 100   [2] *Ibid.* p. 81
[3] *Essays Ancient and Modern*, pp. 66-7

provincial[1]; for he plainly feels that it does not account for the kind of seriousness which comes into poetry as a result of the poet's 'looking into the Shadow'.

First of all, it is the Shadow of himself and his own emotions; and fine poetry depends upon his seeing these things truly, putting himself as it were outside them, in a position from which to judge. The interest of a poet like Baudelaire, then, is not that he 'expressed' himself, and not that he provides in his poems a neurological or sociological case-history, but that he 'sees truly' his own condition:

> We cannot be *primarily* interested in any writers' nerves . . . or in any one's heredity except for the purpose of knowing to what extent that writer's individuality distorts or distracts from the objective truth which he perceives. If a writer sees truly—as far as he sees at all—then his heredity and nerves do not matter.[2]

'Sees truly' cannot possibly be made to mean 'holds the correct opinions'. What Eliot is interested in is the poet's way of confronting the reality of his own emotions, and, beneath them, the moral and spiritual reality to whose existence they testify, even when they seem to do so by denial. Seen in this light, a writer's self-investigation is an act at once moral and representative: Moral, because he apprehends, feels his emotions as pervaded by Good and Evil; representative, because at this level he is investigating a permanent human state. Eliot would certainly agree that it is at the level of Good and Evil that men are brothers. It is in this sense, and not only because of Baudelaire's characteristic symbolism, that Eliot finds him 'primarily occupied with religious values . . .'[3]

In this essay, midway between *The Sacred Wood* and *After Strange Gods*, we are already nearing the end of a process of transition: Transition from the almost epistemological interest of the first, to the almost metaphysical interest of the second. A shift is being made from the actuality of the emotions to the orthodoxy of the sensibility which apprehends and judges them. To put it in another way, Eliot is suggesting that the emotions are completely actualised only when the moral reality behind or within them is actualised. In *After Strange Gods*, the emphasis

---

[1] *The Sacred Wood*, p. 43
[2] *Essays Ancient and Modern*, p. 67   [3] *Ibid.* p. 68

falls upon the necessity for an orthodox sensibility and for an analysis of human life at depth. The aim is not to see life steadily and see it whole, but to see it in its depth and to judge it there.

Tradition is associated with orthodoxy; it must be, in Eliot's view, if it is to be preserved as a living force at all:

> Tradition by itself is not enough; it must be perpetually criticised and brought up to date under the supervision of what I call orthodoxy.[1]

And:

> The general effect in literature of the lack of any strong tradition is twofold, extreme individualism in views, and no accepted rules or opinions as to the limitations of the literary job.[2]

And again:

> . . . a *tradition* is rather a way of feeling and acting which characterises a group throughout generations; and [that] it must largely be, or that many of the elements in it must be, unconscious; whereas the maintenance of *orthodoxy* is a matter which calls for the exercise of all our conscious intelligence. The two will therefore considerably complement each other.[3]

Tradition, then, is something given, as much a given as a man's emotions; and orthodoxy is a way of preserving, judging, supervising it. I am not clear whether the sentences I have quoted are intended as prescriptions for poets on the one hand, or for critics and sociologists on the other. Yet, in the logic of Eliot's whole position, the second alternative must be preferred; for, when he comes to speak of imaginative writers, he does not speak of them as supervising, or failing to supervise, a tradition, but of being, or failing to be, within it. He speaks of orthodoxy of sensibility.

This orthodoxy seems to be a matter of the terms in which man and nature are seen and felt. It is guaranteed by the Christian tradition (the 'orthodoxy' within the wider Western tradition), but it is not a mere re-presentation of dogmatic theology. Eliot is now more concerned with tendencies than with individuals. He is less interested in what poets and novelists conceive to be their creative problems than in the spiritual

---

[1] *After Strange Gods*, p. 62. [2] *Ibid.* p. 32 [3] *Ibid.* p. 29

state of society which poses a real (though rarely seen) problem
for all artists, and which gives a sharp point to the problems
they do recognise as their own. He insists so much on the
orthodoxy in the traditional literary order because he can't
see any orthodoxy embodied or exemplified in contemporary
society. Yet it is doubtful what value his prescriptions (if they
are prescriptions) can have for contemporary poets. When he
invokes Jane Austen to set against Hardy, we are made quite
conscious that what he is pressing for is *not* another Jane Austen;
but we are left wondering just what sort of artist he does hope to
see. Joyce is offered to us as an example of 'ethical orthodoxy';
but I can't suppose that Eliot would want to set him before us
as an exemplar and guide.

The fact is, that Eliot's conception of tradition and orthodoxy
is an inconsistent one. In his opening analysis, he is careful to
distinguish them and to affirm a seemingly definite relationship
between them; but when he comes later to speak of individual
modern writers, he seems to merge the two. It is a case of having
one's cake and eating it too; of blurring, with an almost ritual
movement of the hands, the distinctions which one claims to be
making. We are reminded of his judgment of Racine:

> To my mind, Racine's *Bérénice* represents about the summit of
> civilisation in tragedy; and it is, in a way, a Christian tragedy,
> with devotion to the State substituted for devotion to Divine law.[1]

In what way, then, a 'Christian tragedy'? This judgment seems
to me characteristic of Eliot's attitude. He wants to separate
Christianity from society, and at the same time to merge them;
it is the contradiction inherent in the kind of 'integralism'
expressed by Charles Maurras, who influenced Eliot; and much
of the difficulty latent in his phrase 'orthodoxy of sensibility'
comes, I think, from this fluctuation between terms and definitions. The trouble is that, even where he speaks of sensibility,
his main interest is in the external, institutional qualities of the
tradition which stabilises sensibility. There is a serious lack in
his analysis of 'inwardness with' the thing talked of: a lack of
that *seriousness* without which one can't approach the deeper
levels of literature or the deeper problems relating to the factors

---

[1] *The Use of Poetry*, pp. 41-2

which influence literature. As he says in *Notes Towards the Definition of Culture*:

> It is part of my thesis that the culture of the individual is dependent upon the culture of a group or class, and that the culture of the group or class is dependent upon the culture of the whole society to which that group or class belongs.[1]

Of course we know what he means, and nearly everyone would probably give assent to some interpretation of his terms. But we can see here signs of his whole later orientation towards literature. It differs as much from Arnold's as the two men differ in their literary emphases and intentions. And Arnold is the most important parallel we can find: a great critic of literature who is also a critic of society, and who works within the terms of the same questions as exercise Eliot. Arnold's view of culture is of an interior condition or possession of the person seeking full human perfection, a quality of spiritual being which is at once a possession and a search. Eliot's view is of an external state of society, a healthy tension of institutions and manners supervised by a general agreement on values (the *cultural* significance of dogma). The two approaches may not be necessarily antithetical—Arnold, after all, was not opposed to institutions; he advocated a certain regulating power for the Church in Society, for the State in education, and for the 'academy' in the current of thought—but they are surely at opposite poles in the century-long dialectic between liberalism and orthodoxy. Arnold's approach may be generally characterised, for want of a better word, as personalist, and Eliot's as institutionalist. In the condition of our century, it was certainly necessary that a distinguished mind should question the basis of Arnold's position; but Eliot's is not the only possible approach to that questioning, nor, indeed, the most healthy and convincing one.

In *Notes*, Eliot is openly concerned with the relation of religion to poetry:

> The artistic sensibility is impoverished by its divorce from the religious sensibility, and the religious by its separation from the artistic.[2]

---

[1] Faber & Faber, London, 1948: p. 21   [2] *Ibid.* p. 26

And:

> Aesthetic sensibility must be extended into spiritual perception,
> and spiritual perception must be extended into aesthetic sensibility
> and disciplined taste before we are qualified to pass judgement
> upon decadence or diabolism or nihilism in art.[1]

But these are remarks made by the way, and *After Strange Gods*
would seem to contain a more definitive statement. There, he is
not so much concerned to assert the ultimate equivalence of
poetic and religious standards as to assert a standard of moral
certainty from which writers defect only to the danger of their
writing.

He states his position at some length, and with much care for
qualification:

> I do not take orthodoxy to mean that there is a narrow path
> laid down for each writer to follow. . . . In my sense of the term,
> perfect orthodoxy in the individual artist is not always necessary,
> or even desirable.[2]

For, 'in many instances it is possible that an indulgence of
eccentricities is the condition of the man's saying anything at
all'. What the existence of a tradition, with its orthodox core,
does in such cases is to 'restrict eccentricity to manageable
limits'. And no writer can be fully orthodox, for no one writer
can include within his view of life the limits of the orthodox
vision:

> As for the small number of writers, in this or any other period,
> who are worth taking seriously, I am very far from asserting that
> any of these is wholly 'orthodox', or even that it would be relevant
> to rank them according to degrees of orthodoxy. It is not fair, for
> one thing, to judge the individual by what can be actual only in
> society as a whole; and most of us are heretical in one way or
> another. . . . Furthermore, the essential of any important heresy
> is not simply that it is wrong; it is that it is partly right. It is
> characteristic of the more interesting heretics, in the context in
> which I use the term, that they have an exceptionally acute
> perception, or profound insight, of some part of the truth; an
> insight more important often than the inferences of those who are
> aware of more but less acutely aware of anything. So far as we

---

[1] *Ibid.*   [2] *After Strange Gods*, p. 32

are able to redress the balance, effect the compensation, ourselves, we may find such authors of the greatest value. If we value them as they value themselves we shall go astray.[1]

We have only to read this passage to see how irrelevant is the charge that Eliot wants to erect a standard by which poems and novels (as yet unwritten) may be prescribed and a formula for prejudging them by. Yet I have the impression once again that he has shifted his terms of reference. I can't see that what he is referring to here is orthodoxy or unorthodoxy of 'sensibility', but a condition of intellectual attitude and conscious moral insight. He seems to suggest that we can judge writers (though we are not to rank them) by their motivating *ideas*; and he seems therefore to be advocating a kind of critical attention which is 'disinterested' in the wrong sense, inordinately watchful, lending itself to a too final or too explicit attempt to formulate the '*content*' of a work.

The same difficulty occurs, on a different level, in his remarks on Katherine Mansfield's short story 'Bliss'. He says of this story that

> the moral implication is negligible . . . the moral and social ramifications are outside of the terms of reference.[2]

Yet he praises

> the skill with which the author has handled perfectly the minimum material.[3]

The implication is interesting. We may feel impelled to ask what artistic status can be possessed by a work of art which has a 'negligible' moral implication; and Eliot's only gesture towards answering such a question is to speak of the perfect handling of the 'minimum material': by which he means, not material subjected to the minimum possible moral insight, but material conceived as absolutely neutral as to values.

The fact is that 'orthodoxy of sensibility' seems to be less a personal and positive insight into values, and affirmation of

---

[1] *After Strange Gods*, pp. 24-5. See also *The Use of Poetry*, p. 139, where he explicitly denies that poetry can be bound too closely to a total 'scheme of things', whether religious or not.
[2] *Ibid.* pp. 35-6
[3] *Ibid.* p. 36

them, than a sense of belonging to a tradition and of the limitations to human experience which that tradition demonstrates:

> We are not concerned with the authors' *beliefs*, but with orthodoxy of sensibility and with the sense of tradition, our degree of approaching 'that region where dwell the vast hosts of the dead'. And Lawrence is, for my purposes, an almost perfect example of the heretic. And the most ethically orthodox of the more eminent writers of my time is Mr Joyce.[1]

Despite its tendency to decline from the level of statement to that of rhetorical gesture (the 'vast hosts of the dead' do not really consolidate any argument), this is a key passage. We must remember that Eliot is concerned in these lectures to attack the cults of emotion and personality, and to hint at the literary influence of the Devil. Thus, 'orthodoxy of sensibility' seems to be a true *sense* of man's nature and limitations, and of the nature and limitations of poetry. This emphasis, associated as closely as it is with tradition, is another product and proof of Eliot's emphasis on *order*. It is more than a 'classical' leaning, for he has been at some pains to disclaim the relevance of such terms; it is an emphasis on the roots of art in the human image, and on the essentially limited nature of that image. This seems to be his chief ethical concern, as it is his chief artistic one: a concern not with spontaneity, or 'life', or the enlarging consolations of poetry, but with man as limited and subject to law. Thus he asserts that the 'traditional' view of human life, impregnated as it is with Christian awareness, gives a sense of the *reality* of human life which the more heterodox views cannot give:

> . . . with the disappearance of the idea of Original Sin, with the disappearance of the idea of intense moral struggle, the human beings presented to us both in poetry and in prose fiction today, and more patently among the serious writers than in the underworld of letters, tend to become less and less real. It is in fact in moments of moral and spiritual struggle depending upon spiritual sanctions, rather than in those 'bewildering minutes' in which we are all very much alike, that men and women come nearest to being real.[2]

To *being* real, not merely to *appearing* real as components or subjects of an artistic vision. There is a curious kind of spiritual

[1] *Ibid.* p. 38   [2] *Ibid.* p. 42

snobbery here, and it is hard to see what to make of it; for Eliot himself goes on to reproach Pound with making a hell 'altogether without dignity'; and he emphasises the flashy and accidental nature of Yeats' mythology:

> Thus, in Yeats at the age of sixteen (or at least, as in retrospect he seems to himself to have been at sixteen) is operative the doctrine of Arnold, that Poetry can replace Religion, and also the tendency to fabricate an *individual* religion.[1]

In Yeats' early poetry, the supernatural world

> is not a world of spiritual significance, not a world of real Good and Evil, of holiness or sin, but a highly sophisticated lower mythology.[2]

He acknowledges that, in the later poetry, Yeats purges his work of this excrescent mythology, that he 'has discarded, for the most part, the trifling and eccentric, the provincial in time and place'; but he does not even hint at the positive spiritual and moral qualities which inform the poetry of Yeats' middle period, and which thus superseded their eccentric predecessors. We can see quite clearly that Eliot is concerned with the restriction of eccentricity of vision, and with the poet's sense of the limitations both of humanity and of art. It would be wrong, of course, to accuse him, in his treatment of Yeats, of condemning a mythology because it is not the Christian 'mythology'. He is merely saying that Yeats' mythology has nothing to do with the essential moral struggle and spiritual insight with which poets in the Western tradition have commonly dealt; it is at best a decoration placed over the spiritual facts, at worst a distraction from those facts.

Eliot's position on the relation of poetry to truth and belief is relevant here. As I have already said, he plainly sees the relation of the poet to any intellectual formulation about the world as receptive, and even passive. In his terms, a view of life (not merely a philosophy in the narrow sense) is for the poet a given, something to be absorbed and used. So he prefers Dante to Shakespeare because the given philosophy which Dante used is superior. The poet's task, then (one hesitates to father on

---

[1] *After Strange Gods*, p. 44   [2] *Ibid.* p. 46

Eliot the word 'duty'), is to apprehend through feeling whatever in the common ('traditional') wisdom is relevant to his
present artistic purpose, and to reproduce it in the modes of
feeling. The process, of course, may be an immensely complex
one, involving unconscious factors as well as conscious, and it
is not to be expected that it should ever have a completely
'orthodox' result. But the tradition, supervised by orthodoxy, is
the authoritative factor, the standard for the poet's work even
when he is seen as modifying and re-arranging it by his own
activity. It is 'there', objective, a given. We get the impression
that Eliot is summoning up a silent presence which is also a
pressure, not only providing a standard to which poetry may
be referred but, to the extent that the poet consciously or unconsciously consents to it, somehow acting as a stabilising and
controlling influence on his work. Eliot's thought has consistently, from first to last, demanded the recognition of such an
objective presence and pressure. But in his early criticism its
character of an orthodoxy is understressed, even concealed,
because he avoids moral judgment or prescription, confines
himself so closely to an analysis of poetry as process, and
measures poetic intactness so largely in its own terms. But it is
there, and it is there as a sort of orthodoxy, the nature of which
remains undefined. It is to the accumulated wisdom represented
or embodied in it that the poet must 'sacrifice himself' in the
interests of maturity and impersonality; it is this which makes
artistically necessary his 'continual extinction of personality'.
Here we see the reason for the stress, in *The Sacred Wood*, on the
poet as a 'medium'. The poet's activity with regard to the
'tradition' is to accept and re-create it in terms of his own
sensibility, his 'individual talent', which in turn infinitesimally
modifies the tradition itself.

In the later work, in *After Strange Gods*, for instance, the stress
shifts from the value of the 'medium' to that of tradition. And
now we find the additional suggestion that the poet's very
sensibility is to be judged by the extent to which it is informed
by the tradition. In addition, the nature of the tradition is
openly affirmed. It is a vehicle or embodiment of the moral and
spiritual wisdom of Christianity.

I can see that the artistic process may involve a process of self-surrender; but it would seem truer to the general experience of poets to speak of this in terms of self-involvement rather than surrender. To prefer such a term is to emphasise that the poet's mind and sensibility become implicated with a current of life and art and not with a mere sanction; the tradition comes to be seen not merely as a tradition, a given, but as an enlivening part of the poet's whole experience. Eliot himself insists that it is 'Beliefs as felt' that are important in poetry; may we not insist that it is *tradition as felt*—and that is, ultimately, tradition as *lived*—that is an important influence in poetry. And tradition as felt will hardly be seen as tradition at all, but as something else. In this perspective, the term 'orthodoxy' is an unhappy one, for it leaves out of account the extent to which poetry involves the depths of human responsiveness to a whole range of presences and values; and it leaves out a necessary stress (particularly necessary in our age) on a personal vision of whatever values are affirmed. The creative process may, or perhaps must, involve an implicitly creative response towards the tradition; rather, to remove the stress further in the direction of life, towards whatever reality is signified by the tradition.

The condition of adequately *feeling* an objective spiritual reality is that we feel ourselves, our own humanity, its unique as well as its representative quality. The 'instressing' of the self is surely another road to impersonality, as it is to sanctity; and it would seem to be a more apt one, where poetry is concerned. If a philosophy or a tradition may be felt, experienced, may become subject to the play of sensibility, it is surely by being *personalised*, not by the experiencing self becoming *depersonalised*.

Eliot, of course, does not openly support any process of depersonalisation; but it is indicated by the stresses which he places, and it is indubitably carried by his tone. There is in all his writings on orthodoxy of sensibility a remarkable lack of vitality, an absence, not so much of positive recommendations (which are hardly in place), as of a sense of positive self-involvement in life. He may have such a sense; but if he does, it lies not in but behind the critical writings, in his private life. In the writings, the sense which he communicates is of an objective check, a regulator, a guarantor of balance, rather than of any positive vision which can *include* ordinary human living and re-create it in poetry. Even when we are Christians, trying to fulfil the maxim 'sentire cum Christo', it is with our own eyes we see, and our sensibility is our own. Personal vision is not necessarily private judgment. Yet Eliot nowhere distinguishes between them; nor does he show much interest in the need for such a distinction. 'Order' is a demanding mistress, and 'impersonality' an exacting friend.

The view I am supporting is associated with the name of Hopkins among others. And Eliot's view of Hopkins' poetry is significantly reserved: Hopkins is over-rated, he operates 'within a narrow range', and his metrical innovations, which are interesting, sometimes appear 'as lacking inevitability . . . in that a whole poem will give us *more* of the same thing, an accumulation, rather than a real development of thought or feeling'. But, most important, Hopkins is merely a 'devotional poet'.

> Hopkins is not a religious poet in the more important sense in which I have elsewhere maintained Baudelaire to be a religious poet; or in the sense in which I find Villon to be a religious poet; or in the sense in which I consider Mr Joyce's work to be penetrated with Christian feeling.[1]

The reduction of Hopkins to a 'devotional' poet, incapable of reaching a religious dimension of which Villon and Baudelaire and Joyce are naturalised citizens, is a curious manœuvre. What these three writers have in common is a sense of spiritual and social corruption disproportionate to their sense of positive spiritual, or even affective, life; they are all sardonic in their approach to the human dilemma, and it is as the victim of a dilemma that they see man; their feelings are centred on, though of course not exhausted by, the fact of limitation. What Hopkins possesses is a sense of the unique life of things, which becomes, in certain poems, a sense of the 'sacramental' quality of the universe. To consider him less 'religious' than Villon and Baudelaire and Joyce is indeed an odd way to give greater currency to the ideas of Hulme.

The essay on Baudelaire (1930) gives confirmation to my

---

[1] *After Strange Gods*, pp. 47-8. See also *American Literature and the American Language* (1953), in which Hopkins is said to be a lesser poet than Whitman.

reading of Eliot's intention, and of his consequent deficiencies. He makes, it is true, some serious criticisms of Baudelaire's work, but the burden of his judgment is that Baudelaire is a profound religious poet. Despite his frequently shoddy imagery, he is an important renovator of language; he 'discovers Christianity for himself', and even his Satanism is 'a dim intuition of a part, but a very important part, of Christianity'; he universalises the condition of the man of the cities, raises it to a 'first intensity'. But more than anything else, he reveals in human life, and particularly in human love, the pressure of Good and Evil as the ultimately real forces in experience:

> He was one of those who have great strength, but strength merely to *suffer*. He could not escape suffering and could not transcend it, so he *attracted* pain to himself. But what he could do, with that immense passive strength and sensibilities which no pain could impair, was to study his suffering . . . such suffering as Baudelaire's implies the possibility of a positive state of beatitude. Indeed, in his way of suffering is already a kind of presence of the supernatural and of the superhuman. He rejects always the purely natural and the purely human; in other words, he is neither 'naturalist' nor 'humanist'. Either because he cannot adjust himself to the actual world he has to reject it in favour of Heaven and Hell, or because he has the perception of Heaven and Hell he rejects the present world: both ways of putting it are tenable.[1]

Both ways of putting it may be 'tenable', but they certainly do not amount to the same thing, as Eliot seems to think they do. And the suggestion that there are regulating *positives* at the heart of Baudelaire's vision is made in a curiously off-hand manner. Baudelaire's poetry, as Eliot sees it, may imply the existence of 'beatitude', of positives, but does it in any way embody them, indicate their vitality and make that vitality current in the vitality of the poetry? I am not pretending to answer this question, I am merely asking why Eliot does not ask it, or even, apparently, see its relevance. When Baudelaire's technical mastery is in question, he is careful to illustrate by quotation; but where this much greater issue is in question he does not quote at all. In addition, his attitude to Baudelaire's acceptance of damnation is a baffling and distasteful one;

[1] *Selected Essays*, p. 385

> To a mind observant of the post-Voltaire France . . . the recognition of the reality of Sin is a New Life; and the possibility of damnation is so immense a relief in a world of electoral reform, plebiscites, sex reform and dress reform, that damnation itself is an immediate form of salvation—of salvation from the ennui of modern life, because it at last gives some significance to living.[1]

One may assent to this—especially if one recognises that its wording is that of a deliberately engineered paradox—and yet find unacceptable the critical conclusions which he draws from it:

> Having an imperfect, vague, romantic conception of Good, he was at least able to understand that the sexual act as evil is more dignified, less boring, than as the natural 'life-giving', cheery automatism of the modern world. For Baudelaire, sexual operation is at least something not analogous to Kruschen Salts.
>
> As far as we are human, what we do must be either evil or good; so far as we do evil or good, we are human; and it is better, in a paradoxical way, to do evil than to do nothing: at least we exist.[2]

This borders on the ludicrous. It is an odd kind of snobbery which finds evil less 'boring' than what we might call the theological innocence of those who are seemingly not aware of the supernatural order. And, whether dignified or not, the sexual act is hardly affirmed as valuable when it is described as 'operation'. Again, it is a confoundedly 'paradoxical way' in which it is better to do evil than to do nothing. In the Christian terms which Eliot himself invokes, to do evil is in fact to assert nothingness and chaos against the order of positive being; and in Christian terms, it is *impossible* to do nothing, for to do nothing would be to cease to exist as a human being.

It is as though he were congratulating Baudelaire on being not only conscious of, but subject to, Original Sin: a debilitated echo of St Augustine's cry of 'O felix culpa'. And it is surely an anomaly that the man who praises Baudelaire (an avowed diabolist) in these terms should, four years later, in *After Strange Gods*, hint with disdain that Hardy's novels were written under diabolic influence.

The essay on Baudelaire ends with a quotation from Hulme,

[1] *Ibid.* p. 389   [2] *Ibid.* p. 391

a quotation from that passage in which man is said to be 'essentially bad'. What Eliot is interested in, what his study of Baudelaire exemplifies in such a desperate manner, is the notion that the tradition of the West sees man as limited, and that at its best it sees that limitation as the stake in a remorseless struggle of Good with Evil, the metaphysical realities which give urgency to moral choice. And he asks of poets and novelists not that they endorse this view, not even that they openly examine it, but that they work within it as within a given framework, consent to have their sensibilities stabilised by a sense of tradition in which this view is embodied.

It seems to me that Eliot has here developed a very important insight into and approach to literature, superior in some ways to his splendidly disinterested and alert (yet rather contradictory) early criticism. Human life *has* metaphysical significance; and the greatest literature invokes that significance. Yet there are factors which go to neutralise its value as a *literary* insight; and if it is not a literary insight, then I don't see that it can be a useful insight into literature. Yet is it one's experience that the work of the great writers affects one essentially as being a report on the human condition, in this sense? Or would any creative writer, in scrutinising his purposes, honestly say that this was his chief interest? As well as this, there is the negative attitude in Eliot's own poetry to certain areas of human experience: a matter which I cannot deal with here. There is his conception of his rôle as (apparently) a pastoral one. And there is his failing grasp on poems and novels as they are actually presented in their living intactness.

It is an important insight; but he has suffered a loss in the power to actualise this insight in the normal work of criticism which, however much analysis or generalisation it may use, takes account in its progress of the whole text. So even people who share Eliot's view of the metaphysical roots of literature may decline to share his characteristic practical preoccupations (indicated in the passage on Baudelaire which I have quoted), may insist on choosing very different writers for commendation, and may place very different stresses in the valuing even of those writers for whose work they share Eliot's admiration. In other words, to have put the position which I have just indicated to be Eliot's is not, in itself, to have made very definite choices at all, or to have established any very discernible conclusions of criticism. One cause of Eliot's failure to take these facts into account is not hard to find. He has come to consider other things more important than poetry; and one can possibly sympathise with him in this. But he continues, despite it, to deal with literature, and one sees in his recent dealing always a holding back, a somewhat irresponsible abstraction of some aspect of a given work, a recurrent 'deflection of interest' from literature itself to its background, or its possible effects, or even, as in the case of Baudelaire, to certain personal preoccupations which also occur in his own poetry. Such an approach is very far from his earlier determination to stress the relatively autonomous status of poetry, and from the praise of Blake for his honesty and 'naked vision'.

It is idle nevertheless to accuse him of maintaining a narrow dogmatic test for poetry, as Mrs Kathleen Nott accuses him throughout her book, *The Emperor's Clothes*. An 'orthodoxy' which includes Greek Tragedy, Dante, Virgil, Villon, Donne, certain of the Elizabethans, Baudelaire and Joyce, is not narrow; nor is it in any limiting sense 'dogmatic'. It is surely not dogmatic to assert that such a wide tradition shows a central concern or concerns. What is deficient is not Eliot's conception of the breadth of the tradition, but his feeling for the positive vitality which at every point quickens it, for its *incarnational*, and hence its affirmative character.

If Arnold seems, in a way, to expect too much of poetry, Eliot seems, in a different way, to expect too little. I hope I have sufficiently characterised in what way I mean. It is not that he hopes for too small or too restricted an effect, but that he expects too little of affirmation in it.

What he seems to expect of it, finally, is a report on the human condition.

The French term is perhaps more adequate: 'la condition humaine'; for it is with something permanent, something perhaps essential in man's lot, that Eliot sees poetry as dealing. One can't help concluding that he sees man's life on the earth as merely a *trial*, and that he sees poetry as a report on the inner drama of that trial. He is not interested at all in the spectacle of man-in-nature, as Arnold was. For Arnold was in, and partly of, a Romantic convention, which saw man as having his complement, almost his other voice, in nature; it is partly because of this that Arnold was able to expect poetry to offer consolation and sustenance; the seeing life steadily and whole involved for him seeing man in nature and nature in man. Eliot, however, has chosen a different convention, a convention at whose modern emergence stands Hulme, with his devitalising insistence on the complete discontinuity between man and nature. In Eliot's early criticism, the attention is directed, where it is not a matter merely of analysing poetic 'technique' or the responsibility of the individual to the 'tradition', on poetry as the record of man's attitude towards his own emotions or his own society. In the later criticism, these emphases are supplemented, and so changed, with the emphasis on a relationship between man and God, a relationship conceived always as a purely vertical one.

Therefore, where we find him asserting that poetry expresses some 'permanent human impulse', we should not take the reality indicated by this phrase as equivalent to, or even first cousin of, 'the great primary human affections' of Wordsworth and Arnold:

> But the essential is that each expresses, in perfect language, some permanent human impulse. Emotionally the latter is just as strong, just as true, and just as informative—just as useful and beneficial in the sense in which poetry is useful and beneficial, as the former.[1]

And he sees in Middleton:

> the same steady impersonal passionless observation of human nature . . . a vision of things as they are and not 'another thing'.[2]

For:

> underneath the convention there is the stratum of truth permanent in human nature.[3]

That, however, is in 1927, at a point midway between *The Sacred Wood* and *After Strange Gods*. In *The Sacred Wood*, he sees the poet's, and even the dramatist's, grasp of other lives as a

[1] *Selected Essays*, p. 137   [2] *Ibid.* p. 167   [3] *Ibid.* p. 163

matter less of moral insight than of sensibility. This is the period in which he sees poetry largely as the dramatic objectification of actuality, the actuality of things and of one's own emotions:

> What the creator of character needs is not so much knowledge of motives as keen sensibility; the dramatist need not understand people; but he must be exceptionally aware of them.[1]

A rather gnomic utterance, when we reflect that the proper 'object' in other people for the play of sensibility is precisely that which is also the object of moral insight. However, we must see it as an insistence on the minimal prerequisite of a dramatist's equipment; for in 1921, in the essay on the Metaphysicals, he formulates the notion which has been constant in his work ever since: that the proper subject of the poet's insight is the whole depth and complexity of the human being:

> But that is not deep enough; Racine or Donne looked into a good deal more than the heart. One must look into the cerebral cortex, the nervous system, and the digestive tracts.[2]

What one may find there is not stressed until later: it is the struggle of Good with Evil, the metaphysical realities whose co-existence gives point to moral choice. Poetry at its finest gives not merely the play of sensibility on people seen, as it were, at the stature of dramatised *objects*, but part of the essential truth about man. So we get the rebuke to Matthew Arnold, which I have already quoted at greater length:

> But the essential advantage for a poet is not, to have a beautiful world with which to deal: it is to be able to see beneath both beauty and ugliness; to see the boredom, and the horror, and the glory.[3]

To see human life, in other words, as a *trial*. In fact, Eliot's stress falls on the poet as enduring the contradictions of human life, and on poetry as an analysis of them. He sees poetry as a report on the human condition by one who has been 'there', by one who can say:

I am the man; I suffered; I was there.

[1] *The Sacred Wood*, p. 132   [2] *Selected Essays*, p. 290
[3] *The Use of Poetry*, p. 106

The contradictions are inherent in man's metaphysical status. The 'boredom, and the horror, and the glory' seem in Eliot's work to be of metaphysical authority, but hardly as metaphysical *forces* struggling against each other: rather, as juxtaposed conditions, in the context of which man must live, and from the contiguities of which he cannot escape. That is one of the reasons why he sees emotions as a chief subject of poetry; it is in emotions that the metaphysical forces find a record and a stress. The task of the poet, apparently, is to recognise their existence and to analyse them either as they appear in society or (and more particularly) as they exist in himself. The main pledge of the poet's greatness is the extent to which he is aware of the metaphysical reality within or behind the merely human. We have seen this in the study of Baudelaire, where all sorts of relevant considerations are pushed aside to give room and air to this one insight. Eliot never speaks of that almost tidal sympathy and feeling of being representatively involved in an issue of possibilities, a communion which many poets feel at the spectacle of the world, and which is among the motivating forces of their art. Eliot's sense of metaphysical reality in art is never a sense of 'oneness with . . .', but rather a sense of something almost clinical in its determination not to shirk reality. He compares Goethe with Baudelaire:

> But after this lapse of time the difference between 'health' and 'morbidity' in the two men becomes negligible. . . . We have passed beyond both fashions, of health or malady, and they are both merely men with restless, critical, curious minds and the 'sense of the age'; both men who understood and foresaw a great deal.[1]

And he praises in Blake the determination to refuse nothing of the truth about man:

> It is merely a peculiar honesty, which in a world too frightened to be honest, is peculiarly terrifying. . . . Blake's poetry has the unpleasantness of great poetry. Nothing that can be called morbid or abnormal or perverse, none of the things which exemplify the sickness of an epoch or fashion, have this quality; only those things which, by some extraordinary labour of simplification, exhibit the essential sickness or strength of the human soul.[2]

[1] *Selected Essays*, p. 383 [2] *The Sacred Wood*, p. 151

The seeming contradiction between these two passages is due to the ten years which separate them. There are two different manners of speech involved. But what is constant in those ten years and later is Eliot's concern for a poetry which exhibits the sickness or strength of the human soul; and which exhibits it at a level where it is seen to be permanent, 'essential'. It might be expected, then, that he would have a particular interest in the drama of the Elizabethans and Jacobeans. Part of his interest is, of course, accounted for by his early interest in the analysis of poetic language as the expression of sensibility, and also by the demands of his own creative practice. But his chief interest in them seems to centre on their examination of moral corruption, with the accompanying tension between feeling and language, and on the ambiguous relation which their plays have to the spirit of the age. Thus, Tourneur expresses 'an intense and unique and horrible vision of life' based on the kind of experience possible 'to a highly sensitive adolescent with a gift for words'[1]; Ford shows a horror of moral perversion, tending towards sensationalism; in Heywood, moral reality deteriorates into a pattern of sentiment: and so on. But of the Elizabethans generally, he holds that they see the corruption which they depict not as peculiar to their age, but endemic:

> It is indeed in the lack of this sense of a 'changing world', of corruptions and abuses peculiar to their own time, that the Elizabethan and Jacobean dramatists were blessed.[2]

They exhibit both a personal sense of horror and an awareness of representative corruption without being aware that they *are* representative of one era. Consequently they are able to combine confidence in language and a vital sense of human drama with a powerful inner attraction to the perversities of the human heart and will. This sums up Eliot's interest in them. It is an interest in moral complexity not wholly brought into light and deliberately made the material of analysis; and it is an interest in something which shows the essentially limited nature of man concealed by a poetic 'greediness' which is the

---

[1] *Selected Essays*, p. 189
[2] *Ibid.* p. 202

artistic counterpart of the sin of *hubris*. So we can't condemn these poets for their concern with the horrible and revolting:

> nor can we wholly deplore anything which brings with it some information about the soul.[1]

And he iterates, in his essay on Thomas Heywood, the view which he expressed in relation to Baudelaire—that health and morbidity are not the chief moral issues in a work of art:

> The capital distinction is that between representation of human actions which have moral reality and representations of such as have only sentimental reality; and beside this, any distinction between 'healthy' and 'morbid' sentiment is trivial.[2]

This is merely another approach to the emphasis which I have already noted in Eliot's criticism, the emphasis on poetry as a report on the human condition seen at the metaphysical roots of moral choice. It is an emphasis closely connected with his emphasis on the essential limitedness of man, an emphasis which bears down with an almost obsessive pressure on his work. In contrasting, for example, Pascal to Swift, he invokes the criterion of truth to assess the depth of their respective examinations of man. In Pascal, doubt is one stage in a process of self-purging and growth; in Swift, it is the expression of 'a diseased character or an impure soul'. Pascal's despair

> is in itself more terrible than Swift's, because our heart tells us that it corresponds exactly to the facts and cannot be dismissed as mental disease; but it was also a despair which was a necessary prelude to, and element in, the joy of faith.[3]

It is not a Wordsworthian sense of the one-ness of things which purges, then, but a vision of the permanent duality in which human life is lived; and it is a purging, not a consolation. The activity itself is a probing and a re-presenting; its effect on the reader is a recognition and a purging. As we find in 'The Social Function of Poetry', the poet gives people 'words for their

---

[1] *Selected Essays*, p. 79. See also *The Use of Poetry*, p. 104. The commentary on Arnold's view of the Romantics.

[2] *Ibid.* p. 180

[3] *Ibid.* p. 152. See also *The Use of Poetry*, pp. 118-19. The definition of the 'auditory imagination' contains a compelling statement, on the depth at which, and the thoroughness with which, poetry probes man.

feelings', and so 'teaches them something about themselves'. He also tells them of feelings they have never experienced, because he 'discovers new shades and variations of sensibility in which others can participate'.[1] That seems to be as much as Eliot would claim for poetry; and if he is right, it is certainly a good deal to claim. But his concern with it is so persistent, so paradoxical, that one finds it hard to decide how much light his characteristic analysis really throws on the moral stature of poetry. It may be true that 'humankind cannot bear very much reality'; but Eliot can bear more than Arnold. At the same time he self-consciously bears it, with an air of vicarious martyrdom. To 'look into the Shadow' is to be acutely aware of the duality; but there is another tradition in which the human limits are seen 'truly'; So he says of the *Vita Nuova*:

> There is also a practical sense of realities behind it, which is antiromantic: not to expect more from *life* than it can give or more from *human* beings than they can give; to look to *death* for what life cannot give. The *Vita Nuova* belongs to 'vision literature'; but its philosophy is the Catholic philosophy of disillusion.[2]

Here is the 'classical' stress: the insistence on a realism which does not only give us an adequate sense of human life as it really is, but adequately suggests its limitations: the conviction of the omnipresence of the results of Original Sin. For Christianity is a way of confronting the whole of the facts; it does not seek, as Stoicism does, to console:

> A man does not join himself with the Universe so long as he has something else to join himself with . . . and Christians have had something better. Stoicism is the refuge for the individual in an indifferent or hostile world too big for him; it is the permanent substratum of a number of versions of cheering oneself up.[3]

Poetry is then chiefly a report on the human condition, the permanent duality at the core of man's life; this is the ultimate source of the moral force of poetry, so far as Eliot is concerned, and whether he approaches it in terms of order, or of impersonality, or of orthodoxy of sensibility. We can readily see why Villon and Baudelaire are preferred to Hopkins, and

[1] *The Social Function of Poetry, op. cit.* pp. 158-9
[2] *Ibid.* p. 275   [3] *Ibid.* p. 131

preferred specifically as 'religious' poets; for they reveal more of the duality than he does, lead more directly to a conviction of limits. That is the almost universal stress in Eliot's thinking; and it is hardly, by itself, a Christian stress. But he does occasionally offer something transcending it. His view would be (as a guide) intolerable if he did not, because a consistent vision of the duality of experience, and of nothing else, would generate nothing more purgative than a sense of oppression, and ultimately of accidie. Art is, for Eliot, concerned only with the enigmatic realities of man's ambiguous moral position in the Universe; but it can at times suggest to us a 'pattern' behind the pattern which we can see

> the kind of pattern which we perceive in our own lives only at rare moments of inattention and detachment, drowsing in sunlight. It is the pattern drawn by what the ancient world called Fate; subtilized by Christianity into mazes of delicate theology; and reduced again by the modern world into crudities of psychological and economic necessity.[1]

The positive intent of this passage lies in the affirmation that man has a destiny, and not merely a career, that that destiny has its place in a superhuman pattern behind the human, and that art may suggest its existence to us. At no time does Eliot suggest that art is competent to *define* its existence; he does not prescribe a dogmatic test for literature. Not only does he refrain from saying that the artist *should* invoke the mysteries of Christianity, he actually appears to think that the artist *cannot* invoke them. Poetry can suggest the presence of a superhuman order, but can neither define its nature nor embody it as a poetic reality. So Marvell

> takes a slight affair, the feeling of a girl for her pet, and gives it a connexion with that inexhaustible and terrible nebula of emotion which surrounds all our exact and practical passions and mingles with them.[2]

This was written in 1921; yet it is not very much different from the passage with which Eliot concludes his *Poetry and Drama*,

---

[1] *The Social Function of Poetry*, p. 230. See, too, the remarks on Shakespeare in *John Dryden: Three Essays* (1932), p. 32.
[2] *Ibid.* p. 300

delivered as a lecture in 1950. The only difference is that, in the later work, it is not a 'nebula of emotion' which is invoked, but a context of beatitude:

> For it is ultimately the function of art, in imposing a credible order upon ordinary reality, and thereby eliciting some perception of an order *in* reality, to bring us to a condition of serenity, stillness and reconciliation; and then leave us, as Virgil left Dante, to proceed toward a region where that guide can avail us no farther.[1]

This statement seems to me an important one, and, if it were backed up by any consistent demonstration in Eliot's criticism, it would be a quite valuable one. Superficially it seems to echo Arnold; but it differs from his emphasis in almost all significant respects. It does not urge poetry to complete us in any way, but merely to help establish the possibility of self-completion, to make possible for us a final thought, a definitive experience. While it does not urge poetry to be in any way explicitly Christian, it sees poetry helping us to consolidate our experience so that Christianity becomes more relevant to it: not a substitute for religion, nor an expression of it, but a disposing condition. And it is an emphasis on the *order* which poetry can suggest, not on the sentiments which it can convey.

It is an important stress, and it is regrettable that the assumption of a pastoral rôle should have prevented Eliot not only from reaching it sooner, but from exemplifying it more in his criticism. As it is, the sane serenity which it epitomises is singularly missing from a large part of the criticism which succeeds *The Sacred Wood*. Even so, we may say that he does not claim too much for the moral value of poetry; and that the modesty of his essential claim (to the extent that it is represented by his final statement, in *Poetry and Drama*) confers additional dignity on its subject.

[1] *Poetry and Drama*, p. 35

CHAPTER VI

F. R. Leavis: Reality and Sincerity

WHILE drawing heavily on the work of both Arnold and Eliot, and while having strong though limited affinities with both of them, F. R. Leavis as a critic is very different from either. For one thing, he is neither a poet nor a 'man of letters', in the sense in which Allen Tate, for example, announces himself, and as Eliot, in his prose statements, may be held to be; he is a teacher—more specifically, a teacher in a closely defined milieu, that of a great university. This fact may seem to imply a limitation in him; and so, in a way, it does. It obviously dominates his habits of analysis, his way of critical procedure; and it makes it inappropriate for him to take advantage of the kind of freedom of range that is exemplified by Eliot in his occasional addresses and by Arnold in the lectures which he delivered from the Chair of Poetry in Oxford. But after reading Leavis' *œuvre*, we may reflect that such a freedom may be well lost in favour of what is, after all, a greater virtue in a critic: the virtue of 'relevance' of comment. Relevance is a key word throughout Leavis' criticism, and it is a key notion for us in our attempt to understand the reasons for, and the nature of, the self-imposed limitations of that criticism. It is a criticism which always has its eye on an audience, not for the sake of evoking stock responses from them, but for the sake of convincing them that it has its eye on the object in the contemplative scrutiny of which they are collaborators with the critic himself. The result is that, while he seems superficially more limited than either Arnold or Eliot, he is really more rounded, more complete. The limitation is far from being the product of an un-awareness of the critical function; it is really a sort of intensity.

The fact that he is primarily a teacher may lead us to see why so much of his work has been an open plea for, and analysis of, a certain conception of critical education; I mean the conception suggested in the titles of many of his books: *For Continuity, Towards Standards of Criticism, Education and the University, The Common Pursuit.* It may lead us, too, to see the value (and the difficulties) of the critical language which he has evolved to be an aid in the achievement of 'relevance'. This language, in lesser hands than Leavis', can degenerate into a jargon; but in his hands it has usually a curious exactness.

Take, for example, the word 'enactment', which is the first word one must take account of in any estimate of his views. It is the notion that 'works of art *act* their moral judgments'. This notion is stated, clearly and well, both in the essay 'Johnson and Augustanism', in *The Common Pursuit*, and in the essay on Johnson's criticism.[1] It is brought out in an attempt to assess the limitations of Johnson's Augustan mind and sensibility when confronted with Shakespeare's characteristic use of language:

> That is, he cannot appreciate the life-principle of drama as we have it in the poetic-creative use of language—the use by which the stuff of experience is presented to speak and act for itself.
>
> This disability has its obvious correlative in Johnson's bondage (again representative) to moralistic fallacy and confusion. . . .
>
> Johnson cannot understand that works of art *enact* their moral valuations. It is not enough that Shakespeare, on the evidence of his works, 'thinks' (and feels), morally; for Johnson a moral judgment that isn't *stated* isn't there. . . .
>
> Here we have a clear view of the essential tendency of the Augustan tradition. Such a use of language, so unchallenged and unqualified in its assumption of omnicompetence (how it came to prevail with this completeness would be a large and complicated inquiry, taking in more than the English scene) must tend to turn forms and conventions from agents of life into debilitating conventionalities, such as forbid the development of the individual sensibility and set up an insulation against any vitalizing recourse to the concrete.[2]

Here we have the beginning, and the enlivening force, of his critical practice: works of art enact their moral valuations; they

[1] *Scrutiny*, Vol. XII, No. 3, Summer, 1944

It is interesting that Leavis should use a very similar terminology in both of these essays; the notion is clearly a central one if we are to understand the general intention of his work.

[2] *The Common Pursuit* (Chatto and Windus, London, 1952), p. 110

do so generally not by deploying words to enforce a didactic intention, but by a specifically poetic use of language, which Leavis characterises as 'the poetic-creative'; and they lead to, just as they issue from, a 'vitalizing recourse to the concrete'. Leavis is insisting on a conception of literature which has a relevance and a value for other things besides literature; a 'vitalizing recourse to the concrete' concerns living, as well as reading or writing. And it is interesting that, as soon as he has stated his point, Leavis goes on to talk not about moral intentions and the 'correct' way of bringing them into art, but about language, and about the kind of inner life with which it must maintain contact if it is to be at all capable of registering the sort of 'valuations' which literature exists to register.

It is interesting, because it draws us directly away from the often-voiced notion of Leavis as the simple-minded didact of modern letters. In fact, while one is inclined to remember his influence as of a directly ethical kind, one is seldom conscious, in actually reading him, of any separable ethical stress at all. Certainly, there is such a stress; and I shall try to isolate and discuss it; but it does not unmistakably separate and declare itself in a normally attentive reading. One of the reasons for this is the flexibility with which, in practice, Leavis detects the poetic 'enacting' of moral valuation. His concern for 'life', as we see it even in the passages I have quoted, is a concern for a moral-poetic vitality which can have varying manifestations. His advocacy of Pope (not, to be sure, the Pope of conventional acceptance) is a case in point; for surely, or so a superficial reader might exclaim, surely Pope above all exhibits a use of language very far from 'the poetic-creative use' of which Leavis speaks. But Leavis' use of his own implicit principle extends to Pope, whose use of language he shows to be, in a real sense, poetic-creative.

It extends, too, to Keats, whose almost 'muscular' delicacy of sensuous enactment gives his poetry a value that is far more than merely sensuous, and that contrasts well to Shelley's failure to escape from the vagueness, the lack of grasp, attendant on his desire to express an undisciplined emotion. Similarly, Milton's use of language as a sort of hypnotic ritual is implicitly

contrasted, in Leavis' estimate, to the work of Donne and
Marvell. There are literally scores of places in which Leavis
demonstrates the relevance of the term 'enactment', and shows
the flexibility of which, in his hands, it is capable. But it is
impossible, in a study of this kind, to itemise these ways and
assess the variants. I may say, here at the outset, that to consider
Leavis profitably at all, it is necessary to strike to the centre,
even at the cost of doing his varied achievement much less than
justice. For one thing, looking at his work as a whole, I am
struck by the number of (admittedly tentative) headings under
which it could be discussed. If one were writing a book on
Leavis, it would surely include chapters with such titles as
'Alive in their Time—Alive to it'; The Poet and Civilization;
What does the Poet Represent?; Maturity and Moral Poise;
Tradition and Continuity; Criticism and Education. But the
richness and repetition of quotation promised in such a list
combine with lack of space to make it impossible for me to
discuss any of them. They are all important and lasting
emphases (one might justly call them 'themes') in his work;
and his work as a whole can't be properly comprehended and
assessed without taking them into consideration. Nevertheless,
there is a real sense in which they are not of the centre[1]; they
are not central to a brief study of his view of the moral value of
poetry.

Even considering his use of the term 'enactment', one has to
be almost callous in one's selectiveness. It might even be confusing to adduce examples of his practical criticism. The
relevant point at the moment is the implication of the word
'enactment'. It implies, for one thing, that good poetry embodies, enacts a valuation of, a reality at once inner (spiritual)
and outer (social or sensuous). To enact a valuation is to *realise*
whatever is evaluated; it is to bring us into an immediate and
living relation with reality:

> Take, for instance, the idea of 'realization' that was introduced
> with 'realized' and 'unrealized'—terms that will be used again,
> for they are indispensable. Any suggestion that these terms

---

[1] In addition, his treatment of the social representativeness of poetry, as of its
contemporaneity, strikes me as tendentious and, as it were, an unproven case.
It would be waste of space to debate the issues here.

introduce a simple or easily applied criterion may be countered
with the following passage:

> All our service
> In every point twice done, and then done double,
> Were poor and single business to contend
> Against those honours deep and broad wherewith
> Your majesty loads our house.　　　　　(*Macbeth*, I, 6)

This is an ordinary piece of mature Shakespeare. That is,
without exemplifying the more remarkable Shakespearean
complexity, it has the life and body which are the pervasive
manifestation of Shakespeare's genius in his verse. The effect of
concreteness—of being, we might say, 'realized' and not merely
verbal—depends above all on the implicit metaphor introduced
with 'deep and broad'. Those adjectives, plainly, describe a river,
and, whether we tell ourselves so or not, the presence of a river
makes itself felt in the effect of the passage, giving a physical
quality to 'contend', in the third line, that it would not otherwise
have had. Prompted by 'honours' Shakespeare has, in the
apprehensive rapidity of his mind, picked up the conventional
trope of the King's being the 'fount of honour', and, characteristically, in his rapid motion, brought it to life—its life, which is a
matter of its organic relation to the context, being manifested in
the very absence of explicitness. It is this absence of explicitness
in the metaphor—of full realization, one might put it—that
conditions the hardly noticeable shift to the metaphor of 'loads'
in the next line: the common effect of being borne down by
overwhelming profusion covers the shift. Discussing the passage
elsewhere, I have observed that what we see as the inimitable
mark of the poet in it is his ability to control realization to the
precise degree appropriate in the given place—an ability that
clearly cannot be simulated if anything in the least metaphorically
complex is offered. One might, by way of emphasizing that
'realization' is not offered as a technical term, an instrument of
precision, put it this way; it is in the incomplete realization of the
metaphors that the realizing gift of the poet and the 'realized'
quality of the passage are manifested. However we apply the
term, what we have to consider is always a whole of some
complexity; what we have to look for are the signs of something
grasped and held, something presented in an ordering of words,
and not merely thought of or gestured towards.[1]

---

[1] *Education and the University* (Chatto and Windus, London, 1948 edition),
pp. 76-8

This passage speaks for itself. That is my reason for offering it (and at such length) instead of passages in which Leavis' gift of practical exposition is expressed more tellingly. It is explicit and definitive (within its limits) because it is given to us, in the context in which it *is* offered, as almost a set piece of criticism. And it is important because it shows us quite clearly the link between 'enactment' and 'realisation'. A poem enacts its moral valuation by bringing to the appropriate degree of definition some attitude associated with a social or sensible situation; it can do this either through realising the relevance and limits of a sequence of metaphors (as here) or through bringing to a state of balance some movement of sensuous life. To enact is to realise; to realise is at once to embody and to define; it may even be—it *is* in the passage from Shakespeare which Leavis deals with—to hold in check, to check at the 'appropriate' point of development, the flowing of the poetic impulse into metaphor or sensuous detail.

So much is reasonably clear; at least, it should be clear why, and in what way, Leavis uses the terms 'enactment' and 'realisation' to characterise this process. But, after all, to have said as much is not to have justified the view of poetry involved—a view which finds disabling deficiencies in Milton and Shelley. Nor does it immediately bring the discussion to a point at which Leavis' view of poetry and morality can be defined. I shall try to follow it out later, to show how the 'Reality and Sincerity' of this chapter's title are really, in Leavis' work, almost synonymous terms. Reality *is* Sincerity. Leavis himself gives us a hint of this view at the end of the passage I have quoted; 'the signs of something grasped and held, something presented in an ordering of words, and not merely thought of or gestured towards'. It is the fault of both Milton and Shelley, each in his characteristic way, to use language as mere gesture. Because in each case the poetry comes from an impulse which is flawed— what we may for the moment call artistic insincerity—it leads us away from, instead of into, reality. Realisation, that is, has to do with the presentation of some reality; and it is unnecessary at the moment to contest the use of such a term.

But, as I hope to show, Leavis is not a realist in any naïve sense. The word 'realisation' is a very felicitous one; for it suggests the paradoxically dual nature of the quality which he is talking about. It carries a suggestion not only of the creating, the bringing present, of some objective reality, but also of self-realisation, that kind of inner human activity which is perhaps better called, not self-expression, but self-recognition. So he finds in Keats 'maturity, manifested in technique, of feeling in relation to thought, of imagination and desire in relation to actuality'.[1] It is this blend of qualities—looked at, I must insist, from a centre of interest which is recognisably 'literary', and not in any limited sense ethical—that leads him to see Keats' achievement as one of character as well as of intelligence. The word 'character' does not carry for Leavis any connotation of the stiff and the unbending, but rather of flexibility, of readiness to deal with life on its own terms; it is thus not merely an inner disposition, the product of stern moral training, but a readiness to confront reality. Shelley, on the other hand, he judges to be deficient as a poet because his work shows an open divorce between thought and feeling, a deliberate insistence on emotion which becomes emotionality, and a 'rejection of the past', a failure to find his way into his real place in a living tradition.[2] And he brings, as the summation of his assessment, the judgment that, for Shelley, ' "Inspiration" is not something to be tested, clarified, defined and developed in composition'.[3]

Each word here has its obvious importance: the expression of an impulse nurtured in the inner life of the poet by his continuing experience of an outer reality will, if it issues in satisfying poetry, be also a testing, a clarifying, a defining, and a developing. The last word has its significance too; for it shows that Leavis does not see the true defining of experience in poetry as a limiting of that impulse, but as a developing of it; an increase in a recognisably poetic vitality. And the condition of its developing adequately in and through the poem is that *the experience itself* should somehow come to be present there. The notion is that for feelings to be adequately tested and defined in poetry the situation in which they arise should somehow be in the poetry too, to be there tested and defined.

[1] *Revaluation* (Chatto and Windus, London, 1936), p. 8
[2] *Ibid.* p. 8
[3] *Ibid.* p. 209

At this point, before going on to examine two essays in which Leavis' conception is elaborated more or less explicitly, it is as well to re-issue my earlier reminder: This conception is not, in any limiting sense, a didactic one. He associates Shelley's lack of grasp with his emotionality, and that emotionality is plainly associated with Shelley's interest in febrile moralising. And, in speaking of Matthew Arnold, he makes the same point more clearly. He finds that the lack of any compelling grasp of 'the concrete' and of a distinct *inner* purposiveness in the poet himself is the corollary of a moral insistence, an openly didactic stance:

> And what the Scholar-Gipsy really symbolizes is Victorian poetry, vehicle (so often) of explicit intellectual and moral intentions, but unable to be in essence anything but relaxed, relaxing and anodyne.[1]

The two essays in which his view is clearly worked out through the analysis of set poems are 'Thought and Emotional Quality', and 'Reality and Sincerity', both published in *Scrutiny* with the sub-title 'Notes in the Analysis of Poetry'. The presence of the sub-title in both, as in a third essay, which I find less relevant,[2] seems to indicate that they are intended to form a series; though they have not yet been published in book form. I take them for detailed comment because they are something very like set-pieces, almost deliberate elaborations, through a set procedure, of his essential attitudes.

'Reality and Sincerity' consists of an examination of three poems on a similar theme—the theme of irreparable loss: Alexander Smith's 'Barbara', Emily Brontë's 'Cold in the Earth', and Thomas Hardy's 'After a Journey'. The three analyses are not kept separate, but are deliberately linked in an elaborate comparative judgment; and the comparison is made through a subtle discrimination in which 'literary' and moral qualities are effectively blended. It would obviously be foolish to try to follow out Leavis' analysis from step to step, for it is extremely close and detailed; and, after all, the essay is there

---

[1] *The Common Pursuit* (Chatto and Windus, London, 1952), p. 30
[2] 'Imagery and Movement': *Scrutiny*, Vol. XIII, No. 2, Sept. 1945

to be consulted.[1] But a brief précis may be attempted, in the hope of clarifying my exposition of his underlying views.

Alexander Smith's poem is dismissed trenchantly, on grounds that will be familiar to readers of Leavis' books:

> It goes straight for a sentimental debauch, an emotional wallowing, the alleged situation being only the show of an excuse for the indulgence. . . . If one wants a justification for invoking the term 'insincerity', one can point to the fact that the poem *enjoys* its pang: to put it more strictly, the poem offers a luxurious enjoyment that, to be enjoyed, must be taken for the suffering of an unbearable sorrow. . . .[2]

This judgment answers so completely to my own reaction to the poem that I won't discuss its terms. There are two charges— one made, one suggested: First, that the emotion, and so the poem, pretend to be something they are not: and, second, that the emotion is not focussed on any clear situation or perception presented in the poem itself. The poem is insincere because it is, in obvious senses, *unreal*. It is a bad poem because it conduces to, just as it mediates, an emotional fantasy—a disability seen in its very movement and phrasing.

Emily Brontë's poem is judged much more highly; but reservations are immediately brought forward:

> The emotional sweep of the movement, the declamatory plangency, of *Cold in the earth* might seem to represent dangerous temptations; but in responding to the effect of passionate intensity we register what impresses us as a controlling strength. It remains to be seen just what that is.[3]

It is, it appears, a check in the flow of 'plangent' movement, a check provided by a sort of salutary self-recognition:

> . . . .what is said in stanza seven—
>
> > Then did I check the tears of useless passion

—is more than *said*; it represents an active principle that informs the poem and is there along with the plangency. We have it in the movement, in the tough prose rationality, the stating matter-

---

[1] *Scrutiny*, Vol. XIX, No. 2, Winter 1952-3

It is interesting that the criticism which forms the basis of the essay seems, from the wording of the text, to have been undertaken in some sort of collaboration with students.

[2] *Ibid.* p. 90   [3] *Ibid.* p. 90

of-factness of good sense, that seems to play against the dangerous
running swell. It makes us take the suggestion that some strength
corresponding to 'these brown hills', which do not themselves
melt, underlies the poem. And we see an obvious hint at the
nature of the strength in

> Then did I learn how existence could be cherished,
> Strengthen'd and fed without the aid of joy:

the suggestion that something quite opposed to the luxury of
'memory's rapturous pain' is being 'cherished' in the poem; that
a resolute strength of will, espousing the bare prose 'existence',
counters the run of emotion.[1]

I have quoted this passage at some length not only to illustrate Leavis' procedure in the face of a poem which he responds
to but does not quite know how to approve of, but also to enter
a disagreement with some of the details of his judgment. And I
disagree because I feel he is begging a question in practical
criticism for the sake of exhibiting more clearly his critical
principles. I agree that there is some real spiritual strength
informing the poem, and that it is of the kind he suggests. But
it seems to me to be not a matter of a check given through a
'tough prose rationality, the stating matter-of-factness of good
sense', but of a *statement* whose movement carries on the movement of the poem, is part of, and not a recognisable check to,
the exalted eloquence. That statement may involve a conscious
recall of elements of self-discipline in Emily Brontë's past
experience, but it does not seem to *act* that recall, merely to
state it. Such a critical disagreement is useful only if it helps to
point to a narrowness in Leavis, an inability to sympathise with
the sort of exalted eloquence which is the staple of this poem
unless it shows self-discipline. And I feel that he has here
rationalised his approval of the element of self-discipline by
associating it with a kind of check which I do not find in the
poem at all.

Surely, too, what is most obviously absent here is the kind of
'particularity' which Leavis detects, and assesses, so authoritatively in Hardy's poem. In that poem, he finds that reality
is triumphantly a proof of sincerity, and sincerity the pledge of
reality; and he locates the fusion of the two in the 'particularity'

---

[1] *Ibid.* p. 91

with which Hardy's attitude to his own past experience is brought to a point of definition and, indeed, to a point of awareness of meaning, in a present situation:

> There is nothing that strikes us as odd in that 'facing', but it is a use created for the occasion, and when we look into its unobtrusive naturalness it turns out to have a positive and 'inevitable' rightness, the analysis of which involves a precise account of the 'ghost's' status—which in its turn involves a precise account of the highly specific situation defined by the poem.
>
> Then again, there is that noun in the fourth line which (I can testify) has offended readers not incapable of recognizing its felicity:
>> And the unseen waters' ejaculations awe me.
>
> 'Ejaculations' gives with vivid precision the sound that 'awes' Hardy. . . .[1]

The nature of Leavis' procedure, and of the moral-poetic interest which leads to it, is now obvious. It is an attempt to show the complete interdependence of Hardy's inner disposition with the seemingly external details of his poem; and to show, as well, the way in which that disposition charges the details with poetic force and meaning, while the details refine and define the disposition itself:

> In fact, the difference first presenting itself as an absence of declamatory manner and tone, examined, leads to the perception of positive characteristics—precisions of concrete realization, specificities, complexities—that justify the judgment I now advance: Hardy's poem, put side by side with Emily Brontë's, is seen to have a great advantage in *reality*. This term, of course, has to be given its due force by the analysis yet to be done—the analysis it sums up; but it provides the right pointer. And to invoke another term, more inescapably one to which a critic must try and give some useful force by appropriate and careful use, if he can contrive that: to say that Hardy's poem has an advantage in reality is to say (it will turn out) that it represents a profounder and completer sincerity.[2]

Most of the remaining analysis is an elaborate justification of this judgment. And there are other things to be noted later

---

[1] *Scrutiny*, Vol. XIX, No. 2, Winter 1952-3, p. 93   [2] *Ibid*. p. 93

about the lesson that Leavis finally draws as to the nature of poetic value. But here, surely, we have the crux of the matter so far as his actual analysis goes. It would be as well, then, to point out the subtleties of his position, summarising, at the risk of too great abstraction, his critical argument.

It is plain that, for him, poetic reality and artistic sincerity are virtually synonymous. To say even as much as this is to point to the fact that that reality is not in any stultifying sense 'poetic', nor that sincerity merely a matter of artistic intention. Sincerity is attested by the reality which is 'realised' in the poetic detail, as in the structure and movement of the poem as a whole. And the realisation depends on a sort of attention, of inwardness and disinterestedness, in the poet himself. It is this that both Leavis and Arnold call sincerity; another name for it is integrity. Sincerity depends on the presence somehow in the poem of the situation which justifies the emotion. It is the word 'justifies' which springs to mind, since it is so much in keeping with Leavis' mood and manner. But it should be made clear that the emotion is 'justified' by being defined and appraised In other words, there is a great deal of particular detail in the poem, and it is through its presence that the emotion is defined and valued. It is through it that Hardy can avoid vagueness or over-emphasis, and can avoid begging any questions as to the strength or appropriateness of his emotion to the situation in which he recalls and re-lives and judges it. But particularity is not just a matter of specific detail being 'put in' to give the reader something to hold on to while he appraises the emotion and absorbs the evaluation of it. No; it is a matter of inwardness again: of inwardness with a real situation and with the feelings that are proper to it. And the process of realisation involves a re-creation of language:

> 'View', we recognize, is no insensitive perversity; it is the word compelled by the intensely realized situation, and we feel it imposing itself on Hardy (and so on us) as right and irreplaceable. . . .[1]

There is nothing in Hardy's poem, in the thoroughly apt and freshened language, to put beside some of Emily Brontë's

[1] *Ibid.* p. 95

occasional limpness of phrasing, those of her words which are 'of the order of cliché'. In its details of language, as in everything else about it, the poem is the realisation of a valuable state of mind, at once an exercise in, and an example of, integrity.

While we can, with some minor reservations, admit the justice and sensitivity of Leavis' reading, there are other matters to be raised. After all, he makes large claims for this poem; and it is pertinent to ask what considerable value he finds there to be the basis of those claims. We find this value stated in its negative as well as in its positive aspect: an absence of self-inflation, of self-dramatisation, as well as an integrity in the facing of experience:

> Not to take the significance of that 'Trust me, I mind not' is to have failed to respond to the complexity of the total attitude, and to have failed to realize the rare kind of integrity the poem achieves. It is to miss the suggestion of paradoxical insistence, the intensity of directed feeling and will, in 'Nay, bring me here again'. For what in the bringing him here he may be supposed to mind is not the arduousness, for an old man, of the long journey and the ramble by night. 'To bring me here', says Hardy, 'is to make me experience to the full the desolation and the pang—to give a sharp edge to the fact of Time's derision. But I don't mind—I more than don't mind: bring me here again! I hold to life, even though life as a total fact lours. The *real* for me, the focus of my affirmation, is the remembered realest thing, though to remember vividly is at the same time, inescapably, to embrace the utterness of loss'[1]

And he finds that, although 'The rare integrity appears in the way in which the two aspects, the affirmation and the void, affect us as equal presences in the poem . . . (it) closes on the affirmation'. It is an affirmation which is in no sense rhetorical, but 'intimate':

> No alchemy of idealization, no suggestion of the transcendental, no nobly imaginative self-deceiving, attends on his devotion to the memory of a woman. It is the remembered as it was that Hardy is intent on. . . .[2]

It is well known that Leavis thinks Hardy a great poet, on the score of half a dozen poems of which this is perhaps the

---

[1] *Scrutiny*, Vol. XIX, No. 2, Winter 1952-3, p. 96   [2] *Ibid.* p. 97

best. And it seems to me that, while he has given a splendid reading of this poem, he is judging it too highly; and he is judging it too highly because he has a temperamental affinity with the predominant attitude expressed in it. Consequently, in establishing the degree in which the poem realises and defines its own impulses, he overstresses its total value. (I do not myself think Hardy a great poet.) The rewriting of its intention, in the passages which I have just quoted, is Leavis' own. No one could disagree with him that the final effect of the poem is of a certain positive life, and that its life is of this kind— what we may call a determination to live with reality. It is clearly a realistic poem; and the insight expressed in it is also a kind of courage. It is a courageous determination not to be deflected, by the vagaries of memory or of the present scene, from the rôle, the stance, appropriate to the being whom memory and the present scene have presented to him. But is this affirmation of life the valuable, the deeply impersonal one which Leavis' urgent rewriting suggests it is? The 'ethos with which the poem leaves us at the end' is not simply one which the working of the poem itself has established, it implies an ultimate attitude to life. That attitude, on its philosophical side, is a sort of stoicism in a minor key; while its moral expression is a kind of courage. These qualities no doubt give evidence of a 'rare kind of integrity'. But do they result in a great poem? Certainly they do not express an affirmation of life of anything like the intensity and completeness of, say, Yeats' 'Sailing to Byzantium', or Marvell's 'Horatian Ode'—poems which are very different from each other in affirmation, but both clearly great. It seems to me that the very specificity of reference which is so appropriate to it, and which Leavis counts on so much, are actually in this case a barrier to greatness.

It must be obvious that the qualities of the poem which draw Leavis' ardent admiration are analogous to what people usually mean when they speak of qualities of character. When we notice this, we remember how often, and how aptly, he has used the word 'character' of such poets as Hopkins and Keats. It is clear that, for him, not only is Hardy's perception of his own state adequately realised in the poetic detail, but there is something equivalent to a power of character leading to this realisation,

insisting on it. I am not, except for a couple of minor reservations, questioning the degree of realisation which he finds there;
but I am questioning the poetic importance which he assigns to
the realisation of this particular ultimate attitude; and I am
suggesting that it is an 'affirmation of life' in a less valuable
sense than he, through his rewriting of Hardy's ultimate intention, suggests it is.[1]

At any rate, we can agree that Hardy's attitude is valuable
to the extent that it represents a 'rare kind of integrity', a sort
of disinterestedness which goes with a sustained capacity for
realism, in the ordinary sense of that word. To the extent that
the real is faced, it is 'placed', defined and evaluated; and so, in
some sense, it is affirmed. But the real, in this situation as in
most situations which produce good poetry, is not only the
reality of an external scene but also of a particular present
emotion. And to say that an emotion is defined is, for Leavis,
to say that it is *refined*; particularising is a process of refining. So
we find him saying, in another essay in this series:

> We might say that the sonnet gives us 'the Sunset emotion'.
> To say that, of course, isn't necessarily to damn it. But if a poet
> invokes a stock experience of that order he must control it to some
> particularizing and refining use; and refinement and particularity
> are what we look for in vain in *Calais Beach*.[2]

The use of that 'must' may make us pause. But we come here
to Leavis' preoccupation with emotion in poetry, and his
consistent association of it with particularity, concreteness. As
we shall see, his attitude to it is of a very different kind from
Eliot's, or even Arnold's. But before I examine it, as we find it
asserted in its proper text, the essay ' "Thought" and Emotional
Quality', it would be as well to say something more about the
sense in which he uses the word 'particularity'. It is not a word
worn loosely in order simply to cover a multitude of inexact-
nesses; it is an attempt to come close to the different workings
of poetry by relating them all to a common characteristic. And,
as Leavis uses it, it may range in meaning from Shakespeare to

---

[1] I would disagree with him, too, about some details of the poem's life.
[2] *Imagery and Movement: op. cit.*
In considering these three essays it is as well to remember that they are closely
linked, and even overlap.

Johnson. It applies to the almost muscular 'enacting' of sensory perception which he finds in both Donne and Keats; to the controlled metaphorical vitality of Shakespeare; to the exploration of spiritual states and meanings through the concrete that is to be found in Hopkins and Eliot; to the flexible run of Pope's lines among changes of tone and of pointed reference; and even to the weighty generalising of Johnson. It is, in short, nothing like a formal definition of poetry—nor even part of such a definition—but a word which is flexible enough to be used, with an appropriate relevance, of a wide variety of poetic modes.[1]

It is obvious that such a term, if it is to be of any real use, must be capable of flexible handling. For Leavis does not see the realisation of an insight in the concrete only as a way of defining (and so 'refining') emotion, but as the natural result or concomitant of emotion and thought working together. Particularity, then, connotes a sort of realism; it is the result of an approach, through a unified sensibility, to the real. This is the theme of his essay, ' "Thought" and Emotional Quality', which it is worth while analysing in a little detail.

His procedure in this essay is to do a comparative analysis of four sets of paired poems; and his critical principles are to be located in the conclusions which he draws from each comparison. First, he compares 'Heraclitus' with Scott's 'Proud Maisie', and goes directly on to clarify his conclusions by comparing 'A slumber did my spirit seal' with 'Break, break, break':

> When we look at *Heraclitus* we see that the directly emotional and personal insistence distinguishing it is associated with an absence of core or substance: the poem seems to be all emotional comment, the alleged justifying situation, the subject of comment, being represented by loosely evocative generalities, about which the poet feels vaguely if 'intensely' (the 'intensity' of this kind of thing is conditioned by vagueness). Again, the emotion seems to

---

[1] Even so, I feel that Leavis sometimes uses it in a tendentious way. There is no room to discuss the matter here; but I invite the reader to a careful reading of *The Common Pursuit*, p. 102. There, in a statement on the specific qualities of Johnson's poetry, Leavis finds a kind of 'concreteness' which he tries to specify by calling it a poetry 'remarkable for body'. I must comment that I don't find the 'weight' of the passage which he quotes to be of this kind at all; and I find Leavis' use of his critical terminology in this context evasive.

be out there on the page, whereas in reading *Proud Maisie* we never seem to be offered emotions as such; the emotion develops and defines itself as we grasp the dramatic elements the poem does offer—the data it presents (that is the effect) with emotional disinterestedness. For 'disinterestedness' we can substitute 'impersonality', with which term we introduce a critical topic of the first importance.[1]

In the context provided by my discussion of the previous essay, most of this does not need explanation. But there are two or three elements in it which are new, emphases which we have not encountered before. It is interesting that Leavis should himself introduce the word 'justify', which imposed itself on me in dealing with an earlier passage: Emotional comment should not be merely about itself; and it *will* be about itself, will be vacuous and unreal, unless the poem contains in some manner the situation which the emotional comment implies and points to. If that situation is not somehow *in* the poem, somehow 'justifying' the emotion, that emotion itself will impress itself on us as something detached, external, 'out there on the page': something ultimately mechanical, unrelated in any organic way to the poet's personal grasp of reality.

So much is clear. And Leavis ends his paragraph with the mention of the word 'impersonality'. An emotion which 'defines itself' through the detailed actuality in the poem is an impersonal emotion: not in the sense of being depersonalised, removed from the inner life of the poet, but in the sense of being 'distanced' from him, of being made fruitfully subject to a play of intelligence. 'Emotional quality' is valuable in poetry only when it is the concomitant, and in part the subject, of intelligence. The elaboration of this judgment, and the analysis of its possible variants, provide the theme for the rest of Leavis' essay.

He continues by meeting the possible objection that the impersonality of 'Proud Maisie' is not very impressive, because it is the facile product of a conventional balladist's gift which required no emotion behind it in the first place. If this objection were allowed, then the term 'impersonality' would be rather an empty one. So Leavis offers Wordsworth's 'A slumber did my

[1] *Scrutiny*, Vol. XIII, No. 1, Spring 1945, p. 53

spirit seal' as a poem which is certainly not liable to such a charge. Here, he says, is an impersonal poem which 'unmistakably derives from a seismic personal experience'.

> No one can doubt that Wordsworth wrote his poem because of something profoundly and involuntarily suffered—suffered as a personal calamity, but the experience has been so impersonalized that the effect, as much as that of *Proud Maisie*, is one of bare and disinterested presentment. Again, though the working this time doesn't so obviously prompt to a diagrammatic schematization, the emotional power is generated between juxtaposed opposites. It is generated between the two stanzas, or between the states represented by the stanzas: 'she was, she is not'—the statement seems almost as bare and simple as that. But the statement is concrete, and once the reading has been completed the whole poem is seen to be a complex organization, charged with a subtle life. . . .[1]

In dealing with a better poem than 'Proud Maisie', Leavis is able to take his analysis of the meaning and importance of impersonality one step further. And he is pointing to a truth about the *process* of impersonalising as well as to the fact of an impersonality achieved. The struggle to come to poetic terms with, to deal intelligently with, an emotion so deeply felt as Wordsworth's must involve an activity, a struggle, which is dialectical. Wordsworth, in his presentation of his emotion, achieves a balance between a felt life and a felt death, a presence and an absence, something equivalent to 'the affirmation and the void' whose co-presence Leavis detected in Hardy's poem. And he sees that balance as achieved only through the concreteness of the poem: intelligence playing urgently upon an urgent emotion makes itself felt in terms of things, presences. The balance once achieved, the result is a poem 'charged with a subtle life'. The poem is a representation, in its own, particularised terms, of the spiritual vitality with which the poet can bring himself to contemplate such a personal situation at all.

In contrast to vitality of this kind is the imperfectly controlled emotionality of the two poems by Tennyson which Leavis goes on to deal with. It is unnecessary to look at his analysis in detail; but it should be remarked that the quality which he

[1] *Ibid.* p. 54

finds in Tennyson to oppose to the spiritual courage and emotional vitality of Wordsworth is essentially a sort of complacency:

> . . . there is no attitude towards the experience except one of complaisance; we are to be wholly in it and of it. We note, too, the complete absence of anything like the particularity of (a): there is nothing that gives the effect of an object, or substantial independent existence.

and

> it is plain that habitual indulgence of the kind represented by *Tears, idle Tears*—indulgence not accompanied and virtually disowned by a critical placing—would be, on grounds of emotional and spiritual hygiene, something to deplore. There is nothing gross about the poem; it exhibits its author's highly personal distinction; but it unquestionably offers emotion directly, emotion for its own sake without a justifying situation. . . .[1]

'Emotional and spiritual hygiene' is an ugly phrase; but it is easy to see what Leavis wants; he wants a poetry which is the expression, the representative, of an integrated person. As with Shelley, so with Tennyson, he sees emotionalism going with lack of particularity, lack of feeling for objective reality: and in this failure he sees feeling divorced from thought, sentiments left undefined, all leading to sentimentality. This sentimentality is the result not only of a failure of personal integration, but also of a failure to face reality. Emotional and spiritual wholeness inevitably go together; and intelligence operates fully when it is the agent of this wholeness. Leavis is here very close to making an open statement on the sense in which poetry is *moral*; its moral value resides in the 'emotional quality' which, when integrated with the workings of intelligence, is the index of spiritual vitality.

There are many of us who would say that spiritual vitality extends further, and means more, than this analysis would suggest. But within the chosen limits of his approach, Leavis has come to a truth of obvious importance in life as in poetry. He is not interested in carrying his analysis further, prodding it into becoming an open judgment on moral questions or on

[1] *Scrutiny*, Vol. XIII, No. 1, Spring 1945, p. 59

'life in general'. But he does acknowledge that, in considering the use of emotion in the poetry of Shelley or Tennyson, the critic is led to point to qualities which may seem to an aesthete to be non-literary:

> . . . in the examination of his poetry the literary critic finds himself passing, by inevitable transitions, from describing characteristics to making adverse judgments about emotional quality; and from these to judgments that are pretty directly moral; and so to a kind of discussion in which, by its proper methods and in pursuit of its proper ends, literary criticism becomes the diagnosis of what, looking for an inclusive term, we can only call spiritual malady.[1]

And he finds this spiritual malady expressing itself, in the case of Shelley's poetry, in 'a virtual abeyance of the thinking mind': not only a failure to face reality in life and in poetry, but also a failure to show any convincing interest in it at all. Not that Leavis, as he declares, wants to make Metaphysical poetry the norm; he sees the danger of such poetry for what it is—'the cultivation of thought for its own sake', which is another way of refusing to face reality or to undertake the task of self-integration. But the action of intelligence in poetry (Leavis significantly uses the term 'energy of intelligence') is more properly an activity by which the poet defines emotions and things by facing them in their reality and complexity. Leavis elaborates this by comparing Lionel Johnson's 'By the Statue of King Charles at Charing Cross' with an extract from Marvell; and he does so while using for immediate background his own judgment that

> The activity of the thinking mind, the energy of intelligence, involved in the Metaphysical habit means that, when the poet *has* urgent personal experience to deal with it is attended to and contemplated—which in turn means some kind of separation, or distinction, between experiencer and experience. 'Their attempts were always analytic'—to analyse your experience you must, while keeping it alive and immediately present as experience, treat it in some sense as an object. . . .[2]

This is obviously reminiscent of Eliot's famous dictum about poetic impersonality; but Leavis gives it a distinctive emphasis

---

[1] *Ibid.* p. 60   [2] *Ibid.* p. 61

in his second sentence. He makes it clear, too, that he regards such impersonality as characteristic of 'the strength of all the most satisfying poetry'. Marvell has this; in him it is a kind of 'poise' (a recurrent word with Leavis) representative of his society as well as of his own judicial balance. It is a kind of poise which expresses itself in judgment: but in judgment of a specifically poetic, not of an easily didactic kind: 'Much as the ode seems to be a matter of explicit statement, its judgments are conveyed concretely, in terms of feeling and attitude.'[1] To say this means, for Leavis, to say that they are the products of the whole man; in this case, apparently, almost the products of a whole civilisation.

Lionel Johnson, on the other hand, is seen as relying not on any wholeness of personal experience, but on the workings of a special poetic faculty: that of a mistaken spiritual exaltation:

> It must be plain at once that such impressiveness as Johnson's poem has is conditioned by an absence of thought. This is poetry from the 'soul', that nineteenth-century region of specialized poetical experience where nothing has sharp definition and where effects of 'profundity' and 'intensity' depend upon a lulling of the mind. . . .[2]

The essay concludes with a further analysis of the meaning of 'thought'—an analysis which is especially valuable in that it is concerned with Blake. Leavis finds Blake's shorter poems charged with intelligence working in a different way, because engaged with a different object, from any that he has so far examined;[3] and his interest in Blake gives him the opportunity to make a further statement on the rôle of thought in poetry with reference to the Prophetic Books:

> Just what 'ideas' are would be an interesting and fruitful inquiry. It is enough to say here that their weakness as poetry is their weakness as thought. Their generality is of a kind that makes them illusory and inefficacious. They are lacking in grip on the data they are supposed to organize, and they betray a lack of grasp in the poet for such undertakings. Instead of serving as instruments of clarification, they tend to function as a kind of

---

[1] *Scrutiny*, Vol. XIII, No. 1, Spring 1945, p. 66
[2] *Ibid.* p. 63   [3] *Ibid.* pp. 68-71

ritual, rote, or game—a game that could have given no satisfaction
to the poet if they hadn't blurred the experience they were meant
to interpret.[1]

It is clear that he finds emotional health to be inescapably
associated with the workings of intelligence; and he sees intelligence as associated with a firm grasp of, and feeling for, what
he calls particularity, or the concrete. In fact, he refuses to have
dealings with any working of intelligence that is not expressed
in and through the concrete. This, of course, limits the ways in
which he can openly extend his critical findings into the business
of living; for it disqualifies him from following certain of the
poets into the theological or philosophical territories from which
their poetry derives some of its power, and into which it leads.
Theological and philosophical discourse is inevitably, in some
sense, abstract; and I should certainly argue that the poetry of
Eliot, or Blake, or Dante, for example, prompts the reader to
reflection on life in terms of that discourse.[2] Leavis would
presumably reply that, in so far as he is a literary critic, he can
be concerned with the terms of such a discourse only as they
are 'realised' in the concrete particulars of a poem. This is
virtually the reply which he gives to René Wellek in his essay
'Literary Criticism and Philosophy'; it is in fact the whole
burden of that essay. In it, he makes one statement which is a
fierce defence of the principle that, in discussing anything, the
man trained in the discipline of literary criticism should not
stray at all from the concrete:

> If I had to generalize, my generalization regarding the relation
> between poetry and 'direct vulgar living' or the 'actual' would
> run rather in the following way than in that suggested by Dr
> Wellek: traditions, or prevailing conventions or habits, that tend
> to cut poetry in general off from direct vulgar living and the
> actual, or that make it difficult for the poet to bring into poetry
> his most serious interests as an adult living in his own time, have
> a devitalizing effect. But I cannot see that I should have added
> to the clarity, cogency or usefulness of my book by enunciating
> such a proposition (or by arguing it theoretically).[3]

[1] *Ibid.* p. 70
[2] This question is taken up from different angles in Appendices A and B.
[3] *The Common Pursuit, op. cit.* p. 215

This states his position in negative terms; and I have already tried to suggest how he might care to formulate it in positive terms. And yet I wonder how much more, what greater depth, is implied in his positive standards than the values suggested in that phrase 'his most serious interests as an adult living in his own time'. To be an adult living in his own time *is*, for Leavis, to have a firm grasp of the particular experiences and values of an individual life; and those 'serious interests' are obviously the moral interests which a writer brings to his particular experiences, and tests there. I say 'writer' rather than poet; because the position which I have clumsily interpreted is a position more clearly implied in *The Great Tradition* than in any other of his books. I don't want to step outside my elected subject to discuss this book, in which the analysis of significance is so closely bound up with human character (as distinct from the mere 'creation of characters'). But it is the book which, more than any other, has won for Leavis the undeserved reputation of a simple didact. And it is interesting for my purpose because it shows that he has come to find the central tradition of English literary values, as it is exhibited in the past hundred years, exhibited in the novel more forcefully and completely than in formal poetry. 'The mantle of Shakespeare' has descended to the novelists; and Leavis' favourite novelists have given us the opportunity to see 'the novel as dramatic poem'.

What are these literary values which he sees as central to the English tradition? The whole burden of *The Great Tradition* is that they are moral values made literary through the prolonged exercise of a sensibility which is in touch at once with important human issues and with the writer's own 'most serious interests' (to echo the passage which I have just quoted). The values which he detects are implied in the mention of self-knowledge leading to self-control; of richness of the novel's pattern; of the adequacy of that pattern to express the writer's 'essential interests' and his central insights into human behaviour; of a flexibility of tone with which the writer controls his insight within that pattern. Leavis plainly associates mind with sensibility; and he plainly sees them operating together with most precision and richness (both words are important) when they deal with deeply felt moral interests and issues. He would no doubt prefer the term 'engage with' to the term 'deal with'; for the former expresses more completely the notion of an inner grasp of, and commitment to, human life.

It is obvious that this position is not a didactic one; in fact it is, in a real sense, an anti-didactic one. For to transform the feeling for moral interests and issues into works of literary value on this level is not to use words to persuade the reader of some pre-conceived moral truth; it is, in a way, to *create* values. No matter how traditionally the creative writer holds his moral values, his re-creation of them in literature removes them from the level of conventional acceptance or rejection. It creates new terms of discourse.

If this is so, then in what sense are we to call Leavis' view of literature a moral one? He sees the whole process of a fine literary work as a process of definition, even of self-definition, which we cannot call anything else than moral; and he sees its effect as that of stimulating in the responsive reader a 'sense of life' which is also a readiness for self-definition. In this he is different from both Arnold and Eliot. He sees his great writers as concerned above all with an exalted normality, 'human centrality'. So he says of novelists, in words which could be as easily applied to poets:

> Is there any great novelist whose preoccupation with 'form' is not a matter of his responsibility towards a rich human interest, or complexity of interests, profoundly realized?—a responsibility involving, of its very nature, imaginative sympathy, moral discrimination and judgment of relative human value?[1]

And again:

> *Nostromo* is a master-piece of 'form' in senses of the term congenial to the discussion of Flaubert's art, but to appreciate Conrad's 'form' is to take stock of a process of relative valuation conducted by him in the face of life: what do men live by? What *can* men live by?—these are the questions that animate his theme. . . . The dramatic imagination at work is an intensely moral imagination, the vividness of which is inalienably a judging and a valuing.[2]

[1] *The Great Tradition* (Chatto and Windus, London, 1948), p. 29
[2] *Ibid.* p. 30

And yet again:

> There is nothing sentimental about George Eliot's vision of human mediocrity and 'platitude', but she sees in them matters for compassion, and her dealings with them are assertions of human dignity. To be able to assert human dignity in this way is greatness: the contrast with Flaubert is worth pondering.[1]

I shall return to these questions in the next chapter. What is worth pondering here is the general condition which Leavis posits of the relation of form to 'moral imagination'. We have seen that, for him, thought in poetry is inseparable from emotional quality, and that reality and sincerity are so inseparably twined as to seem synonymous. He is not in any ordinary sense a didact. For him, the whole poem is 'moral': in great poets, as in great novelists, the interest in 'form' is all of a piece with the interest in 'human centrality'. They are not teachers, but artists. The notion of a poem as 'enacting' its moral insights and its sensuous perceptions of the external world involves Leavis in estimating the whole of a poem or novel, and not only what it 'has to say' to us.

This brings us back to the word 'impersonality' which Leavis himself introduced as a key term in the opening of his essay ' "Thought" and Emotional Quality'. It is a word, he said, with which 'we introduce a critical topic of the first importance'; and it may seem strange that he should not have gone on to take up his own challenge and discuss that topic. Instead, he probed its possible meanings by a typical process of comparative criticism. But I can't feel that this is good enough. The word is an important one, a recurrently confusing one, in modern literature. And it is necessary to try to distinguish Leavis' understanding of it from all the others which have had so much currency: from Hulme's, or Eliot's, or Wyndham Lewis', or Joyce's.

We may take Leavis' view and Joyce's (or, rather, Stephen Dedalus') as the two antithetical poles between which discussion of the term might flow. In *A Portrait of the Artist as a Young Man* we find Stephen the amateur aesthetician enunciating his luciferian conception of the artist:

[1] *The Great Tradition* (Chatto and Windus, London, 1948), p. 60

... the personality of the artist ... refines itself out of existence, impersonalises itself, so to speak.

The artist, like the God of the creation, remains within or behind or beyond or above his handiwork, invisible, refined out of existence, indifferent, paring his fingernails.

The number of seemingly careful prepositions, the apparent scrupulousness of the adjectives, may conceal the real tendency of this passage. It is not an attempt to define exactly; it is a gesture of defiance. Whether or not we find the artist 'within' his 'handiwork', certainly he is not of it; he is aloof, contemptuous of the issues which his work has disposed of, perversely enjoying the power of being disengaged. It is a conception of art as power and, ultimately, as refusal of responsibility—a 'Non Serviam' in art as in life. There is a real sense in which it is luciferian.

Leavis' position is the exact opposite. For him, art is a struggle to define oneself and one's values at the heart of the issues which one feels most deeply. To start paring one's fingernails would be an admission of defeat: of defeat, because defection, in the face of life. The impersonality of art consists, for him, in having found, while remaining at the heart of human problems, a point of rest from which to estimate them and to define one's own life, one's possibilities of full living, in relation to them. Thus, as we have seen, he is intensely concerned with emotion, feeling, and thought in poetry; and he sees the artist's emotional life as being 'impersonalised'. By this he does not mean what Eliot means: that poetry is a form through which we can escape the pressure, the actuality, of our emotions. Nor does he mean what Arnold seems to mean: that poetry is a means of turning emotion into ennobling sentiment. He seems to mean two things: that the emotion is universalised, its general import for men discovered: and that it is directed, made subordinate to what we might call a general line of living, a servant of the poet's 'essential interests', which are basically moral.

CHAPTER VII

F. R. Leavis: Impersonality and Values

Of course, the account which I have given of Leavis' view of 'impersonality' is far from exhaustive; and it may not have established any very valuable conclusions about that view. But I hope I have shown fully enough how his use of the term 'enactment', his virtual equation of reality with sincerity, and his analysis of 'thought' in the establishment of emotional health, lead on to his conception of impersonality. That conception, because of the critical care and sense of life behind it, cannot be anything like the conception of Stephen Dedalus or T. E. Hulme. And, in its turn, it leads outward into the consideration of other qualities, qualities both of literature and of the kind of attitude to life which Leavis is trying, in his resolutely unobtrusive way, to establish. It is my purpose in this chapter to try to formulate his view of those qualities. In the process, I shall be examining a trend in his development which I feel to be most important, but which seems to have so far escaped much notice. It is a trend which leads to a position of an almost religious kind. And it is very important in his criticism, especially if we hold, as I do, that his chief contribution to critical thought comes in *Revaluation* and in the works which follow it, rather than in the earlier and perhaps more obviously exploratory works.

We have seen that, for him, the impulse to artistic creation reaches satisfying artistic results only when it is the correlative of a deep ethical preoccupation: the imagination, in great writers, is moral; the form of a great work is a moulding of deeply felt ethical concerns into pattern. But as soon as this is said, there are questions to be asked; and they are questions which Leavis, from his own developing point of view, answers not Theoretically but in his actual criticism. So we find him speaking, in that same introduction to *The Great Tradition* from which

I have already quoted, of 'writers who are significant in terms of the human awareness they promote; awareness of the possibilities of life'.[1]

This is a constant and developing theme; a theme in which we can see, perhaps, his debt to Arnold. But 'awareness of the possibilities of life': what can this mean?

Certainly it means something more than Arnold could make it mean; and I shall try in this chapter to analyse that meaning. At the moment we may note his general burden in *The Great Tradition*. It is a constant theme in that book that the writers with whom he deals exhibit, at crucial moments in their art, a victory of 'life' over its ever present enemies: over self-deception, disabling conventions of art or life, a devitalising scepticism. And this victory is always seen to be associated with a process of self-recognition, of self-definition through the recognition of 'mutuality in human relations', on the part either of the author or of his characters. Self-discovery of this kind is seen as the essential means to an affirmation of life which can be recognised by the reader as really answering to the facts of life as he knows them and at the same time as involving a moral discrimination among the forces and choices presented to human beings. In this respect, *The Great Tradition* looks forward to the book on Lawrence. Its hidden theme is this: That to know oneself *ethically* is to learn to *be* oneself, in the only important sense: as a moral agent capable of asserting certain developing values in the acts of living.

There are certain facets of this position that we may find obvious. For example, Leavis finds Dos Passos' claim to greatness vitiated by his failure to offer us the presence of that hope which his characters discuss: hope of a creative escape from the valueless and chaotic world which he analyses.[2] His characters are not meaningful enough to make the hope of revolution, which they express, into a real hope for valuable human living. And this failure happens because the work 'does not express an adequate realization of the issues it offers to deal with'.[3]

Hope, then, is needed, though Leavis does not ask any

[1] *The Great Tradition, op. cit.* p. 2
[2] *For Continuity* (The Minority Press, Cambridge, 1933), p. 106
[3] *Ibid.* p. 107

writer to state openly his grounds for hope: some kind of hope is, after all, the prerequisite of living fruitfully at all; to hope is to realise that life does have possibilities. And although this judgment is elementary enough, although it is marginal to Leavis' work, it does help to initiate the discussion which I want to follow out. It offers a way of linking up the theme of the artist as ethical man, which I examined in the last chapter, with the theme of affirmation of life, which I want to examine in this. Unlike Eliot, Leavis does not really separate the writer as artist from the writer as man experiencing his values, and defining them in his art. Impersonality is the effect of the work; but it cannot be achieved by a retreat from the artist's deepest values, which are inevitably personal:

> What Lawrence offers us is not a philosophy or an *œuvre*—a body of literary art—but an experience, or, to fall back on the French again, an *expérience*, for the sense of 'experiment' is needed too. In him the human spirit explored, with unsurpassed courage, resource, and endurance, the representative, the radical and central problems of our time.[1]

Leavis was later to reverse the judgment expressed in certain phrases of the first sentence; his book on Lawrence is devoted to demonstrating that Lawrence is precisely an artist, and his work 'a body of literary art'. But I quote this passage *because* it is from an early work, and can therefore provide another early link in the chain. It shows that, for Leavis, life can only be affirmed in art if its 'radical and central' problems are first squarely faced. An easy optimism does not lead, particularly in our time, to great art. The chaotic world of machinery and mechanised people which Dos Passos faces is, after all, not so unlike the mechanical life which Lawrence faces. But Lawrence faces it with all the ethical resources of the human spirit, and attains an affirmative vision in the face of it; Dos Passos' view fails at the point of spiritual crisis, and never becomes vision.

The same resources of the human spirit which are necessarily engaged in the attempt to *live imaginatively* an answer to human problems are also engaged in the struggle with artistic form. And here again we may note, in parenthesis, that while Dos

---

[1] *For Continuity* (The Minority Press, Cambridge, 1933), p. 180

Passos' trilogy is formally ingenious, and in a way adequate, it has no formal power capable of aiding him to attain to a level of vision. Hopkins is the obvious contrast:

> . . . Hopkins's genius was as much a matter of rare character, intelligence and sincerity as of technical skill: indeed, in his great poetry the distinction disappears; the technical triumph is a triumph of spirit.[1]

A 'triumph of spirit', yes; but a triumph over what? The answer must be that it is a triumph over the intractability which life and language both present to the ordinary sensitive man, but which the great artist, by an extraordinary labour of discovery, makes tractable. A triumph which seems to be merely one over language may also be one over the resistance which human experience may offer to the imagination; it is then an affirmation of life. Similarly Leavis, wrongly I think, praises Bottrall:

> The poet glimpses here a recovered spontaneity, a readjustment to life, an ability to ride it easily. . . . Must we despair of attaining a new naturalness at the far side of the experience of disharmony?[2]

In these two extracts, both from an early book, the theme of affirmation is coming to be openly announced. They show two possible aspects of such an affirmation. And they lead us on to see what he is after: a literature which affirms life while never ceasing to re-create literary forms; not an annunciatory literature, but a formed and patterned one. It is not easy—it could not be easy—to see what he means by the 'affirmation of life'. But we can already say that he certainly means the creation of a sense of human dignity, as his remarks on George Eliot attest; and he means, as well, a sense of the inner development of the human individual leading to the recovery of an organic social life, which once stimulated and guided such a development, but which has long since ceased to do so.[3] It is

---

[1] *New Bearings in English Poetry* (Chatto and Windus, London; new and enlarged edition, 1950), p. 182
[2] *Ibid.* p. 209
It is Leavis' conviction that such a sense of spontaneous life must be recovered, together with his conviction that English poetry since Eliot has neither aided in nor achieved the 'recovery', that have probably led him to his preoccupation with Lawrence, to his preference for the novel, and to the emergence of an almost religious quality in his later criticism.
[3] v. *Culture and Environment* (The Minority Press, Cambridge, 1933)

easy to see why, in a chaotic world, Leavis should consider a certain impersonality, a certain detachment, necessary if an inner development is to take place in the individual. It needs great reliance on one's personal judgment, and a careful refusal not to be self-deluded in reaching that judgment, if a man is not to sink under the weight of chaos in the world. But such a detachment is not of itself sufficient; detachment without 'reverence' leads to a kind of scepticism which drains the springs of vital feeling. That is why Leavis' judgment on Isaac Rosenberg, for whom he has an exaggerated admiration, may be instructive:

> His interest in life, in fact, is radical and religious in the same sense as D. H. Lawrence's. It has to be added that we must credit him, on the evidence of his best work, with an extraordinarily mature kind of detachment such as is not characteristic of Lawrence—to say this first gives the right force to the observation that of the two Rosenberg was much more an artist.
>
> The spiritual strength manifested in the detachment of his poetry was needed in an almost incredible degree for the writing of it.[1]

The relative estimate of Lawrence and Rosenberg is, of course, completely changed by the time we come to *D. H. Lawrence, Novelist*. And I quote this passage to show another variant of Leavis' attitude to art as the affirmation of life. I have quoted all these extracts, marginal as they may appear to the real issue, for the purpose of showing how flexible is his handling of his own preoccupation, how many variants his theme of affirmation may have. We have noticed the idea of literature as a struggle with intractability both in life and language; as a reverence before experience; as a form establishing the 'possibilities of life'; and as a spiritual strength showing itself as a detachment from a painful milieu—a detachment which, backed by that strength, creates positives out of the milieu and its pain.

All these variants enable us to carry the notion of impersonality from a negative to a positive pole: from the idea of directing emotions and feelings under the guidance of ethical

---

[1] *Scrutiny*, Vol. VI, No. 2, September 1937, p. 231

perception to the idea of an impersonal art as being, and not merely stating, an affirmation of life. I have purposely quoted Leavis' judgments on poets who are, for the most part, minor; for even in their work he sees the re-creation of feelings by the 'moral imagination' leading to such an affirmation. But the mention of these writers is little more than a background to his more important statements and analyses: to his statement on Henry James, for example:

> It is true that our judgments ought to come from an impersonal centre in us, and that we shouldn't have been able to make them but for a truth the statement of which would be a generalized form of Mr Anderson's proposition: 'If James had not felt in himself the very impulses which he saw crystallized in American manners he would not have understood American manners.' This possibility of impersonality and this measure of 'community of consciousness' are implied in the existence of art.[1]

This is a more inclusive statement than any we have so far had; even though it seems at first sight a more baffling one. And certain things are clear. Leavis is not speaking only of James as artist, but of the critical-creative mind as it may be possessed by anyone. The 'judgments' are judgments in life as well as in literature. The impersonality of which he speaks is a lived one, an inner detachment from personal desires which is also a communion with other minds; the similarity with Eliot's view of the relation of the individual talent to tradition is as significant as the difference. That impersonality, whatever we are to think of it, is the guarantee of the maturity of those judgments; and the fact that they come from an individual consciousness—not, we may notice, a mind—that represents a living community is their sanction. Their only sanction; but enough of a sanction, one supposes, for art.[2] Although the actual wording of the statement is ambiguous, we may see its general drift; and it is a drift in a religious direction. The 'impersonal centre' is clearly not a mere individual detachment, a centre of hard-won rest peculiar to one person; it is the personal equivalent of the common consciousness which, in a really organic community, binds men together.[3] And Leavis

---

[1] *Scrutiny*, Vol. XV, No. 2, Spring 1948, p. 100   [2] v. Appendix B
[3] v. Leavis' interest in this theme in *Culture and Environment, op. cit.*

maintains that the possibility of such a bond is implied in the very existence of art. We may expect, then, that great art reflects and defines it.

If this is so, what are we to think of an art which is the product of a purely anarchic consciousness, a consciousness which, in its determination to use art to assert its own autonomy, disdains communion with other minds? It is this case that Leavis takes up in dealing with Swift. His analysis is superb, though we may find its development charged with paradox. He begins with the statement, conventional enough in itself, but startling in the context provided by his subsequent analysis, that 'Swift is a great English writer'.[1] And he proceeds to examine Swift's aims and sensibility—his attitude to life. He finds that attitude essentially negative:

> But even here, even in the *Argument*, where Swift's ironic intensity undoubtedly directs itself to the defence of something that he is intensely concerned to defend, the effect is essentially negative. The positive itself appears only negatively—a kind of skeletal presence, rigid enough, but without life or body; a necessary pre-condition, as it were, of directed negation. The intensity is purely destructive.[2]

His 'satire', that is, is of the opposite kind from Pope's, whose enmity towards his targets is of a piece with, and subordinated to, his zest in creation; and this zest in turn is backed by Pope's acceptance of, his enjoyment of, the positive aspirations of the culture which he represents.[3] Swift has no such zest in creation; nor does he, as a man whose interest in life is anarchic, represent the culture which he shared with Pope.

We must ask, then, where we are to find in Swift the affirmation which, on Leavis' general view of literature, could alone guarantee his greatness. If Dos Passos misses greatness through a failure to offer his reader a hope realised in the created detail of his work, how are we to call Swift a great English writer? In the passage quoted, Leavis speaks of his 'intensity', and characterises his 'negation' as 'directed'. But directed to what end, what literary value?

[1] *The Common Pursuit, op. cit.* p. 73
[2] *Ibid.* pp. 74-5
[3] *Scrutiny*, Vol. XII, No. 1, Winter 1943, p. 75

> Swift's [irony] is essentially a matter of surprise and negation; its function is to defeat habit, to intimidate and to demoralize. . . . If one had to justify this irony according to the conventional notion of satire, then its satiric efficacy would be to make comfortable non-recognition, the unconsciousness of habit, impossible.[1]

Its value, then, would be to shock people into a fulfilment of the precept 'Know thyself'. But Leavis advances this judgment very tentatively; and it is plain, from the way in which he approaches Swift's work, that this is not the aspect of it which most interests him. He seems troubled by the realisation (which we all share) that there *is* an extraordinary kind and degree of life in the satires; and he has to find some way of accounting for it. He defines it in terms of energy:

> The dispassionate, matter-of-fact tone induces a feeling and a motion of assent, while the burden, at the same time, compels the feelings appropriate to rejection, and in the contrast—the tension —a remarkably disturbing energy is generated. A sense of an extraordinary energy is the general effect of Swift's irony.[2]

And

> in his use of negative materials—negative emotions and attitudes —there is something that it is difficult not to call creative, though the aim always is destructive.[3]

Now, I find this judgment not clear-cut enough—if we share Leavis' usual attitude to literature. He is not claiming for Swift what Eliot claims for Baudelaire: a use of 'negative emotions and attitudes' for the sake of analysing them, of revealing and judging the negativity. He simply finds in them a kind and degree of energy which he can't refrain from calling creative. And, implicitly admitting the paradox, he tries to find the key for it. He finds it in the notion that Swift's energy is an energy of self-assertion—of a self-assertion which, because it is not backed by any real sanctions, is essentially anarchic:

> The only thing in the nature of a positive that most readers will find convincingly present is self-assertion—*superbia*. Swift's way of demonstrating his superiority is to destroy, but he takes a positive delight in his power.[4]

[1] *The Common Pursuit, op. cit.* p. 75
[2] *Ibid.* p. 77
[3] *Ibid.* p. 79
[4] *Ibid.* p. 80

What is uncommon is Swift's genius and the paradoxical vitality with which this self-defeat of life—life turned against itself —is manifested. In the *Tale of a Tub* the defeat is also a triumph; the genius delights in its mastery, in its power to destroy, and negation is felt as self-assertion.[1]

It is a splendid account, but I am baffled by a certain ambiguity implied in the use of its main terms. 'Negation is felt as self-assertion', yes. But the underlying suggestion with which Leavis presents these two passages is that a negative is turned into a positive; and that is a different matter. For this self-assertion is an assertion of the destructive will, the will perversely delighting in its own assumed autonomy: the self-assertion of man not at a Faustian, but at a post-Faustian level. Another age might have hinted at diabolism; certainly, if we accept Leavis' account, we would be justified in finding in the attitude he analyses a 'Non Serviam', a refusal to co-operate with any forces for good. It is not necessary to accept his account; and I for one feel that it is, though superb within its terms, radically incomplete. Swift's self-assertion seems to me not so much a way of demonstrating his superiority as of giving some objective form to his self-distrust, self-hatred. But I question Leavis' account at such length because of the place it must take in any examination of his position. In it, he has faced an objection to his position arising at the very heart of that position; and he has tried to overcome the objection by defining it. The result is paradoxical. But to see the ultimate tendency of his criticism we must look at the conclusion of the essay:

> A great writer—yes; that account still imposes itself as fitting, though his greatness is no matter of moral grandeur or human centrality; our sense of it is merely a sense of great force. And this force, as we feel it, is conditioned by frustration and constriction; the channels of life have been blocked and perverted.[2]

The essay remains paradoxical in its development; but, as we can see here, Leavis takes away in one gesture of summation what he gave through repeated acts of particular judgment. On this showing, if Swift is a great writer, he is a great writer of

---

[1] *The Common Pursuit, op. cit.* p. 85   [2] *Ibid.* p. 86

an unusual kind, and of a good deal less than the first rank; he can't provide for us a norm or a guide. That is the effect of Leavis' total judgment. He does not see Swift as using his 'force' to deal with any central human preoccupation, to establish a normal image of human life; though he does associate it with the great, even obsessed, *concreteness* of Swift's prose, his 'actuality of presentment'. The effect of his judgment is not to dismiss Swift, but to warn the reader to approach him with a certain detachment, and to realise to what values Swift's genius tacitly invites his assent. Leavis is not waiving his own values for a special occasion; he is making a special deployment of them.

In making a more precise attempt to define the affirmation of life which he asks of great literature, we shall have to turn to two other touchstones: to Eliot and, more especially, to D. H. Lawrence; though there are other judgments to be considered as well.

Leavis' most important criticism of Eliot is to be found in an essay on 'T. S. Eliot's Later Poetry', which is included as an appendix in his work on a literary training, *Education and the University*. In it, he examines the later poems as works in which we find an affirmation of life (though he does not use this term himself) under the aspect of a struggle to define the poet's own spiritual life and its terms. These terms are Christian; but Eliot does not satisfy himself with a re-statement, of no matter how subtle a kind, of Christian truths. On the contrary, he re-creates the truths by an effort to fix and define the nature of his own allegiance to them. His work is a 'technique for sincerity'. And it accordingly involves him in a struggle to hold and use the shifting references which language has to spiritual experience: to re-create language through a definition of his own feelings. It is a struggle with the intractable self, and with the language in which the self conventionally thinks of and expresses its own being. It is thus an affirmation of life which, so Leavis insists, has a particular value for our time:

> The poet's magnificent intelligence is devoted to keeping as close as possible to the concrete of sensation, emotion and perception. Though this poetry is plainly metaphysical in pre-occupation, it is as much poetry, it belongs as purely to the realm

of sensibility, and has in it as little of the abstract and general of discursive prose, as any poetry that was ever written. Familiar terms and concepts are inevitably in sight, but what is distinctive about the poet's method is the subtle and resourceful discipline of continence with which, in its exploration of experience, it approaches them.

Of course, the poet's sensibility being Christian, they lie behind the poetry, as well as being in front of it (so to speak) as something to be recreated; but they are never taken up as accepted instruments for getting to work with.[1]

In other words, Eliot's quite remarkable honesty, his refusal as a poet to take any formulation on trust, has led him to make his beliefs his subject. But he has made them his subject in such a way that their very meaning for him is probed in terms of 'sensation, emotion and perception'; they are re-created, and so established on a firmer basis:

The poetry from Ash-Wednesday onwards doesn't say, 'I believe', or 'I know', or 'here is the truth'; it is positive in direction but not positive in that way (the difference from Dante is extreme). It is a searching of experience, a spiritual discipline, a technique for sincerity—for giving 'sincerity' a meaning. The preoccupation is with establishing from among the illusions, evanescences and unrealities of life in time an apprehension of an assured reality—a reality that, though necessarily apprehended in time, is not of it. There is a sustained positive effort—the constructive effort to be 'conscious'.[2]

This is an extremely perceptive account, and one which has corrected the easy preconceptions of a good number of us. But isn't it, too, radically incomplete? The suggestion is clearly made that Eliot's great honesty has enabled him to reach, within his Christian belief, a new level of sincerity and awareness. In that case, surely the phrase should be, not 'establishing . . .' but 're-establishing . . . an apprehension of an assured reality'. And that reality would surely be *in* the poem, offering itself as evidence for the success of the exploration which led to it. Exploration, no matter how honest and subtle, is not of itself

[1] *Education and the University* (Chatto and Windus, London; new edition, 1948), p. 88
[2] *Ibid.* p. 89

an affirmation; or if it is, it is so only in an analogical sense. But Leavis does not go on to take up the question of that reality as it is expressed and defined in the poem. It is the radical incompleteness of his analysis that he fails to do so; for it would be a specifically literary analysis, not an exercise in theology. Instead, he passes rather abruptly from the challenge to do so which the *Quartets* provide, and goes on to deal with 'Marina', where the reality evoked is a great deal easier to deal with. There is a certain modesty in this refusal; but it is a failure all the same. If 'the sensibility (is) Christian', then the Quartets presuppose what they explore and define: a representative view of experience. For Leavis, the deeper questions about affirmation of life, *in this context*, seem to be somewhat embarrassing. It is the great honesty of spirit, and the great positive charge which it gives to language, that constitute for him the greatness of the poetry. But if that 'assured reality' is somehow apprehended in it, then we must ask how much greater positiveness it derives from that reality's being apprehended. It is the question Leavis shies away from. I have the impression that he is much more at home in living through the kind of 'realisation' of reality offered by Shakespeare, or Keats, or Donne, or Pope —that which has an almost 'muscular' concomitant—than in that offered by Eliot.

This virtual refusal, this seeming incompleteness, would hardly be worth alleging against a critic if it were not for one thing. When Leavis comes, in full maturity, to deal with Lawrence, he takes a different approach. He not only gestures towards the reality which Lawrence's art probes, and which it defines in apprehending it; he brings its nature into the open, and he gives every sign of endorsing Lawrence's attitude to it. Admittedly, the reality in each case is very different; and Lawrence's is much the easier to say something definite about. But his refusal to accept his own critical challenge in dealing with Eliot must strike us as paradoxical.[1]

Leavis' final assessment of the poetry, while not entering the element in it of which I have spoken, is made in terms of its

[1] It would be unfair, however, to suggest that he does not respond to the 'illuminative quality' of Eliot's work. See page 95. It is a remarkable analysis, but it refuses to enter one relevant dimension of the discussion which it inaugurates. See also the tribute to Eliot on page 103.

total positive life. He is concerned less with what it affirms (if that is the right way of putting it) than with the quality of the affirmation. That quality is such as to stimulate in the reader a quickening of his whole individual capacity for living:

> To have gone seriously into the poetry is to have had a quickening insight into the nature of thought and language; a discipline of intelligence and sensibility calculated to promote, if any could, real vitality and precision of thought; an education intellectual, emotional and moral.[1]

It should be clear that, for Leavis, the notion of literature as being an affirmation of life, of lived values, cannot be divorced from the literary values which I looked at in the last chapter. But no very satisfying conclusions can be reached simply by studying his judgments of Eliot and Swift. What his criticism has always pointed to, and has come to point to with increasing authority, is the fact of great literature as transcending a merely individual consciousness, even while it remains firmly rooted in such a consciousness. The universal character of literature is seen to be of a nearly religious kind. Indeed, Leavis himself has come frequently to use the word 'religious'. It is part reason for his championship of Lawrence that Lawrence's examination of human issues takes place, as it were, in a religious dimension, and suggests as an 'answer' to those issues a religious use of consciousness; and consciousness is seen as going far deeper than intellect, and as involving a kind of commerce with reality much more profound than any mere 'knowing'. Accordingly, it is part reason for his mounting irritation with Eliot that Eliot's religious focus on contemporary literature (in his criticism) and contemporary society (in his plays) is of a narrow, even truncated kind. What this religious feeling of Leavis' amounts to is a matter of debate. Perhaps it is most adequately represented for him in Lawrence's great works. One is tempted, by the terms in which he puts it, to think of it as merely another example of that paradoxical late growth, humanism, a religion of man developing his own inner potentialities in a secularised world. But one notices how often he quotes Lawrence's 'Thank God I am not free, any more than a rooted tree is free'; and

[1] *Education and the University, op. cit.,* p. 104

this is certainly not a statement which most secular humanists, of whatever kind, would care to endorse. The difficulty in interpreting him comes, as I have said, from his refusal to raise the question of his own position at all except in dealing with actual literary works; and then it is raised obliquely. But it seems to be a religious conception, a nearly religious focus upon literature, in a very different sense from any suggested in the humanist paradox. We may perhaps see it better by looking at his view of Wordsworth, and at his account of tragedy.

In seeking the source and nature of Wordsworth's greatness, he credits him with qualities with which he would also credit lesser poets, such as Hardy: 'emotional discipline, critical exploration of experience, pondered valuation and maturing reflection . . . the sureness with which Wordsworth grasps the world of common perception'.[1] It is in these qualities that Wordsworth is seen as greater than Shelley. But something more, something perhaps of a different order, is needed to account for his distinctive greatness. Leavis finds it, not in any pantheist philosophy, but in a sense for, and re-creation of, a bond which can only be called religious:

> [The poetry] defines convincingly—presents in such a way that no further explanation seems necessary—the sense of 'belonging' in the universe, of a kinship known inwardly through the rising springs of life and consciousness and outwardly in an interplay of recognition and response.[2]

Yet this is no vague religiosity, no self-willed sense of 'belonging' in a world of generalities through distrust of the actual world. It is a wisdom *lived*:

> What he had for presentment was a type and standard of human normality, a way of life; his preoccupation with sanity and spontaneity working at a level and in a spirit that it seems appropriate to call religious.[3]

He is preoccupied with

> a distinctively human naturalness, with sanity and spiritual health, and his interest in mountains was subsidiary. His mode of preoccupation, it is true, was that of a mind intent always upon

---

[1] *Revaluation, op. cit.* p. 212   [2] *Ibid.* p. 161
[3] *Ibid.* p. 164

ultimate sanctions and upon the living connexions between man and the extra-human universe; it was, that is, in the same sense as Lawrence's was, religious.[1]

Spontaneity, that is, as Wordsworth seeks it, involves no cult of the instinctive and primitive at the expense of the rationalized and civilized; it is the spontaneity supervening upon complex development, a spontaneity engaging an advanced and delicate organization. He stands for a distinctly human naturalness; one, that is, consummating a discipline, moral and other. A poet who can bring home to us the possibility of such a naturalness should to-day be found important. In Wordsworth's poetry the possibility is offered us realized—realized in a mode central and compelling enough to enforce the bearing of poetry upon life, the significance of this poetry for actual living.[2]

There is point in quoting all these extracts, repetitive as they are, for they explain and define each other; and, taken together, they offer us little chance of misunderstanding them. Once again it is a question of an affirmation of life through the 'realisation' of an insight into human issues; but in this case the issues are seized for realisation at the point where they become religious issues: the issues of man and his bonds with the universe. And Leavis' judgment on Wordsworth is particularly interesting; because it shows us that what he is bringing forward is not a religious 'criterion' of judgment as substitute for a literary one; here literary and moral and religious interests cohere in the one judgment. He is not engaged in any attempt to find a ready-made religion sheltering behind the exercises of literary criticism. What he says here is of a piece with his 'moral' preoccupation, the nature of which I have already looked at. He becomes engaged with literature on this deeper level when he contemplates works which are the result of their authors' implicitly facing the question: How is man to triumph over the pains of living, in such a way as to affirm life? He plainly finds the greatest works to be of this kind; and I shall come later to his discussion of tragedy. But there is also an excellent though tendentious account[3] of the way in which personal griefs and an awareness of the world's griefs underlie Wordsworth's im-

---

[1] *Revaluation, op. cit.* p. 165   [2] *Ibid.* p. 170
[3] *Ibid.* pp. 178-9

personality, and challenge him to a spiritual development. He faces the question

> if (and how shall they not?) the sensitive and imaginative freely let their 'hearts lie open' to the suffering of the world, how are they to retain any health or faith for living?

It is the awareness of pain which leads to the greatest impersonality, which (or so he elsewhere suggests) is to be found in tragedy. There is a persistent note in this essay of poetry as drawing its life, and so its moral power, from its source in a long backward of living, which itself is mysterious, and which incites, being personal, to 'sincerity', the kind of sincerity which, if it is representative and critically conscious, Leavis would call impersonality. But that is not the whole of the matter. For it is suggested that this backward of living is seen fully only when it is seen as leading into depths, as involving bonds, which are more than personal: the awareness of which is the beginning of religion. It is a very different approach from Eliot's; and it arises because Leavis is coming increasingly to deal with writers whose case is very like Dr Johnson's, as Leavis sees it:

> It was a tragic sense of life that was, at the same time, both moral centrality and a profound commonsense: '*Vivite laeti* is one of the great rules of health', he wrote to Mrs Thrale.[1]

And the struggle to find some grounds for living joyfully drives us into the modes of discourse which he sees Wordsworth's poetry as representing.

But it is in that curiously tentative essay 'Tragedy and the "Medium" ' that his view is found at its most suggestive. It is a reply to Santayana's essay 'Tragic Philosophy'; and I call it curiously tentative because it deliberately, and in 'the abstract', raises issues which it does not follow out. Yet it is an interesting endorsement of his usual critical practice that he should begin his querying of Santayana's account not with a statement of his own *a priori* views on the general issues, but with a statement about the observable nature of poetic language.

> ... to demand that poetry should be a 'medium' for 'previously definite' ideas is arbitrary, and betrays a radical incomprehension.

[1] *The Common Pursuit, op. cit.* p. 115

199

What Mr Santayana calls 'Shakespeare's medium' creates what it conveys; 'previously definite' ideas put into a 'clear and transparent' medium wouldn't have been definite enough for Shakespeare's purpose.[1]

One can only agree wholeheartedly; poets do not, the best poetry does not, work in the way which he stigmatises. He is speaking of the poetic-creative use of language which he elsewhere charges Johnson with misunderstanding. And it is not only a question of language; for Leavis, literature, by 'realising' its insights, in a sense creates new values in the face of life. Accordingly, he passes on from considering Santayana's view of poetic language to consider his view of the tragic effect which, in the greatest poetry, that language leads to; and again he finds the account deficient. I am forced to quote at length, for his development of the charge contains many hints and subtleties:

> It will have been noted that in the former of the two passages just quoted Mr Santayana gives us an account of tragic catharsis. It is particularly interesting because in it he associates the cathartic effect with a poetic use (as he understands it) of language. We are bound to question his understanding, and in attempting to provide our own account of a poetic use we find ourselves exploring for a profounder and more satisfactory account of Tragedy—of the tragic—than he implies here, or offers elsewhere in his essay. This at any rate is what, in my experience, gives the essay its peculiar value.
>
> The view of the tragic implied in Mr Santayana's account of catharsis seems a very limited one. Does Shakespearean tragedy, does the tragic in *Macbeth*, amount to no more than this? If so, where can we look for anything profounder? For surely the tragic experience is, or can be, a more important and serious matter than Mr Santayana here suggests?
>
> To postulate a 'tragic experience' or 'tragic effect' and then seek to define it is to lay oneself open to the suspicion of proposing a solemn and time-honoured academic game. Yet the critical contemplation of the profoundest things in literature does lead to the idea of such an experience, and we can see to it that the attempt at definition shall not be the kind of futility we associate with the Grand Style or the Sublime and the Beautiful. It need

[1] *The Common Pursuit, op. cit.* p. 124

hardly be said, for instance, that what we are concerned with will not be found in all tragedies, or in most. And next, it is well to put aside the term 'catharsis': its promptings don't seem to be at all helpful. . . . If 'calm' may properly be predicated of the tragic experience, it is certainly not 'calm of mind, all passion spent' in the natural suggestion of that phrase. According to what seems valid in the current notion of the tragic there is rather something in the nature of an exalting effect. We have contemplated a painful action, involving death and the destruction of the good, admirable and sympathetic, and yet instead of feeling depressed we enjoy a sense of enhanced vitality.[1]

This passage is perfectly clear; and I for one find that it answers perfectly to the facts. But to speak of an 'exalting effect', or a 'sense of enhanced vitality', is not to settle the question of value. For, as Leavis recognises, the sense of exaltation and of an enhanced vitality can itself be the product of self-delusion. What is necessary, then, is to define these qualities more exactly and more positively—to find a possible account of them which will see them taking their place in the full moral and affective life of the person. So far as Leavis is concerned, the reader as well as the poet should be able to make his exaltation part of his labour of self-recognition, of self-definition. Therefore, he reproves Santayana for other defects in his formulation. The greatest tragedies are not to be seen as expressing, or inducing, a merely stoical disdain for humanity or a defiance of death conceived as an arbitrary force. They do not encourage 'an indulgence in the dramatization of one's nobly-suffering self'.[2] Nor are they the vehicles for an attitude of complacent self-justification pretending to be a stoical indifference to fate: 'the calm of the tensed and self-approving will'.[3] They offer neither emotional self-indulgence nor a moralistic self-approval. Both of these attitudes, far from being the natural results of the tragic experience, are actually 'incompatible with the tragic experience'.[4]

At any rate, it is an essential part of the definition of the tragic that it breaks down, or undermines and supersedes, such attitudes. It establishes below them a kind of profound impersonality in

[1] *Ibid.* pp. 126-7   [2] *Ibid.* p. 128
[3] *Ibid.* p. 131   [4] *Ibid.* p. 129

which experience matters, not because it is mine—because it is to me it belongs or happens, or because it subserves or issues in purpose or will, but because it is what it is, the 'mine' mattering only in so far as the individual sentience is the indispensable focus of experience.

The attainment in literature of this level, and of organization at this level, would seem to involve the poetic use of language, or of processes that amount to that.[1]

With this statement, Leavis' case about the necessity for a poetic-creative use of language in drama is virtually complete. But it is interesting to note that his determination to press it is the result of an interest which goes far beyond what most people would automatically regard as a 'literary' one. Our attention is held by that phrase, 'or because it subserves or issues in purpose or will'. Tragedy does not, apparently, lead to a steeling of any practical purpose or to a buttressing of the *will* to continue living. It touches the person at deeper levels; and it vivifies him in a way which may be fairly called *anti-stoical*. It does not endorse the habitual stance of the ' "established ego" '; on the contrary, it frees the reader from the constriction of his ego, and from the striking of attitudes to which egotism leads; that is why its language must be that of 'exploratory creation', not that of the 'lucid arrangement of ready-minted concepts':

> The attainment of the level of experience at which emancipation from the 'ready-defined self' is compelled involves an essentially different order of expression; one in which heightening is deepening, exaltation has nothing alcoholic about it, and rhetoric (as in *Othello*—for those who take what Shakespeare offers) is 'placed'.[2]

The tragic poet, then, re-creates language in re-creating his insights into experience; and the effect of his work on a responsive reader—the tragic experience—is a 'sense of heightened life' which is also 'a transcending of the ego—an escape from all attitudes of self-assertion'. But the question remains to be asked: A transcendence to what effect? An 'escape' into what realm of value? Leavis answers it in his own characteristic terms—terms which many people may find vague, though inescapably so:

[1] *The Common Pursuit, op. cit.* p. 130   [2] *Ibid.* p. 131

Actually the experience is constructive or creative, and involves a recognizing positive value as in some way defined and vindicated by death. It is as if we were challenged at the profoundest level with the question, 'In what does the significance of life reside?', and found ourselves contemplating, for answer, a view of life, and of the things giving it value, that makes the valued appear unquestionably more important than the valuer, so that significance lies, clearly and inescapably, in the willing adhesion of the individual self to something other than itself.[1]

This is an unmistakably religious conception; and it is worth reflecting that, while it is applied here only to tragedy, it is implicitly associated in Leavis' mind with 'the profoundest things in literature', of which he has spoken some pages before. It is not necessary, it would be an impertinence, to try to specify further the religious faith to which this conception approaches as a norm: as though one could detect an unstated religious adherence hiding shyly behind what is actually said. But it is a religious conception in a remarkably full sense; if 'the significance lies . . . in the willing adhesion of the individual self to something other than itself', then it is clearly this 'something other' that is defined and vindicated by death. It is in the contemplation of this process being brought to artistic completion that the 'impersonality' resides. And it is the deepest kind of impersonality, an impersonality arising from the shared contemplation of a poetic *fact* which is itself religious.

The significance of Leavis' virtual self-commitment to this position does not lie only in the general statements to which his analysis leads him, but also in the passages which he quotes from other writers. He quotes from other critics a great deal more in this essay than I can remember him doing anywhere else; and he sets them against one another: Yeats, Lawrence, Harding, and Traversi are deployed favourably against I. A. Richards and Bertrand Russell; while Santayana comes to seem, in the end, little more than the occasion for this deployment. The amount of quotation might puzzle the reader who did not realise that it was part of a tactic: a tactic conscious or unintended, but a tactic nonetheless. I suspect that it is a tactic for ensuring that he does not commit himself to any

[1] *Ibid.* p. 132

203

formulation which he would not feel safe in defending on philosophical grounds. In other words, he can use these critics for the purpose of suggesting positions which he does not want openly to occupy. They can suggest possibilities of further alternative commitments which Leavis need not endorse; but, since they are quoted at such length, they have the effect of receiving the endorsement which he in fact withholds.

I can understand this move; for Leavis' religious conception is far from a definite one; and it may even be harmed by the adjective 'religious', though I am sure that is what it is. But it is not a settled position, an inner position which can, when faced with works of different kinds, translate itself readily into a habit of procedure and analysis. It is, rather, a reaching out to stabilise, in terms which vary with the works under discussion, an insight which is not a criterion for judging those works but a standpoint from which to get an adequate focus on literature as a whole: On the nature of its deepest expressions, and on the possibilities which it offers or stimulates for the deepest possible commitment to human issues. It is a sign that the sanction for which he is reaching out is a lived one,[1] and that for him to try to formulate it more explicitly would be to disturb its equipoise and undermine its efficacy for literary criticism.

Yet I can't help finding the tactic which he employs in the closing pages of his essay a frustrating one. It is seldom enough that he ever enters upon a literary discussion 'in the abstract' (to use his own sometimes scornful term); and when he does so, as here, it is frustrating to have the normal development of the argument interrupted, the natural exercise of definition deflected. After all, if the *search* for the meaning of the 'tragic experience', the search for a sanction, can be made as explicit as he here makes it, surely it would benefit from not suffering deflection at the point where some more definite *goal* comes to invite definition. And I mean a goal: not a clearly thought-out theoretical framework, still less a rule of thumb.

In any case, we are again reminded that reality and sincerity are the same. But now it is the deepest possible kind of sincerity that is in question; and so it is to the highest level of reality that we are led by a contemplation of that sincerity and of its

---

[1] v. Appendix B

workings in poetry. The apprehension of reality is of the kind to which we give the name 'tragic'; but its effect in poetry, the source of the 'tragic experience', is of a kind which we must call religious. Leavis does not go on to ask, as Arnold did not go on to ask in a similar context, what religious reality answers to this effect. He deliberately limits his account to a view of what we might call the 'moral' aspect of it: to the increase of a specifically moral energy arising out of the religious apprehension, and to a refreshment, from an appeal to an impersonal power and connection, of the personal roots of morality.

This gives us some idea of the position—or it might be better to call it a directing interest—which Leavis seems to have been reaching as a standpoint from which to survey the greatest literature. And it provides an excellent background against which to see his attitude towards Lawrence, with whose creative works, and the values which they represent, he has become increasingly preoccupied. Lawrence stands, above all modern writers, for the spiritual and emotional health which he champions:

> Lawrence stood for life, and shows, in his criticism, tossed off as it was, for the most part, in the most marginal way, an extra-ordinarily quick and sure sense for the difference between what makes for life and that which makes against it. He exhibits a profound, and for those who come to the criticism knowing only the fiction, perhaps surprising centrality.[1]

But this is a judgment earlier than the extended judgment offered by his book on Lawrence. In that, we find an elaboration of its terms. In fact, we can find in it, if we care to search, a more elaborate statement of what his religious position amounts to: a more elaborate one, though perhaps not a more definite one.

D. H. Lawrence, Novelist was published recently enough to put any account of it in danger of becoming a belated book-review. The danger is all the greater since it is so packed with matter relevant to my present interests, it so obviously endorses the chief values which Leavis detects in Lawrence, and it accordingly offers so much invitation to debate. It would deflect me from my main interest to be caught up here in debate and

---

[1] *The Common Pursuit, op. cit.* p. 284

disagreement, even if I were sure enough of my feeling for Lawrence to attempt it. But it is only fair to record that, while the finest sections are authoritative and persuasive, I find much of the other comment distracting; and it is generally comment directed to certain conclusions not only about literature but also about life. I simply do not agree with Leavis in finding 'spiritual and emotional health' in some of the passages which he investigates; and the tactic of the book as a whole (its profusion of adjectives, for example) strikes me as making it tendentious. I make this reservation here to show that I am very far from agreeing with all his critical conclusions, or with every detail of the view of life which he so obviously has come to share with Lawrence.

He states very clearly in his account the conviction that prose fiction has now supplanted 'formal poetry' as the successor of Shakespeare; and he goes on to deliver a perceptive but unfair comment on Eliot's creative work, which he ranges alongside Flaubert's as the antithesis to Lawrence's. It is a passage which is well worth quoting, as a background to the later discussion of Lawrence's standards:

> One may not have thought of comparing Eliot's creative work to Flaubert's, but Eliot's attitude to life is, not less than Flaubert's, one of distaste and disgust. His art, consequently, is involved in the contradiction of which Flaubert is the great example. For it is, surely, a contradiction that Flaubert's case presents classically— all that would-be creative intensity, that intensity of 'doing', devoted to expressing attitudes in which distaste, disgust and boredom have so decisive a part; a cult of art that amounts to a religion, and the directing spirit of it a rejection of life.[1]

He goes on to suggest that Eliot's Christianity, so far from providing a form of life in which these 'rejecting' attitudes are negated, is actually tainted with them; and he comments further

> Eliot's 'standing-off' from life . . . is certainly not a less intense or a less radical sickness of the spirit than Flaubert's.[2]

The only thing one can do with this statement, offered as a judgment of a writer *tout court*, is to deplore it. Much of Eliot's

---

[1] *D. H. Lawrence, Novelist* (Chatto and Windus, London, 1955), p. 25
[2] *Ibid.* p. 26

work certainly does suffer from these disabling deficiencies; and the temptation to them is certainly a constant one in his poetry and plays alike. But it seems impossible, as Leavis himself has elsewhere shown, to apply this as a definitive account to the best of the poetry since 'Ash Wednesday'. If we speak of *Four Quartets*, for example, or even of 'Ash Wednesday' . . . ? Such a tendentious account, offered so early in the book, may lead us in advance to expect that his account of Lawrence's achievement will be an exaggerated one; for it may lead us to suspect that Lawrence's work is being set up as the completely realised norm from which Eliot so disastrously defects. And I for one find this suggestion most unsatisfying.

The Lawrence whom he offers us is not Lawrence the possessed preacher, but Lawrence the artist, whose art triumphantly vindicates certain important values. He is an artist:

> . . . the dramatic poem unfolds—or builds up—with an astonishing fertility of life. This life, so much of which commands the imagination at the first encounter, is all significant life; not a scene, episode, image or touch but forwards the organized development of the themes.[1]

It has, that is, complexity, organisation, richness, direction: the virtues which Leavis finds in so much poetry. But in having them, as a condition of its having them, it testifies to and expresses a sense of life which is extraordinary in its penetration and grasp of values. That sense of life may be conveniently summarised in one phrase, where Leavis speaks of 'art as serving "spontaneous—creative fulness of being" '.[2] As serving it, because it embodies it. And we may note the religious suggestion of the word 'serving'; it alone would be a hint to the directing interest which Leavis has come to share with Lawrence.

But 'spontaneous-creative fulness of being' needs to be defined; and Leavis sees Lawrence's greatest works as defining it in the most satisfying way. He sees Count Dionys, for example, as representing it:

> Representing, in his dark unknownness, the profound energies and potentialities of life that the conscious mind can only either

[1] *Ibid.* p. 151   [2] *Ibid.* p. 172

serve or thwart, he represents, not the absence of 'consciousness', but rather the necessary vital intelligence that, serving the whole life, can detect and expose the usurpations of will and 'idea'.[1]

This spontaneous life of the whole person feeding and guiding the intelligence leads, in Lawrence's case, to 'an almost infallible sense for health and sanity'[2]; it is not an entrée into any Carlylean Cloud-Cuckoo Land, but 'a passionate sense for what is real, and a firm allegiance to it'.[3] Leavis agrees that it is not easy to explain what one means by 'real', but he clearly associates it with the 'fine jet of life', with that consciousness whose focus is ' "body" as Lawrence opposes it to "mental consciousness" '.[4] And a person in touch with the real as Lawrence was will hold out his values as the enemy of any mechanical conception of human life. Those values, lived vitally, may even have a redemptive power. Or so it seems; for Leavis sees Lady Daphne being freed, by her contact with Count Dionys, into a new life in which self-awareness is an instrument of full living.

These are the skeletal terms of Leavis' position, as he interprets it in and through Lawrence; but of course they do not exhaust it. It is necessary to show that Leavis is deriving a rounded view of life (and not merely a collection of fragmentary dicta), from Lawrence's works. That view of life is religious, in a sense not yet adequately suggested; it is moral yet, because of its religious roots, it goes beyond what is normally thought of as moral; it is a view of life-as-a-whole, of universal forces, yet it is intensively centred on an attitude to individual lives. It is moral; but its morality is not one conceived in conventional terms:

> But what the tale brings into discredit is the spirituality of *The Cocktail Party*. It is preoccupied (being in this profoundly representative of Lawrence) with defining the nature of a true moral sense—one that shall minister to life.[5]

We have seen, though indistinctly, what 'life' means: a kind of awareness, of inner vitality, of capacity for growth, existing in a man who is not only unified in his being but has brought

[1] *D. H. Lawrence, Novelist, op. cit.,* p. 62
[2] *Ibid.* p. 70   [3] *Ibid.* p. 78   [4] *Ibid.* p. 78   [5] *Ibid.* p. 82

that unity to focus on 'body'. And that unity is not merely a unity within the individual but a means of uniting him, at some profound level of his person, with certain supra-personal forces. I personally often find Lawrence's way of imaging those forces rather totemistic, as in the short story 'Sun'. But it is not of itself a totemistic conception. And certainly, as Leavis insists, it is no mere question of a surrender to vague but exalting generalities, against which human life is measured and found insignificant. For 'the intuition of the oneness of life' expresses itself

> in an intensity of preoccupation with the individual. No one could have been more profoundly possessed by the perception that life is a matter of individual lives, and that except in individual lives there is no life to be interested in or reverent about, and no life to be served.[1]

Because of this, 'it is only by way of the most delicate and complex responsive relations with others that the individual can achieve fulfilment'; and, as a corollary, 'fulfilled individuals' are the only ones who are capable of 'lasting and satisfactory' relations.[2] With these statements in mind, we can see the fittingness of Leavis' judgment on Lawrence's much misunderstood attitudes to love and sex:

> Love for Lawrence is no more an absolute than sex is his religion. What, in fact, strikes us as religious is the intensity with which his men and women, hearkening to their deepest needs and promptings as they seek 'fulfilment' in marriage, know that they 'do not belong to themselves', but are responsible for something that, in transcending the individual, transcends love and sex too.[3]

So that true lovers are means to a religious awareness in each other:

> Either lover is for the other a 'door'; an opening into the unknown, by which the horizon, the space of life, is immensely expanded, and unaccepted limits that had seemed final are 'transgressed'.[4]

We can readily see why Leavis should judge Lawrence's attitude to his characters to be fundamentally religious, while George Eliot's is (merely) 'ethical'.

[1] *Ibid.* p. 102   [2] *Ibid.* p. 103   [3] *Ibid.* p. 111   [4] *Ibid.* p. 115

In fact, Leavis' analysis leads naturally to the point at which he can associate artistic impersonality with religious belief. When he comes to forge this link in our minds (for he does not openly state or suggest it), we see that the association is a means of defining both impersonality and belief. Impersonality is now seen not merely as a quality of the literary effect, but as a condition of the literary process; Lawrence is seen as living through his art as part of a process continuous with his living through of his life; the reaction against Eliot could not go any further, within the valid limits of the term 'impersonality'. Leavis sees the 'peculiar Laurentian genius' in

> the extraordinary power of the impersonalizing intelligence to maintain, while the artist, in an intensely personal exploratory way, is actually living the experience that goes into the art, the conditions that make creative impersonality possible.[1]

We have seen that that personal exploration is made in a realm of values which is itself extra- or supra-personal. Now Leavis shows us that it leads to a capacity for belief. He sees Lawrence's art as defining 'a norm with which he is preoccupied',[2] and his concern as to vindicate, among other things, 'the capacity for real belief'.[3]

Belief in what? Belief, surely, in the values which we have already tentatively defined. And Leavis sees that, as soon as this question is raised, we have raised also the question of the truth of those values. Yet he seems to suggest that Lawrence's art *answers* that question in the very act of raising it:

> What his art *does* is beyond argument or doubt. It is not a question of metaphysics or theology—though no doubt there are questions presented for the metaphysician and the theologian. Great art, something created and *there*, is what Lawrence gives us. And there we undeniably *have* a world of wonder and reverence, where life wells up from mysterious springs. It is no merely imagined world; what the creative imagination of the artist makes us contemplate bears an unanswerable testimony.[4]

I feel considerable diffidence in dealing with this passage; for it half-states, but merely half-states, a position with which,

---

[1] *D. H. Lawrence, Novelist, op. cit.*, p. 143
[2] *Ibid.* p. 220   [3] *Ibid.* p. 231   [4] *Ibid.* p. 235

like most men, I am in profound disagreement. If we say that the world of Lawrence's art 'bears an unanswerable testimony', then we must conclude that what it bears testimony to is simply its own truth. Leavis seems to be suggesting, in blunt terms, that the greatness of art is a guarantee of the truth of its own world; and we are never justified in suggesting that. If we do, in this case, then the questions which that art 'presents' to metaphysicians and theologians are presented simply for their endorsement. Here is no mere facet of the question of poetry and belief; it is a matter much more important and much more difficult than that. If we take Leavis literally, we will understand him as saying that art perceives reality and embodies it so completely that it *becomes* reality; otherwise there would be no point in saying that it 'bears an unanswerable testimony'. It is surely a view of great art as needing no sanction; though in point of fact Leavis can say this here with such conviction only because he so obviously assents to Lawrence's attitudes. For there *are* attitudes, within and behind the art; and they are, if not debatable, at least capable of being dissented from. Leavis might reply that works of art as great as this don't offer themselves for debate or dissent; and they don't. But it is he himself who has formulated (in 'abstract' terms) the fundamental attitudes which the works *enact*; and, as formulated, they can be modified, or qualified, or completed, or even rejected. To make any of these responses is not to reject the art; but it *is* to recognise the fact that art is not its own sanction; its sanction is reality; and we respond to works of art according to our prior response to reality, though they can modify or enrich our response to reality by the manner in which they elicit our response to themselves. Leavis may well agree with this; but it is not what he says here. If the attitudes which he formulates express (in an inevitably simplified form, for criticism is not a re-creation) the intention and effect of Lawrence's art, then our judgment of the health-giving powers of that art will be at least conditioned by our view of *their* truth and healthiness. That is my own position. While finding Lawrence a great artist, I find much of his work hateful in some of its tendencies. Great art does modify consciousness, does bring a pressure and a presence to vivify, in modifying them, our fundamental attitudes. Lawrence's art does. But we have a duty to supervise the process so far as is consistent with not putting up a disabling obstruction to the work's genius. Not every reader of maturity will adopt all of Lawrence's attitudes to life, or allow his art, as it were, to adopt those attitudes for him, in his too responsive consciousness.

The fact is, Leavis sees Lawrence's work as touching the springs of reality, the reality which is most important to human life. He sees it therefore as moral, but more than moral:

> It is a familiar situation, a familiar kind of life-frustrating deadlock. The presenting of it transcends ordinary moral judgments [i.e. judgments of right or wrong in behaviour]. . . . The presenting sensibility and the inquiring intelligence engaged are, of course, profoundly and essentially moral; the moral concern goes far deeper than the level of those judgments. What is wrong here? What laws of life have been ignored that there should be *this* situation, this dreadful deadlock, between a man and a woman? These questions give the informing preoccupation.[1]

It is a moral preoccupation which strikes beneath the level of moral discourse to a reality which determines moral values. And here we have Leavis' position in miniature:

> Lawrence is the greatest kind of creative writer; it can be said of him, as of Flaubert or T. S. Eliot it cannot, that his radical attitude towards life is positive; looking for a term with which to indicate its nature, we have to use 'reverence'. But 'reverence' must not be allowed to suggest any idealizing bent; and if we say that the reverence expresses itself in a certain essential tenderness, we don't mean that Lawrence is 'tender-minded' or in the least sentimentally given. The attitude is one of strength, and it is clairvoyant and incorruptible in its preoccupation with realities. It expresses, of course, the rare personal adequacy of an individual of genius, but it is also the product of a fine and mature civilization, the sanctions, the valuations and the pieties of which speak through the individual. . . .[2]

It is, as I have said, a religious conception, and not merely an ethical one. It is Leavis' considered view of Lawrence's importance, his over-riding importance in modern literature, his

[1] *D. H. Lawrence, Novelist, op. cit.*, p. 35
[2] *Ibid.* p. 75

establishment of (in the strict sense) a 'normal' consideration of contemporary problems. And it also suggests Leavis' own values; exalted as his statement is, it constitutes a sort of summation to date of all the qualities which he has for three decades admired in literature, and in which he finds literary greatness.

Criticism and Theological Standards

THE dictum with which Eliot begins his paper, 'Religion and Literature', has been taken by several subsequent critics as a declaration of principle; and it is worth while repeating that dictum:

> Literary criticism should be completed by criticism from a definite ethical and theological standpoint. . . . In ages like our own, in which there is no such common agreement, it is the more necessary for Christian readers to scrutinize their reading, especially of works of the imagination, with explicit ethical and theological standards.

As I have already suggested, Eliot's own concern here is a pastoral one. He wants Christian readers to 'scrutinize their reading' in terms which will help them to protect themselves from corrupting influences: it seems that a Christian, by taking theological thought, can add a cubit to the stature of his sensibility, and turn it thereby into a fortified tower. But if Eliot's concern is largely pastoral and protective, that of his followers[1] has tended to be affirmative to the point of aggression. The principle in whose defence they attack is common to them and to Eliot; and not one of them seems to have been any more successful than he in putting it to illuminating use in works of actual criticism.

The declaration of the principle raises an important issue, the issue of poetry and belief. Most Christians who have considered this problem cannot be satisfied either by I. A. Richards' talk of pseudo-statements or by the contention of such men as Erich Heller that, since the poet usually means what he says, poetry puts on us the duty of agreeing or disagreeing with him. The talk of pseudo-statements is unsatisfactory because good poets do indeed mean what they say, and consider the saying it important enough to demand a lifetime's dedication. But Heller's position is unsatisfactory for a twofold reason: Whatever the poet means or intends to say, the critical reader must ultimately be concerned with what the poem

---

[1] I refer to those Anglican critics who are often called the School of Christian Discrimination, from the title of Bro. George Every's book.

as a whole says; and in fact every critical reader knows that the kind of response elicited in him by poetry is not at all of the kind which asks to be expressed in terms of agreement and disagreement. These reservations made, we find the central question still unresolved. In fact, I have seen no persuasive solution to the problem of poetry and belief; and I do not intend to attempt a solution of my own. What is interesting, however, about the statements of Eliot's Christian followers is the fact that they raise the question not for a theoretical but for a practical reason. They raise it not as an abstract problem but as a question of the practical duties and rights of the critic. Consequently, their work amounts to an attempt to answer not the question: *What* is poetry in relation to truth? but the less exasperating question: *What* is a criticism based on truth in relation to a literature seldom based on truth?

Eliot has defined the purpose of criticism as 'the elucidation of works of art and the correction of taste'. And we may assume that his Anglican disciples agree. But 'purpose' here means 'social purpose', and refers to a social activity and use. The actual *process* of criticism may be defined as a more-or-less formal guidance of the reader, even of a hypothetical reader, to the kind and quality of *life* embodied in a poem or novel. It is therefore a communal matter and, as Leavis never wearies of stressing, it is almost inevitably phrased so as to elicit agreement, modification or enlightened dissent.

It is here, of course, that the difficulty arises with a criticism which claims to be Christian. Christianity is a dogmatic religion, and one which illuminates the whole of man's experience. To the non-believer, therefore, a Christian criticism will seem to be a kind of aesthetic dogmatism making for its own powers of interpretation claims which derive from, and represent, the claims of Christianity itself. To the Christian, on the other hand, it will often seem to be the truest kind of criticism because it derives from a true vision of man. On the one hand it is seen as a particularly demanding and even aggressive ideology thrusting out from the ruck of contemporary loyalties; on the other it is seen as the belief which prescribes the norm for human conduct, and so for art itself.

It is difficult, then, to separate one's attitude to a 'Christian criticism' from one's attitude to Christianity itself. Yet it seems foolish to resent the claims of Christianity in the literary field. It is not simply one ideology among others: It has a special relevance to literature because, beyond all other ideologies, it is incarnational; and it has a special force in proving that relevance, because it is realistic about human limitations. But it is precisely at the point where we admit these claims that confusion is so likely to arise. It arises through the assumption that it is Christianity as such which makes claims for its own relevance in literary criticism, and seeks to prove that relevance. But it is Christians, not Christianity, who concern themselves with literature, who make claims and attempt to prove them. And it is sheer impertinence for any or all of such critics to claim that their criticism represents Christianity.

The question, then, is whether a specifically Christian criticism is possible; and underlying that is the further question whether theological formulations have any relevance at all to works of the imagination. Certainly, whenever those formulations are invoked, they are invoked as a standard, an unyielding norm, something objective by recourse to which the critic may test the validity of his own and his subjects' point of view. So S. L. Bethell writes:

> Dr Leavis has more than once stated that literary criticism involves ethical considerations, and it is obvious that we cannot discuss a writer's 'insight' without having some standard by which to assess it. But Dr Leavis has nowhere said that theological considerations are also necessary; indeed he would seem to believe the contrary. Yet, even apart from the fact that there are insights which are spiritual without being ethical, does not the acceptance of an ethical position in itself involve at least some relation to the systems of theology? If the critic elects to take his stand on 'ethics' without any philosophical examination of the matter, there will always be a chance that his ethics may consist of personal predilections or the assumptions of his own social group.[1]

I think the contention is a helpful one; the warning given in the last sentence is particularly apt. But, taking this passage as a whole, is it not a curiously abstract statement for a practising critic to rest on? Is it not, in fact, a most evasive statement? The term 'theology' appears quite elusive under Bethell's pen; at one moment it is linked with 'considerations', at another with 'systems'; and we are never told in what sense of the word theology is especially relevant to literature. Ethics, too, bear 'some relation to the systems of theology', but we are never told what relation. Mr Bethell's very prose, in fact, reflects the difficulty of his position. And that difficulty arises only because he is concerned to press for a criticism which is specially, specifically, overtly Christian: Christian not only in its inspiration but also in its intention and its terms.

Such a case always seems to be argued in terms of the application

[1] *Essays on Literary Criticism and the English Tradition* (Dennis Dobson, London, 1948), p. 13

of special Christian categories. And I should consider such terms as dangerously inappropriate as the attitude which lies behind them. Whatever criticism is, it is not an 'application' of anything; it is certainly not the application of 'categories'. Nor is it the relating of works to an overt standard which remains independent of both work and critic. This attitude is too mechanical, this language too systematised, for such a delicate operation as that of criticism, which is an act of reverence—controlled and selective reverence—towards the thing criticised. It is therefore not a matter of application, but of a full response—a kind of response which involves not only intelligence but the whole affective personality, and involves it even when the final judgment is a rejection of the values embodied in the work being assessed. It seems to me a fallacy to believe that this response can be made fully conscious, fully articulated, fully fitted into the appropriate critical formulae. To attempt to make it so articulated is, in the end, to drive a wedge between these 'two qualities'—intelligent and affective—of the judging person, and to remove him further from the work of art itself. He will tend to become *detached* in the least happy sense of that word.

There is more to it than that. I cannot see (and I speak as a Christian) why anyone should *want* to apply principles explicitly at all. Of course, it is the whole person who responds to a poem or novel; and if that person *is* a believing Christian, then it is a believing Christian who judges; one can't, without great harm to oneself and to poetry, pretend to be something one is not. But it is not only as a believing Christian that one judges. If it were, then Christianity would be something exclusive; and all intellectual intercourse between Christians and non-Christians would become virtually impossible. But it is not. One's sensibility may be permeated with Christian values, one's vision of the world may be pervasively religious; but I see no reason why this should cut one off from full imaginative participation in the work of any artist, so long as that art has human significance and is complete within its chosen terms. Yet this, paradoxically, is what Bethell's position leads to. To invoke a 'standard' is to elect to stand apart from the work of art which one is measuring against it.

If we regard Christianity, and the literary criticism deriving from it, not as exclusive but inclusive, we shall have to decide at what point it becomes relevant to literary judgment. Eliot himself speaks, we may notice, of 'completing' literary criticism with ethical and theological criticism; he envisages two operations of the critical intelligence, and not one. What he does is to point forward from literary criticism, which may be assumed to have its own procedure and value, to a kind of study which we may call religious-cultural criticism. Yet Eliot does not in fact undertake such a study; and Leavis accuses him, with a good deal of justice, of substituting theological considerations for literary rather than completing one with the other. The same is true of his followers, and they have been criticised for it. R. G. Cox, for example, in reviewing Bethell's book,[1] interprets his subject's positive position as follows:

> His most plausible point seems to be that since all criticism will show the influence of the critic's personal beliefs it is better for these to be explicit rather than unconscious.

Yes, for clarity of mind, for balance of approach; but not everything in the critic's responsiveness can be made conscious, let alone explicit; and certainly it cannot be made so explicit as to merit the name of 'beliefs'. In any case, why should the consciousness of one's beliefs lead to any talk of interpretation, of standards, of categories, and the rest? It is a strange picture, that of a reader determinedly holding his beliefs formulated and ready in his mind while he strives to surrender his sensibility in active responsiveness to a poem or novel. We can inject the colouring of sense into such a picture only if we suppose that the explicit beliefs become operative, grow to the stature of criteria, after the work of responding is over and the work of its formulation begun.

Those really are the *practical* questions, especially for those who regard Christian belief as relevant to literature: In what way is it relevant? And at what point in our response to a work does it become relevant?

In what way? Is it relevant as a standard of moral orthodoxy to which the moral meaning of a work can be referred? Surely not; the activity involved in such a work of reference cannot help being one of undue abstraction; and the more plausibly a moral meaning can be abstracted and held up against a standard, the more we will tend to abandon the moral stature of the work as a whole. Too much is left out. Criticism at this depth is valuable only if it insistently points back to the work, to the fleshed context from which it is abstracting. And while the 'standard' remains the important consideration, while our eye is on conformity to a standard, our critical dealings with the actual work will be in danger of becoming a kind of legerdemain.

---

[1] *Scrutiny*, Vol. XV, No. 3, p. 229

Surely Christianity is relevant as a form (I should prefer not to say 'way') of life guiding and enlivening our own native responses: guiding *because* it enlivens them. If that is so, then it need not involve the erection of a 'standard', which is permanently and unalterably 'there'; and anyone observing the process of our critical judgment from the outside would be hard put to it to see it as a specifically Christian criticism.

There is another consideration. Of course, as a man grows in his view of life he will tend to neglect certain kinds of literary work, and the less he will tend to find literature in itself, as a way or guide of life, completely satisfying. This is not to say that he will develop *special* interests, or become the sophisticated rider of ever more exclusive hobby-horses. But he *will* be selective, and it is the living of his way of life, his being vitally informed by his vision, which will be the agent of selection. Literature may be a meeting-place of many human activities, the nodal-point at which theological and social and musical and psychological realities have their most synoptic and concentrated union. But no man can live by literature alone; and it is what he does live by that will so largely determine his instinct for the works which will be of the greatest value for him. On the other hand, this seems to me as much an instinct or sense as a conscious choice. The point I should want to make, and which Bethell and his friends neglect to make, is that the intellectual basis of his way of life will not wholly determine his reading, nor ought it to determine in advance his response to what he does read.

Christianity is relevant. But at what point does it become relevant? The fallacy of such men as Bethell, Bro. George Every, and even Fr. Martin Jarrett-Kerr, is to make it relevant as a sort of extra preoccupation while actually reading. Christianity thereby becomes an interest directing the person of the critic towards formulating while he should be responding.

But we may for the moment assume a different position. It may be that Christianity, considered as a special inspiration or aid, assumes value only after the work of responding is over. Then it would lead to a special formulation (presumably of a kind other than the literary-critical), which we should call by a separate name. Certainly this seems a proper continuation of the critical faculty, and an immensely useful one, *if it can be done*. The only doubt which arises is a doubt as to its possibility; I cannot myself recall any really illuminating demonstration of it.

One feels in any case that, if it were possible, if it came to be done, it would concern not any separate work or body of work, but a whole stream or tendency, and that its value would consequently be of a nearly sociological kind, of a sociology with a theological ground. Where an individual work or writer is in question, such a sociological use would be useful only to the extent that it was the product of a total and responsive reading. The only true sociologists of literature would be the best critics. And if that is true, then the 'sociological' conclusion would be implicit in any case in the actual response, the process of literary criticism itself; it would be an abstraction and formalisation not from a work of art apprehended in sociological terms, but from a criticism already done, whether mentally or in writing. It would have only a limited point for readers as experienced as oneself, but most point for a class of readers insufficiently responsive to the implications of works of art. If one's experience of a writer is as full as possible, there is no reason for attempting to 'complete' it by formulating it into terms foreign to the experience itself. If it is delicate, experienced, and above all *concerned* with literature, the Christian sensibility will inevitably make moral and theological use of its experience of art; but it will do so interiorly and unobtrusively, changing it into an element of personal growth founded on Christianity. And if it is not, no amount of formulation or abstraction can bring it any closer to art; one's application of explicit standards could have merely a pastoral intention and effect.

This is what, I suggest, Eliot does in his later writings. It is also what Bethell, Every, and Nicholson do. Their function is to provide clues to literature for the benefit of their co-religionists. In exercising their function, they make varying claims for what they are doing, and offer to account for it in varying terms. Bethell and Every, for example, obviously regard themselves as practising critics, using Christian beliefs as a standard of immediate critical judgment. Nicholson, on the other hand, claims to be not a critic but a moralist: the claim which Eliot makes for himself in the opening pages of *After Strange Gods*. As Nicholson says:

> This book is not an attempt to measure modern literature by a Christian yardstick. It is not, fundamentally, *literary* criticism at all. It is rather an enquiry into the assumptions as to the nature and purpose of Man which underlie much of modern writing. . . .[1]

But it is impossible to find the underlying assumptions of a literature unless you assume that they do not merely 'underlie' it, but are actually in some way embodied in it. Nicholson does make

[1] *Man and Literature* (S.C.M. Press, London, 1943), p. 5

this assumption, and he acts on it; consequently his work must be judged as literary criticism, because it searches not behind but within the works with which it concerns itself.

Two things become quite evident in Nicholson's book. The one is, that he *does* use critical procedures; and the other is, that Christianity is for him not an enlivening form of life, not even a standard, but a kind of speciality, an additional intellectual hobby.

We notice, for example, that in his remarks on various writers Christian references and approximations in literature become of special interest, not as demonstrating anything about the quality of the literature or even of its author's unconscious beliefs, but in and for themselves. Here is the hobbyist's mentality, at its crudest and least responsive to literary values.

What happens in the case of the relatively sensitive critic such as Fr. Martin Jarrett-Kerr is a lapse at crucial moments into sophisticated special pleading. It happens, for example, in the book on Lawrence which he published under the name of Fr. Tiverton—at that point where, in considering Lawrence's view of sex, he digresses to give an account of the orthodox Christian attitude to sex, to defend that attitude, and to show how Lawrence at once misunderstood it and unconsciously approximated to it. Here we find, not a 'speciality', a boyish preoccupation with counting references, but a lapse of attention. Fr. Tiverton's general account, in another context, might be just and useful but, in the context of a specifically literary study, it interrupts the free action of the sensibility and tilts towards a kind of special pleading.

What I am attempting to provide, by the use of these examples, is not a series of anecdotes discreditable to one school of critics, but empirical evidence that an ethical and theological criticism of literature which *completes* literary criticism is very difficult to conceive, and that the people who have attempted it in the last two decades have fallen into the pit of divided intention. In each case the intentions have become divided either because the possibilities have not been clearly seen or because the interest has not been kept pure. Nicholson wants to be a moralist on a simple pastoral level, and becomes a bad and tendentious critic with a hobbyist's attitude to his central standard. Fr. Jarrett-Kerr wants to be a literary critic, and becomes at crucial moments an open advocate for his own beliefs. Bethell wants to be a critic, but becomes a polemical theorist at a fairly unsatisfactory level. All three of them suffer from using theology as an intellectual interest and not as the guarantee of inward sensitive life.

What is wrong, for example, with the digression by Fr. Tiverton to which I have referred? It is a fairly long digression and, on the whole, a fairly just one. But it is not just in this context; it belongs elsewhere, and its status as a digression is no status at all. However informative it may be, it can only have the effect in this place of distracting attention from the reality of the creative works which are its very *raison d'être*. It distracts the attention of the reader, and it distracts the attention (or gives evidence of a prior distraction) of the author as well; for it impairs the exercise of sensibility by removing it from any object other than the due process of an argument.

Fr. Tiverton might well reply: 'Yes, but what has sensibility to do with it? I use and test my sensibility when I am in actual contact with the novels. Writing about them is another thing. There I have the right to formulate any intellectual position which will be of use to me.' Certainly, one can understand that his temptation was very strong. But a better critic would not have yielded to it. What the digression shows is a divided intention: an intention to see that Lawrence is understood in the most satisfactory terms possible, and an intention that Christianity should not be misunderstood. The use of the second intention detracts from the effectiveness of the first, which it is the critic's business to ensure. If the reality of the texts one is writing about may be forgotten while a digression on a quite different level is embarked on, the responsiveness of the sensibility is diminished; and the sensibility should be as active in its own way during the business of writing as during that of reading. It *should* be active, because its activity is the only guarantee of critical aptness.

It seems apparent, then, that the Christian critics who have followed Eliot's lead have failed dismally to justify the existence of 'Christian discrimination'. The failure may be partly due to the fact that not one of them is a good enough critic. But there are other reasons. Although their overt aims differ, from Bethell to Fr. Jarrett-Kerr, and from these two men to Nicholson, they have each suffered from a division of aims, a failure to assess them properly before writing. And that failure, in turn, comes from a reluctance to see in what sense theology is relevant to literature, and so in what sense a Christian criticism is possible at all. They have all yielded, in fact, to the temptation to take a short-cut, vaulting on their way the stile of 'theological considerations'.

My own feeling is that the more it declares its own Christian nature the less good a Christian criticism will do. Bethell is rightly concerned to stress that ethical insight is not to be divorced from the Christian view of man and his destiny; but he reveals the hollow-ness of his own critical attitude when he refers to that view as 'theological considerations'. Nor does he once give any justification for believing that a specific writer's literary value is connected with his theological wisdom. I agree with him (I suppose he would agree with me) that there *is* a connection. But it is a connection of such a delicate kind that we merely bedraggle it when we try to dress it in a formula.

Christianity is in general relevant to English literature not only because of the historical development of that literature but also because of the historical nature of Christianity. The contention is too large to defend or even to explain here; and it can be indicated best by the brief statement that literature is incarnational, and so is Christianity. But it is not relevant simply as a body of doctrine. Indeed, the body of doctrine is simply *not there* for the critic to use unless it exists in himself, and it exists in him not merely as doctrine but as discrimination. It can only exist in him as a force in his affective personality as well as a force in his intelligence. It is foolish to try to separate sensibility from conscience; but in the best critics conscience is energised to such an extent that it becomes transformed into terms of sensibility. This is certainly true of critics of the stature of Arnold, Eliot, and Leavis; and Dr Johnson's weakness as a critic may possibly be attributed to the fact that conscience in him was often not energised in this way.

There is another fact. Christianity should not be used merely as an objective 'standard', not because it is too small, but because it is too huge. The attempt to 'complete' literary criticism 'by criticism from a definite ethical and theological standpoint' arises from the desire to have an artist who will offer us an account of life which is totally Christian, a world which is at once orthodox and complete: and that is impossible. No creative artist exhausts art or Christianity; there is not one, as Eliot recognises, who does not actually deviate from Christianity. The life of Christianity is the life of the Church, and this is infinitely greater and more embracing than the whole tradition of literature. All an artist can offer is his personal response to the growth of his personal wisdom, even where the final offering invites us to speak of it in terms of 'impersonality', of self-transcendence. It may be that this response will be more satisfying the more firmly it is rooted in a communal traditional wisdom of a religious kind; but in so far as it is art, it is personal, it is one man's voice. The task of the critic is to the same extent communal and personal. He cannot ask that the artist conform to his own puny grasp of the truth. Nor can he expect the artist to give us a truth sufficient to live by, any more than he can expect ratification of what is special, exclusive, in the faith he already lives by.

So much can be said, by way of indicating that Christianity is more relevant to literary criticism the more inward and unobtrusive it is: by way of indicating, too, how ill-advised have been the attempts of Eliot's followers to promote a school of Christian discrimination. Yet it must be added that, although their short-comings have been amply recognised, in *Scrutiny*, for example, their good intentions have not. They are accused time and time again of the crudest propagandist motives and the most dishonest manœuvres to produce a shoddy result.

The *Scrutiny* writers are no more to blame than anyone else, and they have been faced with considerable provocation. But I raise the matter in the belief that a critic who proceeds, however un-obtrusively and responsibly, in the light of a Christian vision, is apt to be suspect among his fellow critics. It may be that they feel his claim, however implicit, to be informed by an orthodoxy is also a claim to a disproportionate advantage over them in the possession of critical balance. And the point is that, although Christianity is relevant, its relevance may not always be admitted.

There are two cases which strike one as significant. We have, for example, D. J. Enright reproaching Walter Stein with claiming too much for Christianity:

> The only point in saying this is that it reminds us that most of this controversy is at the heart of it a controversy about religion. . . .[1]

Enright may not have intended it, but the clearest implication of his remark is that any proffering of Christian insight as an aid in criticism can only lead to controversy, because it must lead to a debate about the truth of Christianity as a system. So what should be personal insight is reduced towards intellectual system, and what is offered as an aid is treated as an occasion for argument. Is the Christian claim (however it is advanced) so inordinate as this, that it inevitably stimulates not agreement but its opposite? Does the first mention of Christian insight inevitably tend to undermine the 'common pursuit of true judgment'?

It would seem so. Leavis, whose attacks on the school of Christian

---

[1] D. J. Enright: 'Literature and Belief': *Essays in Criticism*, Vol. VI, No. 1, p. 64 (It is interesting that Enright, quite unfairly, applies the term 'tub-thumping on a high level' to Stein's article.)

discrimination are otherwise just, fleers at Eliot for having a definite dogmatic belief behind his criticism:

> Mr Eliot has no need to talk hesitantly about the 'need for a religious sense'; he adheres to a religion, and can point to his Church and recite its dogmas.
>
> Nevertheless, those of us who find no such approach to tradition and orthodoxy possible can only cultivate the sense of health they have.[1]

Leavis is probably right in believing that Eliot's use of his dogmatic belief has harmed his criticism. But that is not the present point. The first sentence of his statement, particularly in its tone, in the imputation of sectarianism to Eliot, is markedly unfair. It is not on the ground of his capacity to recite dogmas that Eliot has ever claimed attention for his remarks. He refrains from doing so even in that most unsatisfactory book, *After Strange Gods*. He hardly ever invokes dogma at all; and when he does so, as in his essay on Baudelaire, he does not invoke anything which one would be content merely to recite. He nowhere rests his case on conformity of that kind; and the picture of him which these words evoke is a ludicrously inexact one. What is wrong with the essay on Baudelaire is not that it has dogma behind it, but that the dogma is too subjectively held, and that it leads to a repellent and rather unbalanced conclusion.

I am sure Leavis would agree. And with *his* final sentence, one can only agree in turn. Literary criticism is as much a personal matter, as much the product of a personal sense of life and value as literature itself. It may be added that Christians differ as widely from one another in their 'sense of health' as non-Christians do. But the question remains: How is Christianity relevant? and Who will recognise the relevance of a literary insight informed by a doctrinal belief?

Certainly any critic who rests his criticism consciously on his own 'sense of health' should be careful to ensure that that sense is as active and expansive as it can be and that it reflects as fully as possible the light of objective truth. Doctrine may be admissible in criticism only as sensitive judgment, but it *is* admissible. It is no answer to say that we can only judge by results; for if Christianity is as urgently controversial as Enright seems to feel it is, surely there will be disagreement about results as well. I am not supporting the 'Christian discriminators', who have obviously shown up very badly. But I suggest that we may have Christian critics of the most honest

[1] *Scrutiny*, Vol. III, No. 2, p. 185

and responsible kind, whose criticism will be as apt to enforce—not, it must be remarked, inculcate—a total insight as Leavis' own criticism is. How far they would be likely to differ from Leavis, or from Eliot, is a separate matter. And certainly they will not work through the 'application' of 'categories', or the mere invoking of a 'standard'; but we cannot confine them, either, to a sort of sociology, to picking up and arranging the crumbs from the table of the real critic.

Note—Leavis also goes on to indicate what is the root of our dissatisfaction with Eliot's concern for doctrine: 'One may at any rate venture that health—even religious health—demands a more active concern for other things than formal religion than Mr Eliot now shows or encourages.' Of course he is right. My point about his previous remark is simply that the use of the word 'recite', the emphasis revealed in the use of '*his* Church' and '*its* dogmas' is sign of a dislike of doctrine as such.

Poetry and Sanctions

It may seem that I have raised this question already, and, indeed, that I have spent two chapters in answering it by an elucidation of Leavis' view of literary values. And certainly no one can consider his view of literature without taking account, at every point, of his view of the values that inform literature. But in the concluding pages of my last chapter I felt bound to raise a new question—the question of a sanction for those values; and it seems only fair, as it is necessary, to follow out that question a little further.

There, I found Leavis carrying his statement of Lawrence's values to a level at which they demanded to be considered outside the framework of the work of art. I know that this way of putting it begs certain questions; but I hope that the mode of my previous analysis may exculpate me from the charge of regarding literary 'form' and literary 'content' as two separate things. What I mean is that Leavis' open formulation of those values puts them into a field of discourse where their expression in a literary pattern cannot be allowed wholly to guide the discussion; and that it is a shock to find Leavis suggesting that it is the work of art itself which is their final sanction.

It strikes me, then, that in considering Leavis' criticism I have left out, through diffidence, something besides the topics which I had voluntarily left out at the beginning. He has come to a view of great literature which must be called religious; but has he also come to bestow on literature a definitive status which belongs, of right, to philosophy or religion?

There is in his work a continuing and organic development which I feel to represent a search for sanctions; that is one way of putting it, and I know no others. I hinted at something of this sort in my text; but a discussion of it could have little place in two chapters which were, after all, chiefly expository.

It is interesting that his work should suggest such a question, a question which it does not openly state. And it is all the more interesting that the attention he has received should have been mostly from a Christian viewpoint. Critics criticising critics generally present a dismal sight; and Leavis has been fortunate in not receiving much of that kind of attention. But several men—few of them much given to unrewarding enterprises—have found it necessary to try to analyse the tendency of his work. Of those studies that I have seen —by Martin Turnell, S. L. Bethell, Fr. Martin Jarrett-Kerr, Ian Gregor, Walter Stein, and William Walsh—five are by professed Christians; and of those five, four are markedly favourable, though not all of them are particularly penetrating.

Why should this be? What is there in Leavis' work, as there is not in, say, Arnold's or Richards', that invites such attention? Part of the answer certainly lies in the earnestness with which he concentrates on a literary quality which is also a 'moral' quality. But part of it also lies, probably, in that lively development in his criticism which most people can sense, if not define, and which I have tentatively called a search for sanctions.

Every critic of Leavis' kind must expect to have these questions asked about him. To adopt a 'moral' viewpoint on literature is to invite questions about one's moral attitudes themselves. And such questions resolve themselves into a question about sanctions: What objective reality sanctions these attitudes? How are they validated? Certainly I hope I have shown that Leavis is not an ethical critic in any of the usual senses; and that his view of a literary work is of something which is an achieved literary-moral-social-religious entity. To call this view 'moral' is probably to undervalue it; but it is also to fix it temporarily for the purposes of discussion.

We can look at any great work of art as a forming of values; or we can look at it as something informed by values. The difference is merely one of terminology; but I use the alternative formulations to suggest that great art is not merely the expression of certain previously defined values. On the contrary, it defines them by expressing them; and it creates a new entity which seems to us to be, in some sense, a new value, because it is a new definition and *embodiment* of values. The question we must ask about Leavis is whether, in the case of his favourite authors, he sees this new 'value' as being its own sanction; or whether, on the other hand, he points to certain values in living which the work of art does not create, which it positively draws on, and which we can draw on in judging it. Sometimes he suggests the first; more often he suggests the second. But they are apt, at crucial moments of analysis, to become confused in his work.

'Sanction', then, can be tentatively taken to imply the following items of discourse:

What does the writer *represent* more than his own individual, and possibly anarchic, reaction to his own experience? And in what way does the fact of representativeness endorse or stabilise the norm which his art offers us?

By what norms are the reader's reactions to art sanctioned?

Into what depth of experience, of a more than merely personal experience, does the artist require us to follow him? And in what extra-literary terms is it proper for us to define that depth, *once we have followed him into it?*

Large enough questions; and I do not propose to answer them; I formulate them to show that, in speaking of sanctions, I am not speaking of an 'orthodoxy' which can be applied externally to works of art. Nor do I ask Leavis to answer them; after all, we have his criticism, and must be grateful for that. But his criticism presents these questions to us, if not to answer, at least to ponder on. And we may reflect, when we look at the poets whom he actually analyses, that he hardly ever mentions Coleridge, never mentions Christopher Smart, shows a certain inhibition in dealing with Blake and Yeats, and almost openly confesses to the embarrassment he feels when faced with the task of probing the depths in Hopkins and the later poetry of Eliot.[1] It is likely that all these poets, despite their differences, present him with a common quality, a specific kind of spiritual or symbolic awareness, which he can't feel at home with. If so, then we will find his suggestion that Lawrence's art vindicates its own values a more than usually strange one.

Perhaps we may find our way into his work by reminding ourselves what were the influences on his early criticism. They were Eliot, Arnold, I. A. Richards, and the writers who supported the 'Calendar of Modern Letters'. These influences were strong on his first books; and they may have deflected, even while stimulating it, his natural development as a critic. In any case, they certainly had a great effect on his conviction that 'poetry is what it is, and not another thing'. They had an effect, too, in stimulating the pressing sociological interests which are revealed, in a relatively 'pure' form, in his early books. That sociological interest did not arise simply because Leavis started to publish at the beginning of the 'Red decade'; it arose, too, from his insistence on poetry as preserving a

---

[1] v., for example, his remarks in *Education and the University, op. cit.* p. 87. It is worth noticing, too, that a disagreement between him and Marius Bewley on James' *Turn of the Screw* is put down by Bewley to the fact that they disagree about the nature of Evil: 'I think the way one senses their presence in the novels may be due to one's conception of them *outside* the novels': *The Complex Fate*: Marius Bewley (Chatto and Windus, London, 1952), pp. 142-3.

certain line of continuity in English life which other agencies could no longer play their traditional rôle in preserving. It was a continuity which comprised not merely a literary convention but also a feeling for values. Because religion is no longer accepted, because philosophy is no longer resorted to as a means of attaining wisdom, literature remains the only possible means of asserting continuity in the face of the increasing atomisation of society and the dispersion of its lived, traditional values. Creative literature preserves and re-creates continuity, and criticism, drawing on creation, openly defines it. The processes of literature, of creation and criticism alike, are thus of nodal importance. Society no longer positively helps literature, but has to be helped by it. For

> It is as if society, in so complicating and extending the machinery of organization, had incurred a progressive debility of consciousness and of the powers of co-ordination and control—had lost intelligence, memory and moral purpose.[1]

The tendency of this is obvious. It does not suggest that our present society provides the 'sanction' for contemporary literature; for society has become atomised, and contemporary poetry, as Leavis shows in *New Bearings in English Poetry*, has made society its chief subject, not its chief support. What provides the sanction is the continuity of lived values that exists in the English past: 'a continuity of consciousness and a mature directing sense of value—a sense of value informed by a traditional wisdom'.[2]

So the task of contemporary literature is to re-create and re-assert this continuity in the midst of a society which has lost it. And the continuity is sufficiently present even now, in a vestigial form, to enable us to enter into an agreement on essential values.[3] The poets whom he sees as taking 'new bearings' are, among other things, engaging in the radical analysis of sensibility which can provide the groundwork of such a re-assertion.

Two things are evident. First, Leavis' stress goes beyond what a traditionalist like Allen Tate expects of the poet: 'he must recreate for his age the image of man, and he must propagate standards by which other men may test that image, and distinguish the false from the true'.[4] It also demands that poetry shall, as it were, re-live the continuity itself, in a pattern richer than any suggested by the term 'the image of man'; that it shall, as it were, re-create the sense of social life which modern society has departed from. Secondly, it

---

[1] *Education and the University, op. cit.* p. 23   [2] *Ibid.* p. 15   [3] *Ibid.* p. 18
[4] *The Man of Letters in the Modern World* (Thames and Hudson, London, 1955), p. 11

now becomes obvious that Leavis' view of such poets as Carew, Marvell, Johnson, and Pope, is not merely the product of nostalgia for a settled society; he finds these poets representing their society and its aspirations in some profound way; and, as a corollary, he sees their society opening before them to be expressed, then closing behind them as they express it: a mutual collaboration between poet and society. *Revaluation* is to a large extent a background study to *New Bearings*, though it is also the later work. And Leavis' treatment of these poets has the effect of providing a sort of unattainable norm for contemporary poets striving, with tragic lack of co-operation, in their atomised society.

Leavis' sense of the breakdown in continuity is very acute, and his sense of the need for contemporary literature tro estore it is very urgent. Quite early in his critical development he writes:

> The fact that the other traditional continuities have . . . so completely disintegrated, makes the literary tradition correspondingly more important, since the continuity of consciousness, the conservation of the collective experience, is the more dependent on it; if the literary tradition is allowed to lapse, the gap is complete.[1]

There is an important truth here, even for those of us who would change Leavis' emphasis, and say that the 'traditional continuities' can't be allowed to lapse, and that, if they do, there can't be much hope for the literary tradition. For the literary tradition is as much dependent on them as they are on it. But Leavis obviously intends us to make further deductions from his statement—to make, for one thing, a deduction about the nature and importance of literary criticism in our time:

> Literary criticism provides the test for life and concreteness; where it degenerates, the instruments of thought degenerate too, and thinking, released from the testing and energizing contact with the full living consciousness, is debilitated, and betrayed to the academic, the abstract and the verbal. It is of little use to discuss values if the sense for value in the concrete—the experience and perception of value—is absent.[2]

This is certainly true. But Leavis is here outlining not only a task for literary criticism, but also what we may reasonably call a sanction for it. It is because literature authoritatively embodies values that literary criticism can provide 'the test for life and concreteness'. And this formulation still leaves unanswered the question whether the testing and energising contact is a sufficient

---

[1] *For Continuity, op. cit.* p. 8
[2] *Ibid.* p. 9. v. also *The Common Pursuit, op. cit.* pp. 184-8

test of values. Are the standards suggested here good enough? They are necessary; but are they sufficient? The view here enunciated obviously links up with the passage on Lawrence which I examined in my second chapter on Leavis. It is associated with the suggestion that, in a disintegrating society, literature, tested only by 'literary criticism', is its own sufficient pledge. Leavis *does* offer this suggestion, though I am by no means sure that he would agree with it as I have formulated it; and I formulate it in this way in order to indicate the unease I feel at a recurrent, but undefined, emphasis in his work.

Society is perhaps not so thoroughly disintegrated as Leavis thought it in *For Continuity*; there are centres of life and health still existing, still growing, outside the expressions of literature. But his suggestion may be phrased in alternative ways. First, we may say that, in a disintegrating society, we have to accept great works of literature as adequately defining their own values without recourse to any 'external' values save those we can bring to them from our own 'sense of health', trained, as Leavis would have it trained, by literary criticism. Or we may say that, in a disintegrating society, literature is the only means of expression which offers us values fully enough formed to be grasped; it is the only thing which offers values to us authoritatively enough to be capable of being tested for 'life and concreteness'. In either case, I feel that a needlessly specialist attitude is being taken. And even if we are as integrally selective as Leavis is in drawing on the life of literature, we may still find that that life is insufficient not only to give us complete nourishment but even to exist as the *forum* within which we are to seek it.

In fact, literature cannot vindicate or define itself; this has to be said bluntly. Literature modifies our sense of value, but neither creates it nor extends it in any unilinear way. Its impact on us is as much modified by our own sense of values—produced as that is by a recourse to other intellectual disciplines as well as by a process of 'living'—as our consciousness is modified by literature; and even that modification is generally accomplished unobtrusively and inwardly. It is only by the most tenuous analogical use that we can speak of literature as creating values; and we can't speak of its creating *value* at all. As I have said, we derive our sense of life from other things besides literature, and from other things *before* literature. And just as we can't expect the work of a great writer simply to confirm our pre-existent sense of values, so we can't expect it to create such a sense where none already exists.

No one who really knows his work would accuse Leavis of thinking that literature is self-sufficient in quite this way. He has a very firm conception of the ways in which our responses to works of art lead outward to other 'subjects', other choices; but they are generally social 'subjects', and the choices are generally seen in moral terms; he shows a certain embarrassment in the face of philosophical or theological choices; and he does not seem to me sufficiently aware of the ways in which a philosophical or theological climate (as distinct from a more narrowly conceived 'social' one) can exert pressure on the creative consciousness. Then, too, he has always regarded literature as a nodal—as *the* nodal—expression of values; consequently, he regards it as of over-riding importance, both as an expression of civilisation and as a civilising influence. One does not want to undermine this conception; true literature is too much scanted in our time. But he passes imperceptibly from this attitude to the position where he acknowledges values only as they are subjected to the test of literature, and to the suggestion, which we can't help taking up from him, that literature offers us a final definition of values. It is not merely an excessively specialist approach, the approach of a man who will not take his eye off his own subject; for this 'subject' is a great deal more than a mere subject. Nor does it in any way imply the doctrine of *l'art pour l'art*; the literature in which he is interested has its source in a profound life, and its effect in living. But I for one find him unnecessarily adamant in relying on literature for the nourishment of our deepest selves. His insistence on having values presented 'in the concrete' is itself a value. But it is an insufficiently validated one. If Lawrence, for example, by the very pressure, the embodied values, of his work, tests our responses to life, we too, without being great creative artists, are in the position of testing Lawrence's values as well as the degree of embodiment they have undergone. We do this not only by referring them to our own personal 'sense of health', but by referring them, as well, to whatever institutions or bodies of belief from which that sense is partly derived, and by which, too, it is tested. Literature, in other words, is not the only test. And it is this that certain emphases in Leavis' work tend implicitly to deny, or at least to confuse.[1] He does not think (in Richards' absurd phrase) that poetry will save us; but he seems at times to think that it will complete us.

[1] v. 'Literature and Philosophy': *The Common Pursuit, op. cit.*
v. also an excellent article by Walter Stein: 'The Northern Miscellany of Literary Criticism', No. 1, Autumn 1953. Despite its occasional nature—it was originally a paper delivered before a body of Catholic intellectuals, by no means all literary men—I agree with most of its contents; and I applaud its exploratory approach to a difficult question.

Printed in Great Britain
at Hopetoun Street, Edinburgh,
by T. and A. CONSTABLE LTD.
Printers to the University of Edinburgh.